21 0426721 6 TELEPEN

Deregulating Telecoms

To the Aged P's

Deregulating Telecoms

Competition and Control in the United States, Japan and Britain

Jill Hills

Frances Pinter (Publishers), London

First published in Great Britain in 1986 by
Frances Pinter (Publishers) Limited
25 Floral Street, London WC2E ADS

British Library Cataloguing in Publication Data
Hills, Jill
  Deregulating telecoms: competition and
  control in the United States, Japan and
  Britain.
  1. Telecommunication policy
  I. Title
  384   HE7645
  ISBN 0-86187-568-0

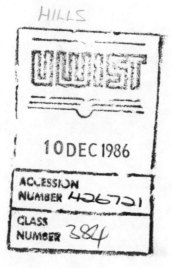
Typeset by Joshua Associates Limited, Oxford, England
Printed in the United States of America

Table of contents

Preface

This book has been written in an attempt to redress the balance of the debate on the deregulation of telecommunications. A great deal has been written on the benefits in general of deregulation and of privatisation but almost nothing on who benefits from the two processes. If the book sparks debate around that issue it will have served its purpose.

Many people have helped directly and indirectly with the book. Part of the research was funded by the Economic and Social Research Council (Grant A23 32 0023) when the Government Department at Manchester University gave me a professional home. My grateful thanks must also go to the Japan Foundation for funding a two-month stay in Tokyo in 1984 and to Waseda University for its hospitality. To all my friends in Japan who made that stay so enjoyable, and to all those who allowed me to interview them, I would like to say 'thank you', but especially to Professor Hideyoshi Tominaga of Waseda University and to Mr Hiroshi Ito then of NTT, who were so generous with their contacts and time. From my students at City University this last year, who will recognise some of the material in this book, I have learnt as much as I have taught.

Finally, without the help of family and friends the time consuming business of writing would have been too much. To my children, Patrick and Christina, for their willingness to take my turn in cooking and housework and to Tonya for her long-distance support, must go most thanks of all.

Deregulating Telecoms

Introduction

This book is about the deregulation of telecommunications in the United States and how the idea has spread to other countries in the form of privatisation and liberalisation in Britain and Japan. In the last two years telecommunications transmission has moved from the status of a virtual monopoly on the part of AT&T in America and British Telecom (BT) in Britain and from the dual monopolies of Nippon Telegraph and Telephone Public Corporation (NTT) and Kokusai Denshin Denwa Co. (KDD) in Japan to one of ostensible competition. Public policy-makers in the three countries have determined that competition should be substituted for governmental control in both the transmission and equipment markets.

The opponents of regulation have dominated the debate in the three countries. The terms of the debate, particularly in Britain and Japan, have diverted attention from the major question of who benefits from deregulation and privatisation. They have also deflected attention from both the national and international transfer of power involved in deregulation—a transfer of power away from elected governments towards private companies.

The book will argue that American domestic telecommunications policy has already had an effect on the rest of the world, particularly Europe and Japan and that its effects are about to spread wider, to the less industrialised world. The trend in the United States is away from the concept of a telecommunications service with rights of public access, to deregulation and privatisation of both terrestial and space communications. The trend is towards increasingly specialised and differentiated telecommunications services for business, with decreasing concern for public access.

But this trend has not come into being by itself. It takes place in a world hit by recession in which the industrialised countries are in increasing competition with each other. Fast communications, and in particular data communications, are seen as a means of increasing productivity and gaining comparative advantage. Both politicians and industrialists have expounded the virtues of new technology as a means by which industrialised countries can rescue themselves from the world slump. It is argued that privatisation and deregulation assist this process of innovation by freeing communications from the dead hand of public control. Hence a Minister of industry in Britain claimed in 1984 that by the liberalisation of BT's monopoly Britain had stolen a march on other European countries. It would lead, he said, to Britain becoming the value added network centre for Western Europe, to it becoming a tele-communications services centre in the same way as it was a financial centre.[1] It is this search for comparative advantage for private industry which is at the centre of the current movement for the deregulation of telecommunications.

The movement to deregulation of public telecommunications monopolies, which has led to *de facto* deregulation in Canada and has been discussed in countries as diverse as Sri Lanka, the Netherlands, Malaysia and Australia, is partly the offspring of ideologically right-wing governments and monetarist economics.[2] But it is also part of the process by which the United States seeks to establish its technological and economic leadership in the world trade in services. Information is now traded in its own right. The majority of records and data bases are centred in the United States, and global business demands the right of free passage of such information around the world.[3] Hence, American pressure for the deregulation of telecommunications monopolies and the activities of American business located overseas in demanding such deregulation, is one of the prongs in a three-pronged attack by the United States to free information services from barriers erected by sovereign governments.[4] Whereas negotiations through GATT have been faced with the resistance of the lesser-developed countries demanding reciprocal trade-offs, the American policies of direct pressure within countries and bi-lateral negotiations with specific countries on telecommunications trade are achieving better results. Had not changes of government taken place it is likely that in both Australia and New Zealand telecommunications monopolies would now be liberalised and privatised. In both Britain and Australia, Inter-national Business Machines (IBM), the American-owned world market leader in data processing equipment, publicly led lobbies in favour of liberalisation.[5]

The knock-on effect from deregulation of AT&T's monopoly in the United States has been both considerable and intentional. Divestiture of its local networks freed it to compete in international markets. For many years the Federal Communications Commission has sought but failed to export deregulation from the domestic American market to the international market. New technology in the form of satellites with point-to-point communications has now incrreased the probability of success. The decision to allow private satellites over the Atlantic takes advantage of the fact that Intelsat, the international consortium with a monopoly of international telecommunications transmission, is locked into older technology and also takes advantage of the burgeoning growth in cable TV markets in Europe. Private satellites would allow cheaper transmission of American cable programming to Europe. And when based on optic fibre networks, as in France, cable TV entities provide possible challengers to PTT monopolies. Private international satellites bring direct pressure to bear on PTTs to liberalise their monopolies.

For the providers of information services and the data processing equipment which goes with such domestic and global flows, the timing is crucial. It is necessary to break the PTT monopolies before they are able to institute their plans for Integrated Services Digital Networks (ISDN), expected to come onstream in the 1990s. Domestic ISDN under public control would not only make redundant the provision of private information networks, but would also introduce higher costs to multinational business. Whereas currently these businesses lease lines from the PTTs and do not pay for the amount of information passed along them, ISDN would instigate a costing of transmission by the 'bits' of information passed. Costs would therefore escalate for the major users of the system—multinational and large business.[6]

It is already accepted that banking was internationalised to escape the rigours of domestic regulation. Similarly there is a knock-on effect in the deregulation of communications by some countries. Multi-nationals, for whom communications is an increasing proportion of expenditure, will relocate or threaten to relocate where regulation is least and prices for international business are lowest. Part of the rationale for liberalisation and privatisation in Britain was precisely to attract this relocation.[7]

Additionally, ISDN transfers power from these private companies back to governments and PTTs. Where the interface between public and private equipment is located in the network will decide how much of current customers' premises equipment is redundant. It is possible that almost all the processing could be done within the public network, leaving equipment companies to supply a public capital market rather than the current consumer market. Liberalisation can be usd to delay the accrual of software capabilities within the PTT.[8]

It is within this international scenario that the book looks at the process of deregulation in the three countries and Intelsat, and examines the beneficiaries of that process. The proponents of deregulation and privatisation have presented regulation as 'political' and deregulation as both 'non-political' and an inevitable result of technological progress.[9] Competition has been lauded as an end in itself rather than as a mechanism for the control of company behaviour. Yet, in its redistribution of resources, the deregulation and privatisation of telecommunications transmission is a political act. Regulation and public control and their opposites, deregulation and privatisation, benefit different interests in society, although the public justifications rarely make these hidden interests public.

Turning to the three countries, in neither Britain nor the United States is a competitive environment for telecommunications something new. In both countries regulation was introduced after a period of competition. But whereas in the United States AT&T was allowed to retain a virtual private monopoly of the telephone service, in Britain after a period when private telecommunication companies were regulated the service became publicly controlled. Hence in Britain public ownership of the service was a substitute for the specific regulatory framework over private companies which was introduced in the United States. Japan, unlike Britain, has had long experience of both forms of regulation. Public ownership has substituted to a large extent for regulatory control in domestic telecommunications whereas international telecommunications have been provided through a regulated private company.

To demonstrate the virtues of competition in the telecommunications market, proponents of deregulation often point to the expansion of the American market prior to 1934. There are lessons to be learned from the experience of competitive telecommunications transmission both in the United States and Britain. In both cases a dominant entity set out to increase its market share by hindering the expansion of its rivals through legal action. AT&T gained dominance by the control of patents and by investing in competitive technologies. In the 1980s in Britain, BT is following that example. Because history can illuminate present controversies, and because in Britain that history is all but forgotten, the book includes a section on the background of telecommunications in the three countries.

Despite differences in historical background the current debate, both in Britain and Japan, has viewed deregulation or liberalisation as synonymous with privatisation. The arguments of proponents of deregulation in America—that competition spurs the provision of new services, that it creates more efficient allocation of resources and that it reduces prices—have been used by the proponents of privatisation in both Britain and Japan. Even some British political science literature conflates the two concepts of privatisation and liberalisation.[10] This confusion is understandable inasmuch as the privatisation legislation in both Japan and Britain has also altered the competitive framework. Just as the final agreement on the Bell break-up has allowed AT&T into new markets, Britain and Japan have also extended the boundaries within which BT and NTT may expand.

In fact the concepts of privatisation and liberalisation can be separated both theoretically and empirically. A market may be liberalised with one or more entities within that market remaining in public ownership or a publicly controlled entity may be privatised (i.e. its assets may be held by private institutions and individuals) with little or no ensuing liberalisation of the market, thereby creating a private rather than public monopoly. Or as in Japan, the sale of the public entity initially may be little more than a paper transaction involving a change in legal status rather than an actual sale of a majority of shares to the private sector. Privatisation *per se* does nothing to liberalise the market.

Regulation is normally justified on the basis that a natural monopoly exists: where it would be inefficient to have more than one supplier in a market because the economies of scale are such that additional suppliers would create additional costs to the consumer. The trade-off which takes place between the monopoly and the government involves the monopoly having its market protected from competitive entrants in return for not imposing monopoly prices on consumers. How far this market protection has been carried differs from entity and in telecommunications from place to place. Although Japan's domestic telecommunications market was until 1985 under the control of a public corporation, NTT, the protection given by regulation to its market was much less than that given to British Telecom prior to the 1981 liberalisation of its market. Conceptually therefore a distinction has to be made between the existing state of liberalisation within a market and ownership of a monopoly supplier to that market.

In all three countries the current round of privatisation and liberalisation has resulted in telecommunications markets in which one private entity has overwhelming dominance and remains regulated. In the United States that dominant entity is AT&T, in Japan it is NTT and in Britain it is BT. The major differences are in the extent of the regulation still exerted over those entities and in the extent to which competition is allowed against them. What we are witnessing at the present time is re-regulation rather than deregulation.

In discussing deregulation or liberalisation it seemed in the past not to be possible to talk of a unified telecommunications market. Transmission markets could be divided into international markets, long-line (or trunk) markets and local networks. Equipment markets could be divided into exchange and customer provided equipment. Each seemed suitable for varying amounts of competition. Michael Beesley and Stephen Littlechild argue that because of their heavy sunk costs local networks may in fact be 'natural monopolies', and this conception is also the basis of the Justice Department's 1982 consent decree with AT&T.[11] Alternatively in the United States, consultants to the Federal Communications Commission in 1977 argued that manufacturers did not need the whole customer equipment market in order to gain the benefits of size needed to decrease unit costs and that no natural monopoly therefore existed.[12] Differentiation of markets formed the base of the FCC's original liberalisation strategy. But experience has shown that liberalisation of one provokes liberalisation of another, and that a unified market now increasingly operates with equipment and transmission feeding off each other. Unification and concentration have followed liberalisation.

The question of whether and to what extent there should be regulation as an alternative to competition revolves around the economic and technical possibility of competition within each sector and the goals of public policy. New technologies may make access possible for competitors, but given the overwhelming sunk investment of the dominant entity, the new entrants may not be able to compete on costs. In that particular case the ironic situation may arise that stricter regulation, perhaps even involving the imposition on the dominant entity of higher prices or imposing access to its network at below cost, may be needed in order to allow competitors to enter and to make a profit. It will be argued that this is akin to the situation in Britain and will be the situation in Japan. Alternatively, although economic and technical access may be possible it may be judged that other political interests outweigh any rights to entry.

Within telecommunications regulated monopoly markets the perception has grown up world-wide that there are cross-subsidies of one set of consumers by another. It is argued that the beneficiaries have tended to be residential consumers on the one hand because most telecommunications monopolies have been under an obligation to provide access to telephones to as many people as possible and also local callers on the other (the majority of residential consumers making primarily local calls). The losers, it is argued by deregulators, have tended to be business customers and trunk callers—also predominantly business users. The movement for deregulation can be understood as a movement to shift perceived costs from business to residential consumers of the telephone service, possibly even to provide a subsidy to some business at a time of recession.

The arguments propounded by the deregulators on the question of the distribution of costs within a regulated system are not altogether as proven as they seem. None of the dominant entities have such transparent accounting methods that it is possible to judge the extent of cross-subsidisation from one service to another. Cross-subsidies are likely to differ according to the type of pricing policy adopted—flat-rate or usage/time sensitive. GTE Service Corporation showed in a study in 1976 that who subsidised whom in a system where there was time-of-day pricing depended upon what measure of costs were taken. If two-way minutes of usage during the busy hour were taken as a measure then residential subscribers subsidised business, whereas if two-way minutes overall were taken the subsidy went the other way.[13] Inasmuch as businesses make more incoming calls and use the network most at peak periods it could be argued that they should take a higher share of the costs than residential subscribers. In Britain BT claims that it loses money on public call boxes and now refuses to install them unless outgoing calls produce a certain amount of income. Incoming calls to call boxes are not counted in its assessment of costs, yet with 25 per cent of households lacking a telephone it is normal for subscribers to phone back those calling from public telephones. Counting two-way minutes of usage might produce a different picture.

Experience in both the United States and Canada suggests that the proportion of fixed network costs and running costs ascribed to residential connections or to local calls is a political decision, taken in the interests of the dominant entity, rather than one on which there are objective criteria.[14] Inevitably in a situation where a dominant entity faces competition on some services but not on others it will attempt to offload costs onto the monopoly service, leading to higher access charges to residential consumers. To take one example of possible cross-subsidisation of specialised business services by other users of the network in Britain, since 1983 BT has run a Sat-stream data communications service to Europe, leasing satellite capacity. By the end of 1985 the service had only one customer. It seems unlikely that the one customer will be paying the costs of the investment necessary and therefore cross-subsidation seems likely to be occurring. Similarly leased private lines in Britain have been cheaper for business than use of the public network—a hidden subsidy to business from residential customers of the network. Other examples are available from Canada where Bell Canada used predatory pricing to see off competition first in local network services and then in long-line services.[15]

The prevailing debate and media hype about new business services has diverted attention away from the costs involved in the deregulation of telecommunications. If, as a result of deregulation access to the network is reduced then the utility of that network to all consumers is reduced by each single user's drop-out. No telephone is useful by itself; it becomes increasingly useful as the numbers of interconnections increase. Although the point is acknowledged by the opponents of regulation, and the difficulties of disadvantaged groups have been a feature of the arguments against deregulation in Britain, the costs are assumed to fall only on those prevented from access to the system, rather than all users.[16] In this context it is pertinent that the British regulatory body, OFTEL, is now moving in the opposite dirction from the FCC, seeking to establish what would be the most 'efficient' use of the network, in order to preclude the costs of the local network being borne solely by local calls and residential subscribers.[17]

It is noticeable in the United States, Britain and Japan that the opponents of deregulation have cited the extra costs likely to fall on rural areas through deregulation, hoping thereby to enlist the support of conservative Politicians, electoral bases are in those areas. A similar argument has been put forward for Intelsat. Yet it is not by any means clear that any of these monopolies have in the past been more than passingly concerned with the rural poor. Services in both Intelsat and the domestic monopolies have been dominated by the demands of the developed and urbanised communities. Low access costs for the poor or geographically isolated have not been a predominant consideration.

Yet it is possible to argue not only from a socialist perspective that reduced access costs ensure that the poor are not excluded from the benefits of new technology, but to argue from a conservative perspective that a tax on consumption is equitable. In the United States, Britain and Japan indirect taxes on consumption are paid as sales tax and ideologically, because they give the consumer a choice, such indirect taxes are preferred to direct income tax. It is possible to consider any subsidy in a telecommunications system which may exist between business and residential consumers as a form of consumption tax, paid to preserve the utility of the telecommunications system for all consumers, and to argue for regulation on that basis.

This book is about the interests which new technology has served and its political role in the redistribution of resources. It is not possible to discuss deregulation of telecommunications without discussing the technological convergence which has taken place in the communications sector. It is the possibility of creating networks with the new technologies at lower costs than those of PTTs which has made deregulation a technological possibility, and it is the convergence of technologies which has raised the political interests which will benefit from deregulation.

Convergence, through the enabling technology of microelectronics, took place first between traditional voice communications and data communications. The digitalisation of switching technology and transmission has ensured that computing and telecommunications are no longer separate components of a communications industry. As voice transmission has become digitalised the distinction between it and data transmission has become artificial, an important point when the regulation of telecommunications is considered.

Second, it is necessary to appreciate the convergence of these forms of communications with image processing and video. Not only is it no longer possible to distinguish technically between voice and data transmission because both can be digitalised, but satellite transmission of voice, data and images is now possible as is the transmission of all three by optic cable. In addition, computers can now store images on compact discs bringing forward the possibility of interactive computerised audio/visual consumer equipment. Interactive cable TV based on optic fibre also provides a possible competitor for traditional telecommunications transmission.

There are now several methods of telecommunications transmission: microwave, coaxial cable, satellite and optic fibre cable. Of these microwave and coaxial cable are 'old' technologies (although research has upgraded the economic possibilities of microwave technology) whilst satellites and optic fibres are 'new'. The first communications satellite, Early Bird, was launched in 1965 and the first production of optic fibre cable took place in the early 1970s. But the problem for satellite makers is that although optic fibres can be directly substituted for coaxial cable, satellites have always been regarded as an intermediate technology because of their cost and lifetime limitations and because the radio spectrum is a limited resource.[18] Even in the 1970s it was anticipated that in the long-term the cheapest method of broadband transmission would be via digital switching and optic fibres. But satellites have one major advantage (or some of them do)—they can be used to break a PTT's monopoly.

The major threat to PTTs has come from satellites. As Andrea Caruso, the Secretary-General of Eutelsat, the European consortium of PTTs has said: 'Could somebody tell me why the coming into being of satellite telecommunications should provoke such "earthquakes" in the discipline of telecommunication services? I do not remember any deregulatory tendency, at least in Europe, before the arrival of satellites.'[19] Caruso provides his own answer to the question—in terms of the profit which both satellite makers and those who can extend their markets or operate their business more efficiently through satellite transmission perceive as possible. The main beneficiaries from satellite transmission in America have been the aerospace industry, cable TV companies, service industries and financial institutions.[20] In seeking to extend the penetration of satellites the American aerospace industry in particular has had a range of useful allies previously excluded by the telecommunications monopoly from the transmission of information.

To explain briefly about satellite transmission: two kinds of transmission are possible for satellites—to earth station and then via cable distribution or microwave to the consumer, or direct to the consumer via satellite dish receivers. These dish receivers can be of two kinds, either receive-only (for TV) or capable of generating messages. Various trade-offs have to be made in the manufacture of each satellite. The higher the power of the satellite, the smaller and less expensive the ground stations need to be. Conversely, the lower the power of the satellite the larger and more expensive the earth stations.

Similarly there is a trade-off between the frequency used and the size of the satellite's footprint. The lower the frequency the larger the footprint. Hence TV satellites in the United States tend to be low power, low frequency using the C band 6/4 Ghz, as do the satellites used by Intelsat. Higher frequencies have the advantage of faster transmission and are therefore suitable for high-speed data transmission but have the disadvantage of a smaller footprint. Again the trade-offs come between cost and demand, a high-frequency space-segment being more expensive but providing the possibility of such services as fast data processing, videoconferencing and other broadband services without interference from other users. This form of satellite transmission using the Ku frequency band can be used both, as Satellite Business Systems has done in the United States, for the transmission of data and voice communications and broadband services, or it can be used for direct TV broadcasts. Crucially, Ku band satellites can broadcast direct to the customer.

But, high-powered satellites are an expensive way of providing programmes in areas which can receive normal TV transmission, so a further intermediate market has developed. Because of developments in receiving equipment technology, the broadcasts of low-powered satellites can be picked up with smallish receive-only dishes, although with some loss of picture clarity. High-frequency broadcasts provide a clearer picture. DBS is a high-frequency service and therefore expensive, whereas in both the United States and Britain, TVRO (TV Receive Only), a market in satellite dishes to put in the backyard, which was at first illegal, allows the reception of unprotected cable TV broadcasts, although with a poorish picture. For the consumer TVRO is less expensive than either DBS, which requires completely new reception equipment or subscription to cable TV.

Low-powered satellite transmissions can also be picked up by a communal receiver dish and distributed locally either by microwave or cable. Cable TV and satellite transmission of programming material have flourished in the United States, where they have provided the bread and butter of the satellite operating industry for the past ten years. Cable TV is now a growth market in Europe increasingly fed by satellite programming.[21]

For some time satellites seemed to provide the new technology which would allow access to the telecommunications market without the enormous fixed cost of establishing a local network. Over long distances satellite transmission was cheaper than coaxial cable. But in order to transmit broadband services, such as teleconferencing, for which the market had not been established, it was necessary to use high-powered satellites in the Ku band, which were expensive. The alternative lower band demanded some form of local distribution and interconnection into the telecommunications carriers' network.

A further problem with satellite transmission is the crowding which comes in the geo-stationary orbit. The problem is not so much physical crowding (although this may be a problem in future years) as overlapping and interference in anyone frequency band. In the United States the lower frequency band used for cable TV transmission is now overcrowded. Moving up the frequency band causes problems in rain attentuation and signal deterioration. The Japanese space industry is attempting to solve the problems associated with the use of the Ka band, which is a band higher than the Ku band currently used for DBS. They are proposing to develop this higher band in conjunction with digital television linked to computerised image retrieval through compact discs, and it is this development which the Americans are anxious should stop.

Because of the various trade-offs necessary between power, frequency, cost and demand, and because launchers can now handle heavier satellites (having more transponders) current generations of satellites have transponders using a mixture of frequencies. 'Spot beams' have also been developed so that there can be differentiation of frequencies between areas with large amounts of traffic and those with less. However, satellites remain 'mirrors in the sky' and in the opinion of some experts it will only be when the satellites are themselves the equivalent of flying computerised telephone exchanges and are capable of on-board processing and of linking with each other that they will be economically attractive for widespread interactive broadband services for large numbers of consumers.[22]

Satellites are in competition with terrestrial transmission provided through coaxial cable and optic fibre cable. Satellites have an advantage under certain circumstances. They are good for:

— mobile communications
— off-shore communications
— rough terrain
— where it is necessary to have a telecommunications system quickly
— broadcasting of stereo and TV.

But they are not economic for distances under about 1,000 miles for telephone transmission. And compared to coaxial cable with a life of twenty-five years, satellites' lives of seven to ten years are short.

Satellites are not therefore the most economical solution to the problems of setting up an alternative telecommunications network which they were first expected to be. Nevertheless, partly because of their linkage with defence and the implications of hegemony in space, those companies involved in their production have close links with governments and form powerful national lobbies.

Within the satellite production market there are three sections: satellites, launchers and ground stations. Each is dominated by different firms. Satellite makers tend to come from defence and aereospace, the market leader being Hughes Aircraft. The majority are American—Ford Aerospace, General Electric of America, RCA and TRW. In Europe there are three groups: Eurosatellite consisting of Messerschmitt, Aerospatiale, ATM and Thomson CSF; Satcom International—British Aerospace and Matra; Unisat, a consortium of British Aerospace, British Telecom and GEC–Marconi.

The European manufacturers have benefited in particular from contracts from the European Space Agency established in 1975, which since 1982 has been the manager of the Eutelsat consortium of European PTTs' satellite provision and transmission. They have also benefited from Inmarsat, a European-led international consortium established in 1981 to provide mobile communications to shipping and latterly to aircraft. The prospect of DBS has also been used by the French and West German governments to enhance their native satellite manufacturers.[23]

The Americans, however, have the advantage of their early experience in the field derived mainly through their contracts from Intelsat satellites, and, despite growing European competition, they still dominate the world market. For Inmarsat satellites European consortia have tended to collaborate with American manufacturers—either Hughes or Ford—because they still lack experience in pay-load manufacture. Between 1983 and the year 2000 the market for satellites is expected to be in the region of £2 billion per annum.[24]

Launches are provided by unmanned rockets—Atlas-Centaur (USA); Delta (USA); Ariane (ESA) or manned by the space shuttle (NASA). Satellites launched from unmanned rockets are cheaper to manufacture because of safety requirements for manned flights. Ariane has established a price advantage both over the shuttle and over the Atlas-Centaur, with a price of $28–35 million quoted in 1984 against the Atlas-Centaur's $42 million. Some private American firms are entering the launcher market, but despite setbacks the major competition is between the space shuttle and Ariane.

Ground stations are dominated by traditional telecommunications firms—ITT (USA) and NEC (Japan) having the largest market share. A variety of small firms cover the receive only market—the largest being Scientifica Atlanta, which claims 40 per cent of the American domestic market.

Coaxial cable, although an 'old' technology is safer than satellite in that there is no risk accruing to launches in which satellites are sometimes lost. A lost satellite can mean years of delay in establishing a telecoms network for a country wanting an instant solution to its problems. Coaxial cable is also more secure than either microwave or satellite transmissions, which are relatively easy to monitor. A recent American defence agency project is specifically directed to making both microwave and satellite transmissions secure. Coaxial cable has however the disadvantage that it can carry relatively few circuits compared to a satellite and that it needs to pass over or under land owned by others. Despite satellites coaxial cable is still a market growing at 15 per cent a year because of its reliability and security.

With the advent of optical fibres, the economics of terrestrial transmission have been revolutionised. Optical fibres have the advantage of allowing digital transmission, of carrying three times the capacity of coaxial cable, of being more resistant to corrosion, of being immune from electrical interference and of being very secure. The fibres have also decreased in price at a very fast rate. In 1973 a metre of fibre cost $5 according to OECD but by 1982 prices were down to $0.50 and $3.50 depending on quality.[25] The fibres have the added advantage of being so thin they can be slipped through existing ducts. Used as submarine cables their lighter weight, increased bandwidth and the increased distance between repeater stations compared to coaxial make them competitive on cost with satellites. The first fibres were discovered in the Post Office at Martlesham but Corning Glass of the United States was the first company to take out patents on their production.

The American market alone is estimated at more than $1 billion per annum by 1990. Corning Glass is the market leader, but other companies, such as AT&T, ITT (USA), NEC (Japan), Northern Telecom (Canada), Fujitsu (Japan) and Philips (the Netherlands) are also contenders. In Britain, BICC the cable manufacturer has a joint venture with Corning Glass and STC (30 per cent owned by ITT), a world market share of about 60 per cent in cable laying, which it is using to enter the undersea optic fibre market. In France, government policy is to increase the output of two smaller manufacturers to fulfill the demand generated by the recabling of the country for cable TV. In all, Europe has eight manufacturers of optic fibre compared to three in the United States.[26]

Cable TV using optic fibre cable can be an alternative to traditional telecommunications transmission via co-axial cable, while new methods of microwave transmission have also made that technology more competitive. Also with the removal of traditional TV broadcasts to a higher waveband, frequencies have been emptied to increase the use of radio for mobile communications. The result of all this technological activity is that a variety of different methods exist for the transmission of information. The convergence of traditional telecommunications, that is voice transmission with data transmission and image transmission, coupled with developments in satellite broadcasting and reception has brought land-based telecommunications into competition with DBS and with cable TV as alternative 'fungible' methods of transmission.

The current telecommunications transmission market can be seen as one in which satellite manufacturers from defence and aerospace, often with the backing of governments and the military, are in opposition to the optic fibre market, the province of the traditional telecommunications manufacturers with their linkage to PTTs. For the traditional telecommunications carriers optic fibre also presents the advantage that it is under their control in a way in which satellite transmission is not. Competition between technologies, particularly technologies which are under some form of government control can best be seen as competition between a variety of companies using government regulation or deregulation of telecommunications as their instrument to gain or keep their market share of telecommunications.

The deregulation of telecommunications monopolies is of crucial importance because transmission represents the filling inside the sandwich of equipment provision on the one side and information provision on the other. Technological convergence has brought the three markets together, transmission being the crucial commodity which allows access to customers for both equipment and information. In addition to the technology changes in the transmission market the telecommunications equipment market has also been undergoing rapid transition. Whereas up to the 1970s computers and telecommunications were separate industries, their convergence can be dated from the entry of IBM into the Private Branch Exchange (PBX) market in the mid-1970s. By 1970, AT&T was announcing its first all-electronic digital exchange followed soon after by ITT, Ericsson, the French and the Japanese. By 1980, most of the industrialised countries had begun the transfer of their telecommunications transmission from the intermediate technology of cross-bar with stored program control to all-digital technology, the British being one of the last to do so. The extent of competition between traditional telecommunications and traditional data processing companies in the United States and Britain is not however simply IBM now manufacturing PBX and AT&T manufacturing computers. Rather it is a matter of how transmission control can limit the choice of competitors' equipment and provide *de facto* control of markets.

Digitalisation has increased the possibility of fast data transmission while the increased numbers of computers used has extended the possible market for data management and other value added network services. Data transmission has in fact been a rather disappointing market, not growing as fast as was predicted in the 1970s. To be economic data transmission services need voice communications as well and once digital transmission is used for voice communication there is no technical distinction between them. It is the prospect of value added networks, expected in the United States alone to be worth more than $100 billion in 1987 which are bringing the computer and software companies (TV programming, data base, financial and other information services) into conflict with PTT monopolies and their concepts of nation-wide ISDN services linked globally. Under ISDN the imposition of network standards will once more allow governments to regulate the entry and behaviour of overseas firms. The interest of these companies is in breaking PTT monopolies before such services can be established.

For Europe and the Japanese much of the post-war period has seen policy directed to reducing dependence upon American companies and technology. From the 1950s when IBM first entered the data processing business, the promise of a tariff-free market has brought American multinationals to Europe. By the end of the 1960s IBM alone had taken a major share of each of the domestic European markets in mainframe computers. In Japan IBM was allowed entry in the late 1950s in return for a technological agreement. There followed a period in which the British, French, West German and Japanese governments used a variety of supportive mechanisms to retain domestically owned manufacture and technology in the mainframe computer market.[27]

As the growth in the market devolved downwards into mini- and micro-computers so European governments have tended to give support to those sectors. But, at each stage they have been faced with the domination of American manufacturers. Until 1981 only in Britain was the attempt to halt that domination successful. In 1983, IBM's dataprocessing revenue in Europe was $10 billion compared to the $1.3 billion of Olivetti or the $1.2 billion of Siemens. IBM's turnover in Britain and France was double that of the national champion companies. The most successful industry in competing within its domestic market against the Americans was the Japanese where IBM's share of the market declined to 30 per cent in 1980. When IBM transferred its Eastern headquarters to Japan in 1984 it was assumed by many Japanese that it was preparing an onslaught on the Japanese market.

In contrast to the computer market in both Europe and Japan in the telecommunications market domestic manufacturers have predominated. Despite the presence of American multinationals, GTE and ITT, in the public sector exchange market national preferences and standards ensured that in the major West European countries the suppliers were predominantly domestic. Siemens and AEG–Telefunken in West

Germany, Italtel in Italy, CIT–Alcatel and Thomson in France (now merged), and GEC and Plessey in Britain were the major suppliers. Although present in the large private exchange market in Britain, IBM was not a major telecommunications equipment supplier. And in Japan, the lack of American procurement by NTT has long been a bone of contention between the Americans and Japanese. While the Japanese manufacturers have solved the problem of oversupply within the domestic market by increasingly aggressive exports, the European industry, fragmented between so many suppliers has lost market share in the world market. It faces the problem that Europe is a fragmented market with differing national standards, which although protecting domestic manufacturers have also prevented them from using the whole European market as a base. In contrast ITT with its eight subsidiaries spread throughout Europe has been able to adapt to different markets. The European industry is now facing a further problem—the cycle of technological innovation in telecommunications is quickening and the cost of R & D for large switching systems is becoming beyond the financial capability of smallish manufacturers. The result has been a movement towards concentration in France and Britain and a movement towards European Community-wide research.

The privatisation of transmission monopolies alters the concern of the PTT for domestic manufacturers. Privatised PTTs become large, powerful commercial companies in their own right anxious to extend their markets domestically and internationally. It makes commercial sense to buy equipment from the cheapest source and to link up with other powerful companies in data processing. Hence both BT and NTT have sought agreements to establish value added networks with IBM, using IBM equipment.

De facto by market dominance in data processing IBM imposed its standards on the rest of the world. VANs provide the opportunity to extend this market share not only within each domestic market, but also globally.[28] Deregulation world-wide opens the possibility of global VANs linking the world's largest manufacturers, banks and retailers outside the regulation of governments. If fast communications increase productivity then in the search for comparative advantage global VANS enrich the largest companies manufacturing on a global scale. Deregulation makes possible increased penetration for information and equipment providers and private international satellites provide the technology which can be used to open access to PTT monopolies.

This book then is about the movement for deregulation and the interests it serves. The three countries began the process of deregulation at different times, with industries in different positions in the world market—Britain's being the weakest—with different traditions and ideologies towards state/industry relations, and with political systems which differ in their centralisation and the strength of their bureaucracy. It is hardly surprising therefore that the terms 'deregulation' or 'liberalisation' or 'privatisation' have produced different political mechanisms of intervention in the three countries. What is evident however in all three is a pattern of the state struggling to retain control over markets which have been formally liberalised and which are therefore more susceptible to foreign penetration. In the United States bi-lateral negotiations with the Japanese have sought to reduce the burgeoning balance of payments' deficit in telecommunications subsequent to the divestiture of AT&T and congressional intervention resulted in a *de facto* re-regulation of the market. Bi-lateral negotiation, threatening West German exports of telecommunications equipment to the USA is similarly being used against the West Germans' policy of controlling information flows in preparation for ISDN.[29]

Deregulation has been an American export to Japan and Britain. In both, the United States was used as a direct model. In Japan, formal privatisation of NTT and liberalisation of the last vestiges of its monopoly have resulted in bureaucracy in the form of the Ministry of Posts and Telecommunications actually increasing its power over the whole telecommunications industry. Privatisation has also resulted in American gains from the sale of satellites to Japan, satellites which will give 30 per cent overcapacity in the domestic market and from the VAN link-up between IBM and NTT. Other American companies have also entered the VAN market while Japanese equipment manufacturers have been specifically excluded from providing services for the lesser developed and newly industrialised countries (predominantly Korea) proposed between NTT and a number of trading houses. In the privatisation process Japanese equipment manufacturers are major losers.

In Britain, IBM was active in pressing for the initial liberalisation of the equipment market and subsequently gained entry to the public exchange market. However, the government's successful desire to sell 51 per cent of BT led to the formation of a private monopoly. British Telecom was given the power to extend its monopoly into competitive technologies in a way that neither AT&T nor NTT have been allowed. Yet, because ideologically the Thatcher government is in favour of competition and the regulatory agency OFTEL has acted in a pro-competitive manner, the government intervened to refuse IBM's joint

VAN with BT as anti-competitive. Nevertheless IBM's subsequent vociferous complaints that BT might be able to cross-subsidise MDNs has resulted in a proposal to open leased lines to any form of added value service excepting resale.[30]

Deregulation is now moving from the United States into the international market for telecommunications transmission. Despite opposition from almost all the member states within Intelsat, the international consortium which has held a monopoly of international telecommunications satellite transmission, the FCC has agreed that four companies may place a private satellite over the Atlantic. The legal arguments concerning the Americans right to place such private satellites on the most profitable Intelsat route revolved around the American definition of what constitutes a 'public' service, the FCC choosing to interpret the wording of the Intelsat international agreement in terms of the 'common carrier' concept used within domestic American law. Because Intelsat already faces competition from two new trans-Atlantic optic fibre cables due to come on-line in 1988, and because under its constitution it may not differentiate prices over various routes, the current financial prospect for Intelsat is gloomy. Although the American administration claims that the less developed countries will not suffer from its intervention, and to the extent that Intelsat's technology has been primarily determined by the needs of the industrialised countries it is true that the disadvantage currently suffered will only be proportionately heightened, the results of domestic deregulation when transposed into the international market suggest that the existing low access for the poor will be further reduced.[31]

The argument of this book is that the deregulation of Intelsat is linked very closely to American industrial and trade policy, to the decision not to break up IBM and the decision to allow AT&T onto the world market. The break up of Intelsat or large increases in its charges would lead to domestic satellites becoming more attractive, with commensurate benefits to American aerospace manufacturers. Just as important, private satellites over the Atlantic will also increase the pressure on European PTTs to liberalise their monopolies. In fact such a breach has already taken place. Despite its single customer the importance of BT's Sat-stream European service is that it has established the principle that direct point-to-point communications, outside the PTT network, can be used by major companies. The European PTT monopolies have already begun to crack.

In conclusion, deregulation and privatisation of communications has not generally been seen as a mechanism of industrial policy. But looked at as part of a process of gaining comparative advantage in the information technology sector, one can see in the deregulation of the telecommunications market a primary mechanism of industrial policy in the United States, Britain and Japan. The goal is the world market. The argument put forward is that innovation lags under public control. 'Technological convergence' is a seemingly politically neutral justification for deregulation. Yet it masks the implication that technology should be allowed to serve private interests, that it should not be under social control. Arguments citing the 'freedom' in technological innovation conceal the political interests of those who develop, manufacture and use that technology. In international markets 'freedom' to develop and use private communications implies a transfer of power from sovereign governments to those best able to use the technology— predominantly global companies.

At the domestic level deregulation is a political mechanism of intervention in markets by governments in order to reallocate the costs and benefits involved in regulation. The richer consumers and sections of manufacturing and service industries in particular have seen themselves as disadvantaged by domestic systems of regulation. Deregulation reverses these gainers and losers and can be seen partly as a response to the world recession. Not only has that recession increased pressure from business along cost-cutting lines, but by reducing the tax-take of governments it has made the selling of public enterprises attractive to public exchequers.

Deregulation and privatisation are part of the strategy of the rich to stay rich and of the large to grow larger. They are part of the swing in the industrialised countries away from government concern with the poor and disadvantaged. They are also part of the American strategy to reduce controls by sovereign governments over the activities of global business.

Notes and references

1. John Butcher, quoted in *Computer Weekly*, 2 February 1984.
2. PTTI, *Privatisation and Liberalisation of Telecommunications Services in the PTTI Asian Region*, PTTI Asian Regional Conference, Seoul, September 1984; H. Janisch and Y. Kurisaki, 'Reform of telecommunications regulation in Japan and Canada', *Telecommunications Policy*, March 1985, pp. 31–40; Robert E. Babe, 'Predatory Pricing and Foreclosure in Canadian Telecommunications', *Telecommunications Policy*, December 1985, pp. 329–33.

3. K. P. Suavant, 'Transborder data flows and the developing countries', *International Organisation*, **37**, 2, Spring 1983, pp. 359–71.

4. Estimates of trade in telecommunications and computer services are almost non-existent. Estimates of world market (i.e. total sales) of $300 billion in 1984 rising to $560 billion in 1990 are given in: W. J. Sullivan, 'Outlook for Telecommunications: Impacts on Labor, Trade and Economic Development', United States Department of Commerce, February 1985, Table 1, quoted in P. Robinson, 'Telecommunications Trade and TDF', *Telecommunications Policy*, December 1985, pp. 311–19. See also: Ron Napier, 'International Services Trade: The Newest Dimension of Trade Tensions', in *US–Japan Relations in the 1980s: Towards Burden Sharing*, Programme on US–Japan Relations, Harvard University, Cambridge, Mass., 1981–8, pp. 63–76.

5. PTTI, *Privatisation and Liberalisation of Telecommunications in the PTTI Asian Region*, op. cit., p.14; Post Office Engineering Union, *Making the Future Work. The Broad Strategy*, London, POEU, 1984, p. 3.

6. 'Telecommunications Liberalisation', *Business Week*, 24 December 1983 quotes Ernst Weiss, Chairman of the International Telecommunications Users Group on ISDN, 'Do we need this elaborate pipeline?'.

7. West Germany's high tariffs are provoking multinational relocation. See: Peter Bruce, 'The High Price of a State Monopoly', *Financial Times*, 11 June 1985. On banking: Brigid Gavin, 'A GATT for International Banking', *Journal of World Trade Law*, **19**, 2, March/April 1985, pp. 121–35.

8. When BT's monopoly was liberalised the proposal that it should retain the right to maintain digital PABX caused enormous pressure from the computing industry, who saw the possibility of the extension of BT's network into software. The provision was removed from the Bill.

9. Sir George Jefferson, Chairman of BT, *Financial Times*, 25 January 1985; Moriya Koyama, Vice-Minister MPT, 'The New Communication Age in Japan', *Telecommunications Policy*, September 1985, pp. 182–4.

10. J. R. Shackleton, 'UK Privatisation—US Deregulation', *Politics*, **5**, 2, October 1985, pp. 8–15.

11. Michael Beesley and Stephen Littlechild, 'Privatization: Principles, Problems and Priorities', *Lloyds Bank Review*, July 1983, pp. 1–19.

12. Chester G. Fenton and Robert F. Stone, 'Competition in Terminal Equipment Market', *Public Utilities Fortnightly*, 31 July 1977, pp. 25–71.

13. Bridger M. Mitchell, 'Pricing Policies in Selected European Telephone Systems', in Herbert S. Dorick (ed.), *Proceedings of the 6th Annual Telecommunications Policy Conference*, Lexington, Mass., D. C. Heath, 1978, pp. 437–75; Leland M. Schmidt, 'Telephone Service Pricing', in *Telecommunications and Economic Development. Exposition Proceedings Vol. 3*, Dedham, Ma., Horizon House International, 1978, pp. 219–27.

14. William H. Melody, 'Efficient Rate Regulation in the Competitive Era', Joint Select Committee on Telecommunications, Washington State Legislature, Seattle, July 11–12 1984; Robert E. Babe, 'Predatory Pricing and Foreclosure in Canadian Telecommunications', *Telecommunications Policy*, December 1985, pp. 329–33; Nina Cornell, Daniel Kelley and Peter Greenhaigh state: 'It has been impossible to determine how large

cross subsidies are, what they accomplish, exactly who receives them, or even whether they exist at all. Internal subsidies defy accountability both in practice and principle. The joint-cost nature of telecommunications service makes it impossible in many cases to determine subsidy from prices.' FCC Staff Report, April 1980, quoted in Ida Walters, 'Freedom for Communications', in R. W. Poole Jr. (ed.), *Instead of Regulation*, Lexington, Mass., D. C. Heath, 1982, p. 127.

15. Robert E. Babe, op. cit.

16. Michael Canes, *Telephones—Public or Private?*, London, Institute of Economic Affairs, 1966 states: '... calls per person go up as the number of telephones per capita increases over an extended range. Since more calls mean more revenue the market tends to reflect the ever-increasing value of service to the subscriber ... Thus a shift in supply causes a shift in demand as long as there remain potential users' [p. 17].

17. OFTEL, *British Telecom's Price Increases—November 1985. A Statement Issued by the Director General of Telecommunications*, London, OFTEL, 16 January 1985, p. 11 (mimeo).

18. On competitive technologies see: Gadi Kaplan, 'Fiber optics, ICs and satellite', *IEEE Spectrum*, January 1984, pp. 38–57.

19. Andrea Caruso, 'Deregulation and Disorder in Satellite Communications', speech to Intelvent, 17 September 1984.

20. W. J. Mellors, 'Commercial Opportunities in Space, a European Viewpoint', in J. L. McLucas and C. Sheffield (eds), *Commercial Operations in Space 1980–2000*, San Diego, American Astronautical Society, 1981, p. 148.

21. Timothy Hollins, *Beyond Broadcasting: Into the Cable Age*, London, BFI, 1984; Raymond Kuhn, *The Politics of Broadcasting*, Beckenham, Croom Helm, 1985.

22. B. G. Evans, 'Towards the Intelligent Satellite', Guildford, Surrey University, unpublished paper, 1985.

23. David Gregory, British Aerospace, 'Future Directions in Space Communications', *Information Technology and Public Policy*, **4**, 1, September 1985, pp. 12–22.

24. For an introduction to satellite technology see: UNESCO, *A Guide to Satellite Communication*, Paris, UNESCO, 1974.

25. OECD, *Telecommunications: Pressures and Policies for Change*, Paris, OECD, 1983, pp. 28–47; other market forecasts are given in: Manley Rutherford Irwin, *Telecommunications America: Markets Without Boundaries*, Quorum Books, Westport, Connecticut and London, 1984; *Financial Times* 27 April 1981; 24 October 1983; 14 January 1985.

26. *Computer Weekly*, 25 October 1984.

27. Rob Van Tulder and Gerd Junne, *European Multinationals in the Telecommunications Industry*, Amsterdam, University of Amsterdam, for Institute for Research and Information on Multinationals, Geneva, 1984 (mimeo); Jill Hills, *Information Technology and Industrial Policy*, Beckenham, Croom Helm, 1984.

28. Peter Robinson, op. cit.

29. *Financial Times*, 13 September 1985.

30. MDN (Managed Data Networks) are variants of basic data communi-

cations. see: revised proposals on VAN: Department of Trade and Industry, London, 1 January 1986 (mimeo).
31. ITU, *The Missing Link*, Report of the Independent Commission for World-wide Telecommunications Development, December 1984, pp. 3–17 demonstrates that nearly three-quarters of the world's population live in countries with telephone densities of less than ten per hundred people. Three-quarters of the world's telephones are concentrated in nine industrialised countries. Tokyo has more telephones than the whole of the African continent.

1 Regulation, deregulation and privatisation—the arguments

The movement towards deregulation

Deregulation, that is a movement away from the regulation of capitalist enterprises by governments has become a world wide phenomenon of the 1980s. In the industrialised West the movement has coincided with the coming to power of right-wing governments. In the United States, in Britain and in Canada also, deregulation is identified with the Reagan administration, the Thatcher government and the Mulroney government. In all three countries market oriented governments have seen deregulation as a means to promote competition and efficiency in their domestic markets and to stimulate them by such competition.

For the Reagan and Thatcher administrations, deregulation is also linked to the issue of political freedom. To these liberal-conservative regimes personal liberty comes with 'freedom from' state interference in private actions. In this context government regulation of the activity of private individuals acting as entrepreneurs rates as political interference. The less the scope of state economic activity, the less regulation in markets, the more these governments consider that political freedoms are extended.

In America this movement towards deregulation of business has built upon the traditional hostility of businessmen towards their state. Beliefs among American businessmen that state regulation costs them money and time which is wasteful and unprofitable are deeprooted.[1] This perceived antipathy between state and business is less evident in Britain, where regulation tends to be based on more consensual bargaining mechanisms.[2] Nevertheless deregulation has been met in Britain with approval from most of the business community, although there has been acknowledgement of the fine line which separates business's liberty from licence to exploit. In both countries the movement has been coupled with hostility to bureaucratic growth, seen as concomitant to the increased regulatory atmosphere of the post-war world. Cuts in bureaucracy and cuts in regulation have gone hand in hand.

But the movement to deregulation has not been confined to those nations headed by liberal-conservative regimes, or dominated by a culture of liberalism and individuality. In Japan where state and business have long, close, historic ties, where bureaucracy has higher status than business and where there is little regard for individualism or liberalism, the Nakasone administration has sought to cut bureaucracy and has privatised both telecommunications and rail transport. And, in developing countries, in South America, Africa and Asia, governments have been selling state owned assets to the private sector.[4]

The reasons for this seemingly odd movement (developing countries would normally be expected to wish to control larger, rather than smaller parts of their economies) rests with the world economic situation. The influence of monetarist policies in the industrialised world, the political pressure of the United States on international lending institutions, cutbacks in aid to the Third World and the burdens of their external debts brought on by the high value of the dollar, have coalesced to increase pressure on domestic spending. In Japan also it is the ideas of monetarist economics which have produced the 'small government is best' policies of the Nakasone government.

These ideas have been brought into favour in the industrialised West by the seemingly intractable problems of a world recession and its domestic consequences. Keynesian economics with its promise that governments might control their national economies through the manipulation of demand and supply, which had formed the basis of much post-war economic management, became discredited in a recession of world-wide proportions. The oil crises of 1974 and 1979 and their inflationary impact on the industrialised West and Japan began a period of retrenchment in economic management. Those smaller nations which attempted to spend their way out of the recession, as did the socialist government in France, soon found themselves forced into deflation of their economies to counter the run on their currency which ensued. Attention became concentrated on the extent and cost of the public sector. Cuts in public spending became the major focus of austerity packages in both the developed and developing worlds.

According to monetarist economics, expenditure by the state fuels government borrowing from the private money markets, which, in turn, raises interest rates and squeezes out 'productive' investment. The alternative—that government should print money to cover its deficit— is seen as fuelling inflation. The control of inflation being the primary target, cuts in public expenditure follow. At the same time it is assumed that lower interest rates will lead to more investment in industry, while unemployment keeps wages down, thereby increasing industry's productivity. Due to the more open post-war international economy in which the industrialised countries primarily compete for exports to each other and to third markets, productivity has become a salient political issue. In addition, it is argued that cuts in public expenditure open the way to cuts in personal taxes and in corporation tax, thereby increasing companies' propensity to invest.

In fact much of this monetarist scenario has been made nonsense of by the actions of governments to defend their exchange rates, and by the American increased budgetary deficit, which has in true Keynesian fashion engined the world economic recovery. But, while acting to increase its own budgetary deficit, the Reagan administration has preached financial rectitude to the rest of the world through the World Bank and the International Monetary Fund. For those countries with dollar debts, the high value of the dollar against their own currencies has threatened bankruptcy. For those, such as Japan, who have the manufacturing capacity to meet demand in the United States the low value of the yen against the dollar has enabled increased import penetration and the export of capital generated into the buying of American companies or investment in green-field sites in the United States. At the same time Japanese monetarist policies at home have kept down domestic demand for imports.

During the period that high interest rates in the United States have been made necessary to finance the increasing budget deficit, the high value of the dollar has affected American industry's ability to export. Those who have benefited have been those who could supply cheaper goods to the American market than the Americans could themselves and who could supply cheaper goods to third markets. Where the exchange rate was kept artificially high, as in Britain, export prices remained high, exports fell and manufacturing industry retrenched, shedding labour. That retrenchment was further exacerbated by government action to reduce public expenditure. As demand abroad fell so did demand at home, leading to further retrenchment by industry, further unemployment and further reduced taxation resources for the government.[5]

It is within this world scenario and its relation both to the ideology of liberalism and to that of monetarist economics that the movement towards deregulation and privatisation needs to be seen. One method of cutting public expenditure is to sell off state owned assets to the private sector. Where the level of the public sector borrowing requirement or budget deficit is considered to be the touchstone of anti-inflationary policy or is used as the touchstone for development aid, the sale of state assets presents several advantages. Sales produce income which can be used in the short-term to reduce the deficit. They also preclude the need for further investment in the enterprise. Hence some state-owned enterprises have been sold specifically because of their need for future investment capital.

The obvious disadvantages are that enterprises (if already profitable) will not generate future income for the state sector. Also, in order for the sales to go ahead, if the enterprise is unprofitable or is burdened by accumulated debt, the government may have to write off many years of public investment. It will also need to pay consultancy fees to stock-brokers to launch the issue. In addition, there is the problem of putting the enterprise up for sale at a reasonable price—too high a price may lead to a shortfall in the sale, too low a price may result in windfall profits. Both have happened in Britain.[6]

A further problem occurs in small countries, where the market may be too small for more than one enterprise to operate profitably. It may be necessary for the government to grant monopoly concessions to the newly privatised company, or to make concessions on import restrictions. This problem is of particular importance in developing countries, but a conflict of interest between making a successful sale and providing a competitive environment is evident also in Britain. The Conservative election manifesto of 1983 stated:

Merely to replace state monopolies by private ones would be to waste an historic opportunity. So we will take steps to ensure that these new firms do not exploit their powerful positions to the detriment of consumers or their competitors.[7]

Despite these fine words, as we shall see later, the conflict between a successful sale on the one hand and the restriction of the privatised company's ability to act as a monopoly, was to be resolved in favour of a successful sale.

The desire of the British government to fund public revenue expenditure from capital is an important reason for the ongoing sales of British public assets to the private sector, just as it is in countries as diverse as Togo, Brazil, Bangladesh and Turkey. In contrast, in Japan, where the sale of NTT will take place over several years, it does not seem to have been primarily motivated by a desire to gain relief for the government's budgetary accounting. In Japan, as in Britain, other reasons are cited for the benefits of deregulation and privatisation. But before discussing those arguments we need first to discuss what is meant by 'regulation', 'deregulation' and 'privatisation' and what the existing literature has to tell us about who benefits from each.

Regulation and deregulation—what are they?

Regulation can be defined as the substitution of rules made by government for the competition of the market.[8] Regulation can either involve setting the framework in which private enterprises operate, or it can mean detailed intervention in their affairs through the setting of their rates of return, or their tariffs or by decisions on which particular enterprises can enter a particular market, or what services may be offered.

In Europe detailed intervention of this kind is normally associated with public ownership of the enterprise, but the two do not always go together. For instance Cable and Wireless was a wholly publicly owned company for many years yet the British government had no greater input into its strategies than the appointment of a Chairman and a couple of directors, whose responsibility was to the company not the government. On the other hand British Leyland, which is a privately owned company heavily reliant on government financial backing, has had very detailed state intervention in its affairs.

Public ownership and regulation are not necessarily the same thing. Nor is privatisation of a public enterprise necessarily a form of deregulation—it depends on the legal and day to day relationship between the enterprise and government institutions before and after its sale to the private sector. Where monopoly rights or near monopoly rights are given by government to the newly privatised enterprise, the traditional economic arguments for regulation remain. Privatisation of itself does not necessarily alter the need for public control. The major difference is that whereas under public ownership the exact extent of regulation may be hidden, the regulation of a private monopoly may be more open—and therefore more rigid. For government, public ownership gives more flexibility and more bargaining power, whereas for the regulated enterprise there is more uncertainty. Once the rules become public and codified, government comes under pressure to alter the rules in favour of certain interests and it tends to have less flexibility. Hence the systems of regulation adopted in both Britain and Japan attempt to retain the flexibility and power of central government by retaining discretionary power to ministers and bureaucrats.

Reasons for regulation

The reasons for the regulation of private enterprises vary and can roughly be categorised into 'social' and 'economic'. 'Social' regulation may be intended to safeguard those interests which the market cannot be expected to meet through the operation of the profit motive. Profit based private enterprises cannot be expected of their own accord to finance uneconomic activities voluntarily. Nevertheless these uneconomic activities may be regarded as important by the community at large. For instance, it may be considered advantageous to the community at large to have rail transport or telephone service in rural areas, although the provision of these services might be uneconomic in terms of the returns on the necessary capital investment. Before AT&T's break-up and before BT's or NTT's privatisation all were under an obligation to provide telephone service to everyone without discrimination. Although AT&T provided few telephones to rural areas, both BT and NTT charged less than the true costs of installation. The effect was a subsidy or transfer of wealth from one set of customers to another.

Another example of 'social' regulation is contained in the bill under which Japanese NTT was privatised. NTT has five research labs which are considered to do work that is an asset to the national economy. Under the legislation which privatised NTT it was forced to retain its research facilities, and part of the sale profits may be devoted to supporting its long-term research.

A second reason for 'social' regulation is the cost to society of 'externalities'—the unpleasant side-effects of profit making. Since the Second World War there has been an enormous increase in this type of social regulation, with all the industrialised countries regulating safety at work, safety to consumers, waste disposal, pollution and so on although the extent and efficacy of this regulation varies from country to country as does the style also. In Europe the style of this regulation tends to be more consensual than in the United States where it tends to be more legalistic, but in all cases this kind of social regulation places the cost and responsibility for 'externalities' onto the producer.[9]

Economic regulation can also roughly be divided into two kinds. On the one hand governments may act to establish rules which make the market function better, the assumption being that a truly competitive market is that which most benefits the consumer. So, for instance, the anti-trust laws in America and Japan and the Monopolies Commission and Fair Trade Authority in Britain act to prevent detrimental loss of competition in a market through mergers and takeovers, or through price fixing and cartels. Secondly, governments have traditionally taken it upon themselves to regulate the activities of particular enterprises where there is a 'natural monopoly' of the market which puts consumers at risk of exploitation.

A 'natural monopoly' is said to exist where the economies of scale are such that to have more than one company in the market would increase unit costs to an extent that would be detrimental to consumers. Traditionally industries where what are known as 'sunk costs' are heavy tend to be considered 'natural monopolies'. So, for instance, both railways and telecommunications demand a great deal of infrastructural investment in terms of local lines or networks which cannot be used for anything else and so are said to have heavy 'sunk costs' and have been considered 'natural monopolies'.[10]

Traditional economic theory suggests that perfect competition in a market in which prices to the consumer will be lowered to the point at which they meet marginal costs of production will only occur if there are numerous companies in competition. If one enterprise has a monopoly of the market its behaviour is likely to be exploitative to consumers and prices will be fixed considerably above costs. For this reason 'natural' monopolies have been considered to be in need of government regulation. Regulation by government is intended to stop monopoly pricing and to benefit the consumer by lowering prices. What is in effect taking place is a transfer of wealth inasmuch as regulation is intended to benefit the consumer at the expense of the producer.[11]

There is however a trade off between monopoly and government within the regulatory process. The cost to the monopoly is in foregoing monopoly pricing but at the same time it gains because regulation prevents the entry of any competitors into its monopoly market. In the United States for instance, the Federal Communications Commission has been asked on numerous occasions to determine whether another company's service or equipment infringed AT&T's monopoly. From 1934 to 1956 AT&T's monopoly remained intact. Deregulation of the transmission market started at that point in 1956 when the FCC, in its *Above 890 decision,* allowed private companies their own microwave telecommunications service, and in the equipment market in 1956 when, in the Hush-a Phone case, the Courts decided that 'foreign' equipment could be used in conjunction with Western Electric telephones (see Chapter Three).

The question then arises: when does a natural monopoly become an unnatural monopoly? New technology can alter what seemed to be a natural monopoly into one which is unjustifiable on economic grounds. If new technology makes it economic for a competitor company to enter the market without incurring higher costs than the original company, then should it not be allowed to do so? For instance, if satellites by broadcasting to individual customers' receivers bypass the heavy sunk costs of local networks, can a natural monopoly be said to exist? Or if the market for equipment expands or diversifies to such an extent that it can accommodate two or more companies without affecting unit prices then presumably a natural monopoly can no longer be said to exist.

To sum up, regulation by government of industry is intended to effect a transfer of wealth from one group to another. In general, that transfer is intended to take place from producers to consumers, and regulation is intended to benefit the consumer. Sometimes the regulation will be deemed to be 'social' inasmuch as it is intended to benefit all consumers by forcing industry to meet needs which are uneconomic, whether these are for certain services or to compensate for the socially detrimental effects of its activities. Sometimes the regulation can be described as 'economic' because it either seeks to make the market work better, or it seeks to control pricing activities of monopoly enterprises.

In fact it is often difficult to separate social and economic regulation. American regulators in particular have seemed to prefer across the board tariffs, rather than tariffs which are discriminatory and profit maximising for the regulated entity. In turn, average pricing may carry hidden cross-subsidies from one consumer to another. In undertaking economic regulation of a natural monopoly the regulators also undertake social regulation of a hidden nature. And this transfer of resources from one group to another may go on for years without any public discussion of the rights and wrongs of such a transfer. Part of the movement towards deregulation in telecommunications transmission can be traced to the profound dissatisfaction of business users who felt that they were losing out to residential consumers within this hidden social regulation.[12]

Deregulation involves the substitution of market competition for the decisions of regulators. Access to a regulated market may be opened, as in the case of telecommunications terminal equipment, on the grounds that it is no longer a natural monopoly. Such liberalisation in the case of publicly owned industries may be followed by their transfer to the private sector. The fear by new competitors of hidden cross-subsidy of services within a state corporation provides a motivation for this privatisation.

Yet the problems for regulators do not end with mere liberalisation and privatisation. Where monopolies have operated for numbers of years, their market share, even after access of competition is allowed, may be dominant. Such dominance may be seen both by its competitors and by consumers as a threat demanding some form of transitionary regulation. John Meyer and William Tye suggest that the:

demands for some form of temporary or continuing regulation during the transition to deregulation can be explained almost entirely as a response to the strength of the entry threat relative to the magnitude of sunk costs incurred by the affected parties in the previous regulatory regime.[13]

They argue that where access to the market after liberalisation is easy, the previously regulated incumbents will demand some form of protection through regulation, to allow them to recoup their sunk costs in infrastructure investment. Where market access continues to be difficult then it is customers who will demand some form of regulation to allow them to amortise their sunk costs. In addition they might have added that where access is difficult, demands for continued regulation will also come from new entrants. The first problem to be met in this transitionary phase is that of who is to bear the overhang of these existing sunk costs.[14]

The problem is compounded by the social regulatory aspects of previous regulation, where tariffs charged may have borne no relation to the actual costs of the provision of services. To allow immediate profit orientated price discrimination of services may impose increased costs on one particular set of consumers, which may be judged unfair. In the United States, the question of what 'access' charges should be imposed on residential consumers, who AT&T claimed had been subsidised by business under the previous regulatory regime, became an issue following the breakup of AT&T. The FCC decided that local consumers should in future bear all the costs of the existing sunk investment in the local network in any one geographical area. In Britain, BT's privatisation has been followed by a regulatory system under which it has undertaken not to raise the price of residential rentals each year more than two points above the rate of inflation, thereby spreading over time a similar loading of sunk costs in the local network onto the residential consumer. Under both systems the intention is to spread 'cost pricing' over a number of years, although the specific 'costs' calculated may be disputed as well as the method of distribution.[15]

At the present time therefore, the deregulation of telecommunications transmission actually involves a new regulatory regime. In

Britain and Japan this re-regulatory regime is imposed on the newly privatised entities, whereas in America it is imposed on the newly broken up AT&T and its operating companies. In none of the three countries has deregulation meant no regulation. But because of the mechanisms of regulation in Britain and Japan the actual distribution of resources implied by the term 'deregulation' away from those subsidised under the previous regime, has been more hidden than in the United States. On the whole customers in Britain are still made aware of shifts in tariff structures only after the event. Tariff rates have not yet been adjusted in Japan to the new liberalised transmission market, but there the unit price of ¥10 is set by legislation making it more difficult to offload the sunk costs of the existing local network onto local callers.[16] In general, however, interim regulation after liberalisation is no more than a mechanism for the redistribution of existing costs.

Regulatory institutions

The actual form that the institutional setting of regulation and re-regulation takes is likely to reflect the historical traditions of state/industry relations in the country concerned and the power of the relevant bureaucracies. In Japan, where state and industry have been close historically and where the bureaucracy has high status, regulation of NTT, prior to privatisation, was undertaken by the Ministry of Posts and Telecommunications (MPT) subject to laws passed by the Diet, and by the Diet itself. Post-privatisation re-regulation is undertaken by the Ministry alone but on a much wider scale.

In Britain pre-privatisation regulation of telecommunications was similarly undertaken by the Department of Industry. Post-liberalisation regulation was also undertaken by the Department, but it proved unequal to the task of controlling BT's new found powers. Post-privatisation regulation is shared between the Department, which sets the rules, and a new semi-independent agency, the Office of Telecommunications (OFTEL) which applies the Department's rules and makes regulatory decisions concerning BT's anti-competitive behaviour. The Director of OFTEL is appointed by the government and it has a small staff of ninety. But it is not constructed along the lines of the Federal Communications Commission inasmuch as it has little autonomous power, nor jurisdiction over broadcasting or radio or the entertainment side of cable TV. Semi-autonomous agencies are a favourite mechanism of British governments when they wish to distance themselves from unpopular decisions, but they have a habit of developing autonomy in such a fashion as to become an embarassment to government.[17]

The United States has a tradition of regulation by independent agency, operating under the general rubric provided by legislation passed by Congress and under the review of the courts. The Federal Communications Commissioners are appointed by the President subject to ratification by Congress and since 1934 have been responsible for the regulation of telecommunications, radio and TV. The courts have often ruled through anti-trust action in a way which would be inimicable in either Britain or Japan, but which has kept the identification of the FCC with AT&T's interests under some control. Most recently it was under such anti-trust action that AT&T was divested of its operating companies, but it is unusual that those companies' activities are still, post-divestiture, being regulated by the court, whereas AT&T's are regulated by the FCC. It is also evident that whereas pre-divestiture regulation was divided between FCC on interstate services and the state public commissioners on intrastate, the divestiture has opened space enough for the FCC to extend its regulatory decisions to intrastate matters. As in Britain and Japan deregulation has provided the opportunity for the wider exercise of power by the central bureaucracy.

It is noticeable however that in recent years the FCC has actually opted out of regulating all the companies in the telecommunications transmission market, preferring to allow competitors of AT&T to be self-regulating.[18] Self-regulation is obviously a cheap form of regulation, demanding voluntary decisions by the regulated enterprises that they will behave within certain guidelines. In Britain the mechanism has been used particularly within the insurance and banking industries and within the professions, all occupying elite status positions where statutory controls have been powerfully resisted. Self-regulation implies that the industry will be conscientious in prosecuting offenders, an unlikely process at the best of times. The abdication of regulation is justified in economic terms where competition can take over from regulation. But abdication may also imply a weak or overloaded bureaucracy, or perhaps a bureaucracy interested only in symbolic action. The FCC regulation of private competitors to Intelsat will be on a self-regulatory basis.

These four methods represent the different forms of regulation which are evident in the telecommunications market in the three countries—public ownership coupled with Ministry regulation; private ownership coupled with Ministry regulation; private ownership coupled with regulation by a government appointed agency and self-regulation. Each has given rise to arguments concerning who benefits from regulation.

Who benefits from regulation?

Economic regulation is intended to act for the benefit of the consumer by creating lower prices than the monopoly would create without regulation. A number of American academics have challenged this view, arguing that the consumer is unrepresented or ignored in the regulatory process, that regulation is ineffective in reducing prices and that the process of regulation benefits the regulated industry or the bureaucracy which regulates it. We shall take these arguments one by one.[19]

There seems little doubt that the consumer finds it difficult to gain a hearing within the regulatory process, whether that regulation is of a private or publicly owned company. A previous FCC commissioner, Richard Johnson has given examples of the FCC's refusal to acknowledge the standing of consumer groups in its decisions to license broadcasting stations until it was ruled against by the courts.[20] In Britain consumer watchdog bodies, often created by legislation and appointed by government to provide some consumer input into the regulation of publicly owned industries, have traditionally had only a marginal advisory function, consulted after decisions have been announced. The Bill which privatised BT transferred the functions of the Post Office Users National Council (POUNC) to the newly created OFTEL agency. Rather than having even a marginal say as a group in overall policy, consumers became dealt with individually on the basis of complaints. And in Japan consumers have always been difficult to organise across traditional group and company allegiances.

The problem is partly that there is no 'general interest' which is represented by all consumers. Business and residential customers are both consumers of telecommunications services. Each has a different interest in reduced rates for the services which it uses most; international business for international traffic; domestic business for trunk calls and residential callers for local calls. In the long-term their only common interest is in low charges for access to the network, but in the short-term none wishes to pay increased usage charges to retain that universal network.

Sam Peltzman argues that all parties to regulation, both producers and consumers, are short-changed by the regulatory process in that bureaucracies will tend to reject cost-based price discrimination in favour of unitary tariff structures, which will be more than competitive cost prices but less than monopoly prices.[21] His argument ignores the fact that consumers are not an undifferentiated mass and that tariff structures benefit some more than others. Where there is true unitary tariff pricing, although John Meyer and his associates argue that there never has been such pricing in the United States, then those who benefit are likely to be those who live in areas where the infra-structural investment cannot be repaid through the traffic generated.[22] In Intelsat's unitary pricing the revenue from the 'thick' routes of the cross Atlantic traffic are said to benefit the 'thin' routes to poorer countries. Nevertheless, because access charges to Intelsat in the shape of expensive ground station equipment are high, the poor benefit less than they might. Unitary tariffs coupled with cheap access charges are most likely to benefit the rural, poorest and least developed areas and countries and the poorest individuals.

There are those who argue that economic regulation is simply another method of transferring wealth from one group to another and that this should be explicit, rather than hidden. They contend that the ending of economic regulation involves the state in making social regulation public through direct subsidies to uneconomic services. In both the United States and Britain deregulation and privatisation of telecommunications has resulted in the idea of social funds to offset the cost of uneconomic rural services and in Britain to offset the costs of emergency services. Some economists argue that if governments want to subsidise residential telephone subscribers then they should do so openly with a subsidy and that all services should be based on cost.[23]

The first quantitative evidence against the benefits of regulation was presented by George Stigler in the 1960s. He argued that the regulation of utilities made no difference in prices to the consumer. His argument was that regulators failed to regulate, whereas they are expected to reduce prices to the level covering marginal costs.[24] Since his work the difficulties of regulating such monopolies as AT&T, where it is impossible to discern exactly how much any one service costs, have become evident.[25] Similar problems face OFTEL, the British regulatory body for telecommunications, in trying to establish whether BT is cross-subsidising a service.[26]

This problem of actually determining how much any service costs is particularly important where a market has been partially deregulated. In telecommunications transmission the major sunk costs come in local networks. Long-distance transmission has fewer sunk costs involved, so competition is likely to want to enter on that long-distance transmission. If competition is allowed on these long-lines or trunk lines, one question then facing the regulators is whether the monopoly should be allowed to reduce prices to meet that of the competition and what are the true costs of the service? Where some services are subject to competition and others are not then the interests of the regulated entity are in off-loading costs onto its regulated service.[27] In Britain when a public corporation, BT, made a loss on equipment sales, thereby opening itself to accusations from the manufacturers that it subsidised this service.[28]

A second set of economic criticisms of regulation point to the ineffectiveness of such a system in fostering innovation and thereby reducing costs.[29] It is argued that the monopoly gains by depreciating equipment over a long time period if it is regulated by a mechanism which allows it to make a percentage return on the capital it has invested. Depreciating capital equipment over a long time period allows it to keep what is called its rate-base high and so inhibits the introduction of more modern technology. In Britain it seems that the poor service given by the Post Office to financial institutions in the City who wanted to upgrade their technological capacity was a major factor in pressure for the liberalisation of its monopoly.[30]

Depreciation over a long time period also produces lower prices, hence one of the first actions of BT, when faced with privatisation was to speed up its depreciation. In the United States AT&T has blamed higher prices to residential consumers on faster depreciation of the local network.[31] But a further problem for regulators enters at the point of new investment. A rate of return form of regulation actually encourages monopolies to invest in over-capacity of hardware on which they gain regulated returns. How are regulators to know whether the network is being used efficiently, or whether any particular network configuration is in the best interests of consumers? The relative trade-offs between cost and quality are political, not technical decisions, yet are dependent on information provided by the monopoly supplier. As a public corporation, BT denied the British Government access to such information, and it is not yet clear that OFTEL will have the power or resources to undertake such investigations.[32]

Another set of criticisms revolve around the reputation of monopolies for being unwilling to meet the needs of the consumer. They are said to be inflexible and bureaucratic, dictating to rather than responding to the market. This charge was levelled at NTT by large users. And one of the major problems facing both AT&T and BT has been to alter their corporate cultures to suit service industries in a competitive environment.[33] Critics therefore argue that competition increases new services and produces greater innovation than a monopoly market.

Yet another set of critics of regulation argue that monopolies may in fact not need regulation in order to stop them exploiting their market dominance with monopoly prices. They argue that the monopolies may already face competition from other monopolies. For instance, although gas may be a monopoly it faces competition from electricity so it will not charge monopoly prices. Recently some members of the American administration have argued that dominant market share does not necessarily bring monopoly power.[34] A further argument is that the best way of regulating a monopoly is to allow it to bid for a franchise for a limited period. The monopoly then has to be competitive in order to gain the franchise.[35]

Economists have also presented arguments based on political analysis to show that consumers do not benefit from regulation. George Stigler followed up his work on utilities with a general theory of regulation. He argued that the bargaining process involved in regulation contained a transfer of wealth between producers and consumers in which the producers always came out best. He based his argument on the bargaining process between regulators and regulated. He contended that the numerically large, but diffuse group of consumers all of whom had a small per capita stake in the outcome of regulation were inevitably outlobbied by the numerically small, compact group of producers, all of whom had a large per capita stake in the outcome. In other words organisational and cost constraints impose a limit on the group size of those who can be successful in the political bargaining process and those constraints favour the producers.[36]

Stigler's work has been followed by others who argue that regulatory agencies have been 'captured' by the producers they are intended to regulate. Such behaviour on the part of the bureaucracies has been variously termed 'clientelism' or 'producer protection'. Much of the evidence, as Paul Quirk has pointed out, tends to rest on assumptions (unspoken) of what the agency would have done without industry influence. Within these critiques there is often an unspoken normative stance on what should have been done—what was in the 'public interest' at that time.[37]

Nevertheless there are a variety of studies which suggest undue influence of regulated industry in regulatory decisions, and a considerable range of overlapping explanations as to why or when this influence occurs. Some commentators emphasise the interdependence of regulators and regulated, where regulators rely on the regulated for information or to work out standards and rules within the general legal framework laid down by Congress or Parliament. Others emphasise the way in which agencies are judged on their success in terms of how their regulated industry flourishes. Detailed intervention in the industry's affairs actually gives the regulator a stake in the industry.[38] In Britain, OFTEL's newly appointed director stated that:

> I want to make sure that BT serves its customers effectively, meets competition fairly and with a sense of economic responsibility, plays its part in developing the UK technological base, accepts its social obligations to the nation. But within these constraints I also want BT to prosper.'[39]

Yet others explain the influence of the regulated in terms of agency structure, arguing that regulatory agencies in the United States may be isolated from the main branches of governments and are therefore more susceptible to industry pressure, although these hypotheses are refuted by others.[40]

A further explanation has concentrated on the actual rulemaking function of the federal agencies and their blend of legislative, executive and judicial functions. Agencies tend to work on a case-by-case decision basis, and this case-by-case approach is said to be more prone to industry influence than would be general across the board decision-making, which would involve interests other than the particular companies concerned in the case decisions. Marver Bernstein and Horace Gray point to the predominantly reactive powers of the agencies—the fact that they have to wait for a complaint or request before acting—and their lack of planning and forward thinking as the main reason for industry influence.[41] Yet in Britain OFTEL started its life by actively soliciting complaints on BT's anti-competitive behaviour so that it might investigate and act, suggesting that the use of given power is as important as the formal structure of that power.

Other explanations have centred on the life-cycle of agencies, stressing that a new agency with popular backing is able to adopt a stronger stance towards its regulated industry than one which has been in being a long time. It has been said that OFTEL gained in authority in its initial advice to the British government from the fact that it was a new agency which government could not afford to undermine. A similar argument can be made about changes in personnel within agencies. It could be argued that new strong chairmen may promote the agency image as a defender of the public interest or, as Mark Fowler of the FCC has done use the agency chairmanship to promote the concept of deregulation, although his critics point out that until the 1980s the FCC's decisions tended to be anti-competitive rather than pro-competitive.[42] There seems little doubt that regulatory atmosphere is affected by the general political atmosphere, with swings in public favour towards regulation and deregulation and that by the latter 1970s opinion had swung away from regulation.

Some explanations of industry influence on regulatory decisions are more particular in suggesting specific gains to be made by regulators. Undue influence can be bought informally through private entertainment and socialising, which make it harder to be aggressive in public. In America there is also the possibility that disgruntled regulated industries may lobby Congress to oppose the regulators' reappointment. In Japan fear of American pressure can bring anticipated reactions from MPT officials. There is also the possibility that regulators may be primarily concerned that such disgruntled industry lobbying could result in budgetary cuts for the agency or that regulators may expect appointments within the regulated industry as their next career step. Quirk produces some empirical evidence from a survey of bureaucratic attitudes to suggest that in some, but not all agencies, prospective careers may influence regulators behaviour.[43]

In Britain where civil servants tend to be the major regulators of industry, for two years after retirement civil servants are not supposed to enter an industry with which they have had dealings. The intention of the rule is to preclude a conflict of interest between present action and future career, but in recent years the guidelines have been regularly breached. In Japan the fact that civil servants retire at fifty into industries which they have regulated has long been a matter of public concern, and is said to be a factor in the close relationship between bureaucrats and industry.[44]

Another set of critics of regulation argue that bureaucratic actions will be aimed primarily at defending their position, in extending their territory, building empires and increasing regulation. Peltzman argues that the regulators will always prefer to set across-the-board prices rather than have a variety of cost-priced services. not because of consumer pressure, but because of bureaucrats' desire to build a broad-based coalition. Cross-subsidisation is an attempt by regulators to keep this broad-based coalition behind them. He argues that they will inevitably tend to suppress cost differences between different services as a matter of course. According to this argument the regulators primarily use regulation to favour their own political survival.[45]

Working from the perspective of organisational and administrative theory others suggest that changes in the behaviour of regulatory agencies are brought about by changes within the environment in which they work. For instance if the regulated industry changes rapidly then regulators are likely to demand increased information from the industry on the grounds that ignorance is the worst crime possible for regulators. Their uncertainty then results in increased flows of information which the regulators may not be able to handle. Commenting on the FCC from a British perspective in 1983 Michael Beesley noted: 'The inference from inconsistency in its decisions is that the regulatory body, faced with an ever-increasing and burgeoning technological sphere cannot respond effectively.'[46] From an American perspective Florence Heffron argues that the FCC's movement towards deregulation of telecommunications reflected an attempt to exert control over its environment. She argues that technological advances brought uncertainties into the FCC's workload, with pressure for entry into AT&T's monopoly from different industries and dissatisfaction from some consumers. Heffron says that the FCC attempted to hold back these technological developments, but as the pressure became more intense the only way for the agency to regain some control over its environment was to deregulate. Her analysis suggests that once regulation had become fraught with perpetual challenges, deregulation benefited the regulators. Her conclusions echo studies of other organisations faced with changing environments which may meet those changes at first with hostility and greater authoritarianism and then with changes in organisational procedures. Her interpretation of events suggests that the regulators eventually benefited more from deregulation than regulation.[47] Similarly in both Britain and Japan regulators initially gained in power.

Privatisation

The question of who benefits from regulation or deregulation has hardly been explored in either Britain or Japan. In Britain the major proponents of deregulation have been economists arguing for privatisation of publicly owned enterprises. In the words of two such influentials:

privately owned companies have a greater incentive to produce goods and services in the quantity and variety which consumers prefer ... Resources tend to be used as consumers dictate rather than according to the wishes of government, which must necessarily reflect short-term political pressures and problems of managing the public sector's overall demands for capital. '[48]

They argued that privatisation would produce benefits to the consumer, both indirect by reductions in taxation and direct, by greater choice and lower prices and increased efficiency. On the question of whether publicly owned industries are efficient, the evidence from British experience is unclear. Partly the problem is the difficulty of comparison. Those enterprises which were denationalised first by the Thatcher government were also, with one exception, profitable—suggesting that publicly owned industries do not necessarily have to be inefficient. Recent figures for those privatised enterprises, most of which show increased profits, do not therefore really prove anything, particularly since most of the managers are the same as when the companies were publicly owned.[49]

Efficiency has sometimes been equated with a shedding of labour of the privatised industry. In Japan, one of the arguments put forward for the privatisation of NTT was that it was overmanned and inefficient, although its return on capital was as good as its privatised counterpart, KDD. In other words, inefficiency, low returns on capital and overmanning, may well reflect monopoly positions in a market and government tariff controls, rather than simply public ownership *per se*. In Britain however the role of the public sector trade unions has been antagonistic to the Thatcher government and privatisation is a mechanism for the reduction in public sector union power and an easing of the public sector pay bargaining process.[50]

Much of the argument in both Britain and Japan has centered around the benefits of privatisation as against public control and relatively little attention has been given to the problems of regulation of the private monopolies thereby created.[51] Privatisation has been seen as a means of ending government interference in the enterprises, yet it has not solved the problem of how a centralised state lives with autonomous companies which affect its policies. Michael Beesley and Stephen Littlechild suggest structural controls through the introduction of competition, rather than through profit-based regulation of a monopoly, but fail to grasp the nettle of how government regulates dominant firms in the intervening period, or who benefits from deregulation in a small domestic market.[52] The British government is already finding conflicts of interest between the shareholders, residential customers, domestic business customers, international business, and traditional telecommunications suppliers of BT.[53]

British academic economists and Conservative politicians have tended to view all activities within the present public sector as suitable candidates for privatisation. However translating recent American work on monopoly behaviour into the British context, Glyn Davies and John Davies argue that whereas traditional economic theory emphasises the ease of entry into a monopoly market, the real problems of entry are related to the cost of capital and to the ease of possible exit. They argue that to expect private industry to choose to sink money into fixed infrastructure for which there is no alternative use is unrealistic—a factor which is of obvious significance in the wiring necessary for cable TV or the local distribution networks necessary for telecommunications transmission to local subscribers.[55]

The theory suggests that prospective competitors to monopolies face huge up-front cash outlays and thereby high exit costs unless alternative uses can be found for the infrastructural investment. One can argue that satellite technology, microwaves and optic fibres have made these costs less onerous and that telecommunications and cable broadcasting provide alternative uses for the same networks. But given the scale of investment needed to set up alternative local distribution networks, it would seem unlikely that private enterprise would voluntarily undertake such massively expensive investment. Hence the theory suggests that while it may be possible to introduce competition on long-distance transmission where up-front costs are lower it is unlikely that such competition will enter the local networks.

Some empirical justification is given to this theory from experience in Britain. Private enterprise was loathe to take on the up-front investment needed for cable TV, even in heavily populated urban areas, until it became evident that cable companies might link with BT's competitor Mercury, to provide telecommunications transmission services in the future. And Mercury itself, despite government pressure, refused to extend its proposed trunk service to an alternative local network. Its investors were unwilling to commit any more money, and certainly not the £2 billion required for a local network, until they saw some returns on their investment. And experience in the United States with SBS suggests that the up-front costs of satellite competition to the established monopoly are greater than those originally anticipated.[56]

The implications of this experience are that competitors will continue to need access to the existing distribution networks and regulation will continue to be needed to ensure that entry and to ensure fair payment by those competitors for that right of entry. The problem then is, as MCI has found in America, that such payments create a burden on their services and reduce their profitability, thereby curtailing the investment needed to duplicate the existing network. The alternative, as has happened in Britain, is that entry is granted at a cut-price level in which case re-regulation involves a transfer of wealth from the dominant entry to the competitors—exactly the form of hidden cross-subsidy that privatisation and liberalisation was said to replace—leading to higher prices for the dominant entity's residential consumers. In Britain and the United States already and in Japan in the future deregulation is likely to involve a transfer of wealth from residential consumers to the shareholders of the dominant entity and its competitors and to those businesses, domestic and international who will benefit from lower prices and customised services.

In Britain opposition to deregulation and privatisation as in Japan came predominantly from trade unions and the socialist parties. Yet, surprisingly, in Britain there has been almost no discussion of possible methods of re-regulation which would ensure the protection of access to the network for the majority of people. The arguments have revolved around renationalisation and what form it should take. There has been virtually no discussion about BT's costings of its services, or its investment strategy or of the implications involved in increasing access charges to the network. Unlike the United States where Congress has become involved in the defence of a universal telecommunications service, in Britain the establishment of a semi-autonomous government agency to regulate the industry has effectively removed discussion from the parliamentary arena. And in Japan the public debate has hardly begun.

Whereas in America it has been recognised that increased residential charges for 'access' and increased bypass of the local network by large business users will increase the costs of those who remain, in Britain there is no such recognition. Yet BT itself estimated that a 10 per cent increase in residential rentals would produce a 2.5 per cent decrease in the network, whilst the Ministry seemed to accept happily that BT's liberalisation would result in 10 per cent increases in rentals due to competition, thereby implying a reduction in the network of more than 2 per cent and implying further increased costs for those residential consumers remaining.[57] The possibility of lowering access charges to increase the spread of the network has not been put forward as a method by which BT might increase its revenues and reduce costs to all consumers. Nor has government funding of access to underdeveloped areas been considered. While pressure was placed on Mercury to extend its trunk network to the north-east, Scotland and Wales—all suffering from economic recession—no public mention was made of the possibility of the government offering a subsidy in terms of social regulation. Hence while in the United States the Rural Development

Bank helps fund telephone access to rural communities, no such development aid exists in Britain.

Nor has there been any discussion by the Labour Opposition in Britain of the social justice issues raised by the exclusion of approximately one quarter of British households from access to a telephone, or their concentration in areas outside the south-east and in lower income economic groups. Whereas in the United States the cost of telephone service is computed within social security allowances, it is not considered a necessity in Britain. Although privatised BT operates a voluntary scheme of reduced charges for low usage (equivalent to the life-line services introduced post-divestiture in America) no socialist justification for regulation has been forthcoming in terms of equity or justice or on the basis of the cost barriers to access of whole sectors of the population either domestically or globally to any form of new technology.[58]

To conclude, while economists seek to peddle their wares on the basis that they are 'objective' truths, the reality of the situation is that they contain normative perspectives. Freedom within a deregulated telecommunications sector, without any form of regulation, is freedom for certain people to benefit from access to transmission facilities and the profits which go with that access. Freedom of choice refers to those consumers for whom competitive services are provided—not consumers as a whole. American research teaches us that regulation acts to the benefit of producers and bureaucrats. American and British experience teaches us empirically that privatisation and re-regulation acts for the benefit of shareholders in the dominant entities and large user companies and against the interests of domestic manufacturers and residential consumers. Japanese experience so far indicates that it is competitive suppliers who have benefited and local manufacturers who have lost under privatisation, but redistribution of existing network costs has not yet taken place.

Notes and references

1. Leonard Silk and David Vogel, Ethics and Profits. *The Crisis of Confidence in American Business*, New York, Simon & Schuster, 1976; *The Costs of Government Regulation to Business*, a study prepared for the use of the Subcommittee on Economic Growth and Stabilization of the Joint Economic Committee of Congress, 95th Congress, 2nd Session, 25–921, Washington D. C., Government Printing Office,1978.
2. See: Alan Peacock (ed.), *The Regulation Game*, Oxford, Basil Blackwell, 1984.

3. Leader, *Financial Times*, 17 July 1985.
4. Anatole Kaletsky, 'Everywhere the State is in Retreat', *Financial Times* 2 August 1985.
5. See: Peter Riddell, *The Thatcher Government*, Oxford, Martin Robertson, 1983.
6. Michael Smith, 'How Maggie sold us £2bn short', *Guardian*, 4 December 1984
7. Conservative Party Manifesto 1979 reprinted in *The Times Guide to the House of Commons*, London, Times Books, 1983.
8. I have taken this definition from Michael Moran, 'Theories of regulation and changes in regulation: the case of financial markets', paper to Political Studies' Annual Conference, Manchester, 1985.
9. On social and economic regulation see: James E. Anderson, 'Economic, Regulatory and Consumer Protection Policies' in Theodore J. Lowi and Alan Stone, *Nationalizing Government. Public Policies in America*, New York and London, Sage, 1978, pp. 61–84.
10. Harold Demsetz, 'Why Regulate Utilities?', *Journal of Law and Economics*, **11**, 1968, pp. 55–65.
11. Sam Peltzman, 'Towards a More General Theory of Regulation', *Journal of Law and Economics*, **XIX**, 2, August 1976, pp. 211–40; Stephen Breyer, *Regulation and its Reform*, Cambridge, Mass., Harvard University Press, 1982, pp. 15–36.
12. John deButts, interview, 'Telephone Monopoly: Good or Bad?', *US. News*, **81**, 22 November 1976, pp. 43–4.
13. John R. Meyer and William B. Tye, 'The Consequences of Deregulation in the Transportation and Telecommunications Sector', *The American Economic Review*, **75**, 2 May 1985, p. 46.
14. Ibid. pp. 46–51.
15. Roger G. Noll, 'Let Them Make Toll Calls: A State Regulator's Lament', *The American Economic Review*, **75**, 2 May 1985, pp. 52–56; Ben Johnson, 'By-passing the FCC: an Alternative Approach to Access Charges', *Public Utilities Fortnightly*, 7 March 1985, pp. 18–23.
16. NTT has not had any mechanism for 'costing' services, so there is no knowledge of possible changes in rates.
17. See for instance: Jill Hills, 'The Industrial Reorganisation Corporation'. The case of the GEC/AEI and GEC/English Electric Mergers', *Public Administration*, **59**, Spring 1981, pp. 63–84.
18. See: 'Remarks' by Dale N. Hatfield, Acting Asst. Sec. for Communications and Information, NTIA, in *Challenges in Telecommunications and Information Handling for the New Administration*, Washington, D. C., Center for Telecommunications Studies, George Washington University, 1981, pp. 204–9.
19. In writing the following part of this chapter I am indebted to the general overview of the literature contained in Michael Moran's unpublished paper cited above.
20. Quoted in: Morton Mintz and Jerry S. Cohen, *America Inc, Who Owns and Operates the United States*, London, Pitman, 1972, pp. 239–42.
21. Sam Peltzman, op. cit., p. 236.
22. John R. Meyer, Robert W. Wilson, M. Alan Baughcum, Ellen Burton,

Louis Caoulette, *The Economics of Competition in the Telecommunications Industry*, Cambridge, Mass., Oelgeschlager, Gunn & Hain, 1980, pp. 85–6, 172–6.

23. Michael Beesley and Stephen Littlechild, 'Privatization, Principles, Problems and Priorities', *Lloyds Bank Review*, July 1983, p. 8.

24. George Stigler and Claire Friedland, 'What Can Regulators Regulate? The Case of Electricity', *Journal of Law and Economics*, V, October 1962 reprinted in D. Grunewald and H. L. Bass, *Public Policy and The Modern Corporation*, New York, Appleton–Century–Crofts, 1966, pp. 147–67.

25. Majority Staff of the Subcommittee on Telecommunications, Consumer Protection and Finance of the Committee on Energy and Commerce, *Telecommunications in Transition: The Status of Competition in the Telecommunication Industry*, US. House of Representatives, 97th Congress, 1st Session, Washington D. C, Government Printing Office, 1981, p. 49.

26. Bryan Carsberg, 'OFTEL—The Challenge of the First Five Years', *Information Technology and Public Policy*, 4, 1, September 1985, p. 2.

27. *Telecommunications in Transition*, op. cit. p. 59.

28. On the relationship between manufacturers and BT, see Lord Weinstock, House of Lords' Debate, 16 January 1984, cols 859–63.

29. John R. Meyer *et al.*, op. cit., pp. 155–172

30. *The Future of Telecommunications in Britain*, Cmnd. 8610, London, HMSO, 1982, p. 4.

31. Charles Brown in testimony to Joint Hearings of Subcommittee on Telecommunications, Consumer Protection and Finance of the Committee on Energy and Commerce and Subcommittee on the Judiciary, 97th Congress, 2nd Session, HR 97-116, Washington D. C., Government Printing Office, 26 January 1982 argued that local rates for telephone service would increase partly because of faster depreciation, (p. 13.)

32. *Report of the Post Office Review Committee*, Cmnd. 6850, London, HMSO, 1977, p. 38.

33. See: Alvin Toffler, *The Adaptive Corporation*, Guildford and Kings Lynn, Gower, 1985; Jeremy Main, 'Waking up AT&T: There's Life After Culture Shock', *Fortune*, 24 December 1984, pp. 34–42; Sir George Jefferson, quoted in *The Sunday Times*, 28 October 84: 'My first aim was to change the prevailing ethos of a public administration in which morale was low, into a market responsive organization . . .'.

34. Commissioner Denis R. Patrick, 'On the Road to Telephone Deregulation', *Public Utilities Fortnightly*, 6 December 1984, pp. 19–21 argues large market share might mean superior economic performance.

35. John Vickers and George Yarrow, *Privatization and the Natural Monopolies*, London, Public Policy Centre, 1985, pp. 26–31.

36. George Stigler, 'The Theory of Economic Regulation', *Bell Journal of Economics and Management Science*, Spring 1971, pp. 3–21; George Stigler, *The Citizen and the State: Essays on Regulation*, Chicago, University of Chicago Press, 1975.

37. Paul J. Quirk, *Industry Influence in Federal Regulatory Agencies*, Princeton, New Jersey, Princeton University Press, 1981, *passim*.

38. See for instance: Louis M. Kohlmeier Jr., *The Regulators. Watchdog*

Agencies and the Public Interest, New York, Harper and Row, 1969; Marver Bernstein, *Regulating Business by Independent Commission*, Princeton, N. J., Princeton University Press, 1955.

39. Bryan Carsberg, op. cit., p. 2.

40. R. W. Lishman, '"Independence" in the Independent Regulatory Agencies', *Administrative Law Review* reprinted in Samuel Kristov and Lloyd M. Musolf (eds.), *The Politics of Regulation*, Boston, Houghton and Mifflin, 1964, pp. 97–101.

41. See for instance: Marver H. Bernstein and Horace M. Gray, 'In Practice is Regulation Consistent with the Public Interest?', Congressional Testimony to Hearings before the Antitrust Subcommittee of the Committee on the Judiciary, 84th Congress, 2nd Session, 1956, reprinted in Samuel Kristov and Lloyd M. Musolf (eds.), *The Politics of Regulation*, op. cit., pp. 223–30; James Q. Wilson, 'The Dead Hand of Regulation', *Public Interest*, No. 25, Fall 1971, pp. 39–50.

42. Nina W. Cornell and Douglas W. Webbink, 'The Present Direction of the FCC: an Appraisal' *American Economic Review*, **73**, 2, 1983, pp. 194–7.

43. Paul J. Quirk, op. cit.

44. Jill Hills, 'Government Relations with Industry: Japan and Britain'. A Review of Two Political Arguments, *Polity*, **XIV**, 2, Winter 1981, pp. 222–48.

45. Sam Peltzman, 'Toward a More General Theory of Regulation', op. cit. pp. 211–40.

46. Michael Beesley, *Liberalisation of the Use of British Telecom's Network*, op. cit., p. 49.

47. Florence Heffron, 'The Federal Communications Commission and Broadcast Deregulation', in John J. Havick (ed.), *Communications Policy and the Political Process*, Westport, Conn., Greenwood Press, 1983, pp. 39–70.

48. Michael Beesley and Stephen Littlechild, 'Privatisation, Principles, Problems and Priorities', op. cit., p. 4; see also: Michael Beesley, 'The Liberalisation of British Telecom', *Journal of Economic Affairs*, **2**, 1, October 1981, pp. 19–27; Stephen Littlechild, 'Ten Steps to Denationalisation', *Journal of Economic Affairs*, 2, 1, October 1981, pp. 11–19.

49. Sue Cameron, 'UK Privatisation. What the Managers Think', *Financial Times*, 20 July 1985.

50. David R. Steel and David Heald, 'Privatising Public Enterprise. An Analysis of the Government's Case', *Political Quarterly*, **53**, 1982, pp. 333–49.

51. David Heald, 'Will the Privatisation of Public Enterprises Solve the Problem of Control?', *Public Administration*, **63**, Spring 1985, pp. 7–22.

52. Michael Beesley and Stephen Littlechild, op. cit.

53. Bryan Carlsberg, op. cit. discusses some of these contradictions.

54. Glyn Davies and John Davies, 'The Revolution in Monopoly Theory', *Lloyds Bank Review*, July 1984, pp. 38–52.

55. *Financial Times*, 15 May 1984.

56. Satellite Business Systems was a consortium of IBM, Aetna Life and Comsat, started in 1973 to provide satellite links for data and transmission to large businesses. After eleven years of losses, and $1. 2bn spent by the

three companies in 1985 it was sold to MCI. See: *Washington Post*, 1 July 1985.
57. *Beesley Report*, op. cit. p. 15.
58. The exception is the Greater London Council which has raised these issues of access. See: Gareth Loxley, 'London calling: A Policy for Telecommunications after Privatisation', *Telecommunications Policy*, September 1984, pp. 178-80.

2 The first deregulator: The United States

Historically the evolution of American telecommunications was a movement from competition between many small companies to gradual concentration into major blocs, each structurally separated by regulatory policy. Western Union dominated telegraph services and AT&T dominated the telephone. Structural regulation of what were seen as 'natural monopolies' froze this concentration for twenty years, while behavioural regulation attempted to offset the excesses of these dominant entities. But against this concentrated power the American pluralistic mechanisms of control were weak. Formal regulation was divided between state Public Utility Commissioners, the Federal Communications Commission and antitrust policy, but state and federal arms of legislature, judiciary & executive branches all hand a hand in the industry. From 1925, AT&T consisted of a vertical monopoly comprising research, manufacturing, the supply of equipment, local networks and toll services, and held a geographical monopoly covering the major urban areas. In the immediate post-war years structural regulation was used to keep AT&T confined to its 'natural monopoly' of telecommunications. It settled for the protection which its regulated status offered in return for being allowed to retain its vertical integration.

It was large business users who first challenged the monopoly. As the importance of computers and digital transmission to large business increased its interests came to be best represented by specialised, private services and by the competition which would increase its power relative to AT&T. The 'natural monopoly' concept of a unitary telecommunications market gave way to the concept of several separated markets. Distinctions were first drawn around the customers' premises' equipment market and then the long-lines data communications market. But the two fed off each other, the liberalisation of equipment increasing the demand for the liberalisation of transmission and the liberalisation of transmission increasing the demand for the liberalisation of equipment. Alliances formed between large users, equipment manufacturers and computer service companies in opposition to AT&T.

Competitors were concerned to take portions of possible AT&T business but were also concerned that AT&T should not be able to use its monopoly profits to compete with them. Large business saw the cost and technological advantages of dedicated communications networks at the same time as competitive technologies produced the possibility of transmission at lower cost than AT&T's coaxial cable. First microwave technology, then satellite technology seemed to offer cost-effective alternative methods of transmission, particularly for data.

Yet business soon found that networks constructed purely for private use were of less value than they would be if interlinked into the public network. And carriers found that the data tranmission market alone was not enough for them to be profitable. Nor for AT&T was voice transmission and voice equipment enough when telecommunications technology overlapped that of data transmission and computing equipment. In time-worn fashion it moved into the new pastures.

Unable to find a compromise which would at one and the same time protect AT&T's monopoly, prevent it from abusing that monopoly and allow the new carriers interconnection, the FCC belatedly moved to structural redefinition of the market. The major divisions in the market were seen as voice equipment and voice transmission on the one hand and computing equipment and data transmission on the other. The one was a natural monopoly, the other competitive. The major contenders became AT&T in the former and International Business Machines in the latter. AT&T's monopoly was nibbled away by decisions of the FCC and the courts which allowed the competitive technologies into the voice monopoly. Yet still AT&T remained the dominant entity, responding to competition with predatory pricing and the refusal of interconnection to its long-line competitors and with the manufacture of equipment which seemed to breach the divide with data communications. As digitalisation made it impossible to distinguish voice and data communications equipment, further redefinition of the divide was attempted—this time between 'basic' and 'enhanced' services. But this divide could also not stand up to technical convergence. Even basic telephone service may be described as 'enhanced' transmission and the 'enhanced' services needed voice transmission to make them pay.[1]

While the FCC moved from a position of growing difficulty in technically defending AT&T's monopoly to one of espousing increased competition, AT&T itself continued to defend that monopoly vigorously with all the tariff and legal weapons which it held, culminating in a Congressional Bill aimed at renewing and expanding its monopoly. Only when it became evident that the concept of a 'natural monopoly' was dead did the trade-offs it gained from its regulatory status become less beneficial than the costs of that status in preventing its entrance into the growth market of data communications and equipment. It became in AT&T's interests to rid itself of its 'natural monopoly' and it settled with the Justice Department in the historic consent decree of January 1982.

The break-up of AT&T in 1984 in which it was divested of its local companies was based on the old structural separation of the 'natural monopoly' of telephones and the 'competitive' market of other services, but this time carried out only at the local level, and policed not by the FCC but by the courts. A non-viable technical distinction is made more vulnerable by the decision to allow the newly created regional companies to sell customer equipment. Inevitably the provision of that equipment will lead to pressure for the transmission capacity to go with it. The same problems are now to be worked out at local level as have occupied the FCC since 1956. The current division of the network is made even less convincing by the acceptance of a unified information communications service embracing telephone, other services and equipment at inter-state level.

For a time at the inter-state level it seemed that post-divestiture AT&T suffered from regulation while its competitors were non-regulated. But, the FCC has chosen to deregulate the market further, releasing both IBM and AT&T to fight with each other on equal terms. Both companies' interests lie primarily with the large users of long-distance communications. Both will now construct alternative local networks for large companies, using the very satellite transmission which previously was AT&T's competitor. AT&T and large business users will compete with its previous local companies by bypassing their networks. Those companies held by regulation to their geographical areas and local telephone service are unable to compete against the long-distance integrated service offered by AT&T. In urban areas they must also compete against the local by-pass possibilities of the broadband services of cable television companies.

Although the largest companies benefit by the construction of private networks and long-distance discounts provided by AT&T and its competitors, the burden of costs for the local networks has been shifted to the residential consumer, both directly and indirectly. As AT&T's smaller long-lines competitors lose money, so it seems that history is repeating itself with progressive concentration in AT&T's favour. Regional companies have demanded increases in local tariffs and increased access charges to compensate for their decreased revenue, hitting the residential consumer and encouraging the by-pass of their local networks. Their interests are also in accommodating the demands of large business users, rather than lose their revenue altogether. Hence large business will be released from any but minimal financial obligation for the continued availability of a national network. Deregulation has provided and continues to provide a massive reallocation of resources in favour of large business. That reallocation has been justified by AT&T's own propaganda that residential services were previously subsidised by long-lines services—a proposition which was never proved. Meanwhile IBM and AT&T have been released onto the world market to fight for the export of integrated information services and large user companies, benefitting from lower domestic costs, gain comparative advantage against their international rivals.

Historical background

When the telephone was first invented in the 1870s by Alexander Graham Bell, Western Union was already the dominant company in telegraph. Unlike Western European countries telegraph was not provided by the government—Congress actually refused to buy the patents in 1846. Bell, demoralised by litigation over his patent from Elisha Gray, offered to sell it to Western Union. That company refused. But as it became clear that telephone would be more than a passing gimmick, in 1878 Western Union purchased Gray's patent. Bell immediately filed a court action alleging patent infringement, resulting in an out of court settlement between the two companies. In 1879 Bell purchased Western Union's telephone equipment, agreed to pay Western Union a small royalty, took control of Western Electric, a manufacturer of telecommunications equipment, and agreed to keep out of the telegraph business until the expiry of the telephone patents in 1893.[2]

During the years of its patent monopoly Bell expanded service, particularly to urban industrial areas. Its primary market was that of business. AT&T was established to provide intercity connections in 1885. Western Electric, which had previously manufactured equipment for Western Union became the sole supplier of the Bell telephone companies.[3]

After its monopoly on patents expired Bell became more aggressive, cutting prices and seeking to gain a monopoly by the alternative means of market share. Hoping thereby to limit their expansion, it refused to interconnect competitors and refused to sell Western

Electric equipment to non-Bell companies. In fact these tactics led to many states passing laws requiring interconnection and resulted in the establishment of independent manufacturers. Despite Bell's attempts to limit their growth independent operators proliferated and by 1907, when Theodore Vail again became president of AT&T, market share was split evenly. The independents owned 3.0 million stations and Bell owned 3.1 million. For the first time telephone service during this period extended into suburban and residential areas and involved competition between two or more companies in half the centres served.[4]

Vail altered Bell's policy to one of absorption of the opposition on the one hand and competition through R & D on the other. Before 1907 the major developments in telecommunications, such as the Strowger switch, took place outside the Bell system. Efforts had been concentrated on buying the relevant patents, rather than creating them. In 1907 Bell and Western Electric's research staff were centralised into one organisation and in 1925 Bell Telephone Labs were incorporated into the AT&T structure. Vail's policy became one of 'occupying the field', defending Bell's territory by R & D in contiguous technologies so as 'to always have something to trade against the accomplishment of other parties'.[5]

Vail also altered policy to allow interconnection and sales of Western Electric's equipment—so that companies could be more easily integrated when they were acquired. By 1912 the relative proportions of Bell and the independents had altered considerably. Bell owned 5.1 million and the independents 3.6 million stations, but Vail's policy of acquisition also slowed growth of the telephone service.

In 1909 Bell took a controlling interest in Western Union. The surviving independent telephone companies and Western Union's competitor in telegraph, Postal Telegraph, petitioned the Justice Department. In 1913 under the Kingsbury Commitment, AT&T agreed to divest itself of Western Union and to cease acquisition of competitive independents. Instead by allowing interconnection to its long lines and giving technical help in rural areas it expanded its network without financial liability. When the Kingsbury Commitment was lifted in 1921 Bell began its pattern of acquisition again.[6]

Vail also began a campaign to extend regulation to telecommunications as a further method of defending Bell's dominant position, both against competitors and against the possibility of government ownership. In 1910 the Interstate Commerce Commission was authorised to regulate interstate radio and wire communications, but largely ignored communications in favour of transport. The uncertain legal position, appeals against regulation, the relation of the operating companies to AT&T and its ownership of Western Electric provided a prescription for weak legislation. It was difficult to determine what were appropriate prices to provide a fair return on capital. Gerald Brock argues that, as Vail had anticipated, the system of competing federal and state regulation coupled with the complex Bell structure prevented any real control of the Bell system, while it provided AT&T with the protection and legitimacy of a regulated utility.[7]

In turn, weak regulation and AT&T's research facilities enabled it to trade its entry into the radio market with Radio Corporation of America (RCA) in the 1920s. While RCA acquired AT&T's broadcasting assets, AT&T retained exclusive rights to wire telephone service and to the transmission of sound pictures by wire. Similarly, AT&T's entry into motion pictures from which it was forced out by anti-trust pressure after 1935 'provided it with bargaining chips to defend its primary area of telephone service'.[8] By 1934 the American domestic market for radio, telegraph and telephone was structurally segmented with RCA, Western Union and AT&T being the dominant entities. The only competition between Western Union and AT&T occurred on private interstate leased lines.

The 1934 Communications Act established the Federal Communications Commission as the regulatory body for telecommunications and broadcasting under Congressional oversight. Section I of the Act sets out the goal: '. . . to make available, so far as possible, to all people of the United States a rapid, efficient, nation-wide, and world-wide wire and radio communication service with adequate facilities at reasonable charges'. Those carriers designated as 'common carriers' under the Act were under an obligation to provide a service to the public. In return they were saved from incursions into their markets. The 1934 Act gave the FCC the power of approval of new services, the power to compel interconnection, the power to suspend rates pending investigation and the power to allocate frequencies. Rates charged were to be 'just and reasonable' but no criteria were set out in the legislation as to what the terms meant. At this time AT&T provided 90 per cent of the telecommunications network through AT&T longlines and through its twenty-two local operating companies, but those companies, concentrated in urban areas, covered less than 50 per cent of the land area of America as it was then. Independent companies covered other areas, but rural penetration was slow.

Just as prior to 1934, the relationship between AT&T, its operating companies, Bell Labs and Western Electric were too complex for regulators to tackle, so after 1934 regulation tended towards a crude 'rate of return' form of regulation. Opponents of this form of regulation argue that it produces no incentives for the regulated entity to cut costs but rather produces incentives for investment in over-capacity. The hardware can then be included in its rate-base, on which its allowed rate of return is computed. In a report in 1938 the FCC alleged that AT&T's ownership of Western Electric allowed it to charge high prices to the operating companies, which then used these costs to increase their rate—base. In effect AT&T's vertical monopoly allowed it to escape regulation. Although this report, drafted by Commissioner Paul Walker, was later disavowed by the Commission, similar allegations were to be made later and to provide the basis for a Justice Department anti-trust suit against AT&T in 1949.[9]

The regulatory system was further complicated by the preference of the FCC and state regulators for average pricing of services, and by the fact that local calls tended to be charged on a flat rate basis rather than the usage sensitive basis of the European monopolies. Until 1930 costs were allocated on what was known as a 'board-to-board' basis, in which all the costs of the local network and its expansion were paid for by local service customers. Long-lines paid nothing towards its usage of those networks. In 1930 the United States Supreme Court rejected Bell's 'board-to-board' system of tariffs, on the grounds that:

'While the difficulty in making an exact apportionment of the property is apparent . . . it is quite another matter to ignore altogether the actual uses to which the property is put. It is obvious that, unless an apportionment is made, [local service] will bear an undue burden . . .'.[10]

In lieu of cost-based pricing, Bell then collected revenues differentially from local 'basic' service and other 'non-basic' services. In view of the company's slogan of 'universal service', the Bell system aimed at obtaining maximum contributions to overhead and earnings from non-basic services so that basic service might be provided at the lowest rates consistent with the revenue requirements of the Bell companies. Local service became the 'residual' service, in that rates were first set for the non-basic services and then local charges were set to make up the residual revenue which would be needed to produce the allowed rate of return on capital.[11] Although there was almost no incentive for AT&T to reduce costs the system seems to have worked well enough while AT&T retained its full monopoly, while new technology decreased the costs of the provision of long-lines and meanwhile the whole system was growing fast.[12]

AT&T has consistently argued that because of the distinction between basic and non-basic services, residential and local services are cross-subsidised by its trunk services.[13] The evidence for this contention came predominantly from the 'separation allowances' used between AT&T and its operating companies. These separation allowances arose after 1930, intended to compensate the local operating companies for the fact that the trunk network used the local network. Network costs were divided between costs associated with usage and costs associated with the fixed investment which was used jointly by all services, with interstate and intrastate toll users contributing to the latter. AT&T's method of allocating separation allowances 'benefited' the local operating companies, in that money passed from one to the other.

The proportion of the revenues of the local operating companies contributed by trunk usage increased as trunk usage increased. However, because higher charges were levied on trunk services than would be necessary had there been no local network to help support it, it was argued that trunks cross-subsidised the local network. Cross-subsidisation was not however proved because local service would only be cross-subsidised if it failed to meet its own costs. In addition a transfer of money took place in the opposite direction since local operating companies had to pay AT&T a proportion of their gross revenues for the 'licence contract', to compensate AT&T for common services.[14] By 1974 the fraction of joint costs recovered by local operating companies through separation payments had risen to 19 per cent and to $3bn. It was argued that without those access costs interstate toll tariffs could be reduced by 29 per cent while rates for basic exchange service would have to rise by 24 per cent. The arguments over 'access' costs and over whether or not local networks were being subsidised increased as AT&T's monopoly was gradually breached in both its provision of transmission and that of equipment.

Neither the FCC nor Judge Harold Greene who ruled on the break-up of AT&T in 1982, nor William Baxter, the Department of Justice attorney in that case, accepted that local networks were subsidised by long-lines, but it has been in the interests of AT&T, particularly since the advent of competition with its long-lines to argue for the existence of that cross-subsidy.[15] By insisting that the subsidy was pre-existing AT&T could reduce tariffs on its long-line service in order to meet competition, but retain its overall rate of return through its local operating companies' monopoly of the local network. Once competition had been admitted into AT&T's monopoly it became important for the FCC to regulate on cost-based pricing rather than on rate-of-return but the task was extremely difficult.[16] A General Accounting Office Report in 1981, which took two years to prepare detailed 'the Commission's inability to accurately allocate telephone companies costs and expenses, rates and to establish a useful accounting system'. Its failure was partly due to lack of resources, partly due to lack of political will and partly due to AT&T's unwillingness.[17]

Between the 1950s and the 1980s, when it was broken up, AT&T defended its concept of 'one system' in an environment where technology was fast changing and growth markets appeared which overlapped with its monopoly. That defence began in the 1950s. In 1949 the Department of Justice brought an anti-trust suit against AT&T with the intention of forcing it to divest itself of Western Electric, its manufacturer. The intention was to promote increased competition in the equipment market and to prevent any possible evasion of regulation through the company's vertical integration. Seven years later, saved from losing Western Electric by the Defense Department's intervention, AT&T agreed to a consent decree which limited its operation to the regulated 'communications' sector. As it had done in the past it traded its right to enter new markets for the safety and legitimacy of a protected monopoly area. The decree precluded it from entry into either data communication services and equipment or into the provision of cable TV services. In the same year IBM in another consent decree agreed not to engage in computer services except through an arms length subsidiary. Later, in yet another private anti-trust suit it sold its computer service bureau to Control Data Corporation and undertook not to compete with CDC until 1979.[18] AT&T was thereby protected from IBM's entry into transmission until 1980 and its Satellite Business Systems venture.

In the late 1950s the first crack came in AT&T's existing monopoly when the Court of Appeals overturned an FCC decision that the Hush-a-Phone device (a kind of cup which snapped onto the handset which was particularly useful in noisy environments) could not be used with Bell telephones. It was the first instance of the defeat of AT&T by the large user companies—in this case the petroleum companies.[19]

Similar cracks began to appear in AT&T's transmission monopoly as new technology made the up-front costs of competition with AT&T less overwhelming and business demanded specialised services. It is normally assumed that competition will enter where excess profits are being made, but to compete with a regulated monopoly demands both a potential market and regulatory decisions in favour of competition. Gradually technological developments, business demand created by the burgeoning numbers of computers and FCC permission contained in a series of decisions during the 1960s and 1970s edged into AT&T's transmission monopoly.

The first such breach came at the end of the 1950s. Despite AT&T's argument that the use of private transmission systems would lead to 'cream-skimming' and would undermine the average pricing of the common carrier systems, in its *Above 890* microwave decision, bowing to pressure from both large users and equipment manufacturers, the FCC allowed microwave transmission for private lines for large business users. It did not however allow sharing of lines or attachment to the public network. The systems were mainly used by power companies, railroads and petroleum companies and by public service licensees.[20] Once private lines were allowed equipment evolved to service them. It was only a matter of time before large user companies demanded that they be allowed to attach this equipment to their public network connections and to interconnect their private networks with the public network.

It was eight years before the FCC's Carter-phone decision in 1968 broke AT&T and GTE's monopoly over attachments to the network. Independently manufactured equipment could be attached to the network provided an interface device was used to protect the network from harm. Again opposition to AT&T's monopoly had come from large users such as the petroleum companies and the National Retail Merchants Association. Opposition also came from the Justice Department, criticised for the lack of effectiveness of its 1956 consent decree with AT&T. Following the 1968 decision on foreign equipment interconnection with the public network of the *Above 890* private lines was allowed. Hence a decision which seemed specifically to relate to breaching the equipment monopoly effectively breached the transmission monopoly as well.[21] This liberalisation of equipment was extended in 1978 to allow customers to buy equipment from independent suppliers and attach it directly to the network provided it met approved standards.

After a six-year battle in 1969, the FCC also approved provision by Microwave Communications Inc. of a microwave link between Chicago and St. Louis. Once again large business users, computer service organisations and equipment manufacturers opposed AT&T and the other land-line carriers. Large users argued that they needed bulk transmission capacity at lower rates than were provided by the land-line companies. Eventually the argument of the common carriers, that they could not: 'lose the only declining unit cost business ... the high-usage toll routes, without destroying the entire average rate-making structures that have enabled the industry to bring subsidised exchange service to millions who would otherwise be unable to afford a telephone ...'.[22] was discounted. The FCC also allowed the inter-connection of MCI's long-distance data lines with the local networks, but it was 1974 before AT&T was finally stopped from inhibiting that interconnection.[23]

AT&T's response to the threat to its monopoly from new microwave common carriers was to file a set of tariffs with the FCC which would undercut its rivals' offerings for heavy users. The ensuing FCC investigation into comparative rates of return for AT&T's various services suggested that for the service for the heaviest users (TELPAK—a bulk lease service) the rate of return was 1.3 per cent. In comparison it was 1.4 per cent for telegraph grade private line, 4.7 per cent for voice grade line and 10 per cent for services for light users. Hence light users subsidised heavy users (a situation replicated in 1985, when AT&T claimed to have been earning only 6 per cent return on private lines compared to the 12.75 per cent allowed).[24]

AT&T countered that the FCC had used the wrong method of costing, but nevertheless had to file new tariffs. This one example illustrates the weakness of a regulatory body which must always respond to tariff filings, and its ineffectiveness. Not only did it take four years to reach a decision that the tariffs were predatory but despite its ruling against the tariffs, following a short period of suspension, they remained in place until new ones were filed.

The technological integration of microchips, of data processing and telecommunications led to digitalisation of transmission and the convergence of two separate markets—data processing which was unregulated and telecommunications, regulated. From the first stand-alone mainframe computer there evolved distributed processing and on-line time sharing. These demanded increased communications capabilities between computers. As the cost of computing hardware fell, by 1969 the cost of the communications portion of a data processing system had become greater than the computing portion, leading inevitably to demands for lower business user costs.[25]

The established carriers were also said to be reluctant to provide other than slow speed data transmission. At the same time the 1956 consent decree became a handicap to AT&T in its efforts to market products incorporating software and to IBM, concerned lest its products were deemed to fall into the regulated market space of AT&T. For equipment suppliers transmission capacity would provide the opportunity of selling more equipment and of locking customers in to their own brand and standards. By the 1970s, IBM had established its standards as *de facto* national standards in data processing, but these standards were not those of AT&T's telecommunications equipment. What was needed was the technology to bypass the up-front costs of establishing a national local network in competition to AT&T. The issues of competitive carriers, of the division between voice com-munications and data processing, and the entry of satellites, all came together in the late 1960s and early 1970s.

The major technological breakthrough came with the launching of the first domestic communications satellite in 1975. Satellites provided the possibility of alternative nation-wide transmission to AT&T's terrestrial network.

Satellite policy

The first geo-synchronous orbital satellite was launched in 1963 but when Congress passed the 1962 Communications Act it was assumed that satellites would be used predominantly for international com-munications. The decision to allow satellite competitors to AT&T in the domestic market took ten years and was the product of a variety of industrial, Congressional and Executive influences. The process began in the early 1960s when an application was filed with the FCC for the provision of a domestic satellite purely for established TV trans-mission, then carried by AT&T. The application was followed by a number of others including one jointly from Lockheed (an aerospace manufacturer) and MCI. Executive influence came first from the Johnson administration's Task Force, in favour of a regulated approach and then from the Nixon administration's White House based Office of Telecommunications Policy favouring an 'open skies' competitive approach. The final decision of the FCC in 1972 demonstrated its staff's concern that a completely open competitive policy would produce over-capacity and leave AT&T, which could fill its satellites with telephone carriage, as the monopoly satellite carrier.[26] The final FCC decision prevented AT&T from owning satellites, and forbade the provision of private lines for three years. A form of transitional structural regulation was therefore imposed on the satellite market, with the intention of allowing others a head-start against AT&T.

By 1970 the FCC had received applications for eight projects involving satellite transmission of either voice, data, or images for the domestic market. Yet, of the eight projects four had been abandoned by 1980, at a total cost to the companies involved of $576 million.[27]

Competitors with AT&T who got their satellites into orbit, RCA Corporation and Western Union, soon found that there were major problems in that competition. Until 1979, when Bell Labs devised an echo-cancelling chip, the echo on satellite transmission was such that conversations could be sent only one-way by satellite. Even AT&T and GTE used satellites in the early years for only a small proportion of their traffic. The other major problem for AT&T's competitors came from the use of the C band and large earth stations. The signals needed local distribution and where these had to be interconnected with the public network AT&T could either delay interconnection or effectively quash competition. By 1975 there were only two domestic satellites.

Because of these problems the early satellites had empty transponders, which were filled with TV Broadcasts. Home Box Office, a cable TV company and the Public Broadcasting Service both provided video services by satellite and as more satellites were launched so cable TV fed from satellite programming grew at a fast pace. At this stage cable TV was predominantly one-way, not interactive.[28]

One satellite could cater for a variety of services provided by a variety of companies. The satellite operator could keep some transponders for its own use, or in case of failure, could lease some to cable companies, could lease some to telephone or data carriers and could lease to individual business users themselves. But all circuits had to be leased.

The lease of transponders was governed by the FCC. As the cost of satellites and their launches decreased, so did the tariff set by the FCC for each transponder. The satellite makers argued that none of them had made a profit from the first round of domestic satellites which had had their leasing rates controlled by the FCC. They argued that the FCC's leasing rates gave a return on capital which made no allowance for R & D. In addition, while cable companies and dish manufacturers such as Scientifica Atlanta were the darlings of Wall Street the pay load manufacturers found it difficult to raise capital, part of the problem being that there were too many manufacturers for the domestic market. Insurance rates had also risen following the loss of RCA's Satcom III in 1979. To add insult to injury, because of the shortage of transponders (less than 160 in 1981) the satellite makers had also seen lessees of transponders sublet them at a huge profit to cable companies.

Dissatisfied with the FCC, Hughes took matters into its own hands and in 1981 organised an auction of transponders. The FCC later invalidated the sale, but in a majority decision in 1982 agreed the principle of the sale of transponders. Their decision based on the view that the shortage of transponders was temporary, saw the sale of transponders as 'opening' the market. Once transponders became private property then companies could claim tax allowances on their investment, so they argued that more companies would be able to afford to utilise the facilities. By approving sales of transponders the FCC was assuming that these companies would 'regulate' themselves. Western Unions's answer—a 'condominium' solution, involving the sale of transponders before the satellite was built—became the norm in the industry, and the provision of satellite communications became unregulated.[29]

In 1980, five years after its first application and following a court decision, the first communications satellite using the higher Ku band was launched by Satellite Business Systems (SBS) consisting of IBM, Comsat and Aetna Life Insurance. The goal was to provide large companies with their own internal communications systems for computer data, facsimile, electronic mail, video-conferencing and voice transmission. IBM's entry into communications was opposed not only by AT&T but also by other computer equipment manufacturers, all of whom feared IBM's domination of end-to-end transmission. They argued that IBM could lock in customers to its standards and that it and AT&T would simply share out the market, rather than compete.[30] The same argument was to reappear in the 1980s in both Britain and Japan.

But IBM's vision of future communications was expensive. By 1981 with a further satellite launched, only 25 companies had signed up, and despite investment of $1.26 billion there was no prospect of a return on capital until 1983 at the earliest. Each satellite could carry 13,000 two way telephone conversations and in 1981, SBS began to downgrade its market to telephone traffic, starting first with long-distance business users, and then a service in 1982 for residential users. It set to undercut AT&T rates by between 14 per cent and 30 per cent. Using the Ku band, SBS was the first satellite to communicate directly to rooftop dishes and by so doing avoid the problem of interconnection with AT&T's network. SBS was therefore the first direct competitor to the transmission monopoly of AT&T.

The technical opening of the Ku band presented the possibility of DBS broadcasting to small rooftop dishes. The FCC gave its agreement to such a service in 1982 and nine companies filed applications. But in competition with local TV broadcasting, with public and commercial TV and with cable TV, the cost and the additional programming have not proved attractive to customers. In 1984 Comsat pulled out of a consortium with Prudential Insurance and United Press International at a cost of $24m. Prudential also announced that it was considering shutting down its existing DBS business, United Satellite, at a cost of $68m. Other previously interested companies such as CBS have also withdrawn plans for DBS services. It seems that DBS came too late for the American market and was too expensive. Also by 1981, with twenty-six satellites in orbit, the C band was already saturated, meaning that there was little possibility for cable or TV programming companies to expand their markets further (cable now reaches 37 per cent of the population). The FCC however gave approval for a further twenty satellites to be launched, thereby generating signal overcapacity.

By 1984 the satellite makers and operators were therefore in the position of having a saturated domestic communications market. The Ku band services of SBS have so far proved too expensive and too far ahead of the market. For TV companies the C band is full, cable TV is suffering privations from the advance of video recorders and the Ku band DBS lacks demand. In addition the Intelsat upgrading programme of which the United States has been the prime beneficiary is coming to an end with Intelsat VI and will be only a replacement market in the future. In this context the bulk traffic crossing the Atlantic has obvious attractions, as does the opening of the cable market in Europe. Competitors to AT&T's international carrier status had already been allowed, and BT seemed to be breaching the international monopoly of Intelsat with its agreement with SBS, so, in 1983, the first application for a private satellite to challenge Intelsat's monopoly was made to the FCC. (See Chapter 7)

Basic and enhanced services

Whilst the FCC was deliberating its domsat policy, it was also embroiled in the increasing overlap between the digitalisation of voice communications and the transmission of data. AT&T's first electronic exchange was developed in 1964 bringing closer the prospect of the digitalisation of the telephone network and the integration of customers' computing and telecommunications equipment. With voice communications regulated and data processing unregulated and with AT&T restricted by the 1956 consent decree to regulated activities, there was considerable pressure from the computer industry and large users to clarify the boundaries between the two markets. In its Computer I Inquiry, begun in 1966, the FCC attempted this distinction, but finding it difficult to determine a technical definition of the boundary resorted to concepts of 'hybrid' data communications systems which it intended to regulate on a case by case basis. Roger Noll argues that the FCC was still at this stage thinking in terms of a natural telecommunications monopoly which had to be protected.[31]

The issue tied in not only with the question of domestic satellites but also with the repercussions of the MCI decision. MCI became operative in 1972. The decision in its favour was followed by a further influx of potential private line competitors filing for permission to begin service. Backed by the users and equipment makers, but opposed by the common carriers and the state utility commissioners, the FCC decided in 1971 to open AT&T's monopoly to competitive carriage of data communications. First in 1971, unregulated data transmission networks for private use were allowed. Then customers who leased lines or long-distance facilities from AT&T were allowed to resell their spare capacity to third parties. Since these private lines could not interconnect into the public network this decision allowed the entry of resale carriers only in a small way. After 1976, these private carriers were allowed to interconnect with the public network. Despite the reopening in 1974 of an anti-trust case against it by the Justice Department, AT&T tried to make (and often succeeded in making) life as difficult as possible for these new entrants by mimicking their services and delaying interconnection.[32]

The FCC still clung to its attempts to protect the voice monopoly of AT&T and it was only following two court rulings in 1977 and 1978 on the MCI's Execunet service, and after years of losses, that MCI was allowed to provide competitive competition in voice long-line service. As a result of its experiences at this time MCI filed an anti-trust suit against AT&T and its operating companies, which was awarded in its favour in 1985. Finally in 1982 the FCC decided that those who leased voice lines in bulk from AT&T could resell their lines to third parties, thereby opening the door to the proliferation of resale voice carriers.[33]

Many of the new competitors served only limited geographical areas and, in particular, resale carriers were vulnerable to changes in AT&T's tariffs. Other private line competitors were able to cut prices on AT&T's long-distance routes partly because they did not have to contribute to the retention of the local network through separation payments. AT&T protested that it was handicapped by the necessity for it alone to support the local network through its long-lines revenue. Its competitors argued that they did not receive equitable access to the local network. Not only did their customers have to use push button telephones and dial twenty two numbers to access their service in comparison to AT&T's customers use of dial phones and ten numbers, but they operated in a situation of nation-wide uncertainty, with the quality of their interconnections much poorer than those of AT&T.[34] During the 1970s the new carriers agreed to the Exchange Network Facilities for Interstate Access which allowed them to pay a share towards the joint costs on a flat-rate basis, which meant they payed less than AT&T which payed on a usage basis. [35]

It seems to have been the entry of IBM via its SBS consortium into direct competition that altered AT&T's attitude from formal toleration of competition to outright aggression in defence of its monopoly. Action switched from the FCC to Congress as AT&T under its chairman, John de Butt, set about raising political consciousness of the FCC decisions. AT&T's supporters introduced into Congress a bill which would have re-established AT&T's monopoly and would have given it the right to purchase its competitors. Fierce lobbying over the Bell Bill, which found 175 House members to sponsor it, and from the competing interests of cable TV and broadcasters over successive attempts to rewrite the 1934 Communications Act resulted in a stand-off situation. Attempts to rewrite the Act against AT&T opposition ended in the 97th Congress.[36]

Nevertheless Congressional hearings raised political consciousness of AT&T's dominant position. The Staff Report to the House Sub-Committee on Communications under the chairmanship of Timothy Wirth dissected that dominance, showing that MCI, the original independent competitor with AT&T's long-lines had only 1 per cent of the market, and AT&T had a 90 per cent market share.[37] The report is said to have been crucial in convincing AT&T management that the legislative avenue back to its previous monopoly was closed and that it should settle its anti-trust suit with the Justice Department.

The House Bill, prevented from reaching the full House by the Justice Committee on the grounds that it pre-empted the anti-trust case, is also said to have influenced the FCC Computer II decision.[38] In 1980 the FCC issued the result of its Computer II enquiry, which had become necessary because of its inability to technically distinguish 'hybrid' data communications from other communications. Under the Computer II decision the Commission made a distinction between 'basic' and 'enhanced' services, the latter being those which added some value to basic transmission services. The 1956 consent decree was abnegated and AT&T was allowed to compete in enhanced services and customer-provided equipment through a separate subsidiary. The Computer II separation also forbade the subsidiary to use software developed by Bell Labs, so as to minimise cross-subsidisation. AT&T itself was split into two companies, AT&T Communications, covering phone calls (regulated) and AT&T Technologies which included Bell Labs and Western Electric. This second company was to be responsible for making and marketing all types of telecommunications and data-processing equipment, including AT&T's 1984 microcomputer products. For the first time AT&T was officially allowed to compete outside its telephone monopoly.

The FCC decided also that except for minimum safety requirements, all equipment attached to the network should be deregulated and that in future it would regulate only voice transmission—the basic telephone service. This latter decision was probably helped by the FCC's chronic shortage of resources and the increased workload which deregulation had brought—for instance, 17,000 applications for cellular radio licences alone. It was carried further in 1984 when the FCC decided that although other carriers besides AT&T were 'common carriers' as defined by the 1934 Act it would choose which companies it should regulate and in future would choose to regulate only AT&T.[39] Hence, within a period of ten years the equipment market and all but AT&T within the transmission market had become deregulated.

On 8 January 1982 it was announced that a settlement in the anti-trust case between AT&T and the Justice Department had been reached and that the Justice Department's thirteen-year-old case against IBM had been dismissed. The 1982 settlement between the Justice Department and the company forced AT&T to divest itself of its twenty-two operating companies. However AT&T kept Western Electric and Bell Labs, seemingly because of the international advantage that would be given to AT&T as an equipment and network supplier by Bell's technological and Western Electric's manufacturing capacity.[40]

Within the domestic market AT&T remained responsible for inter-state and intrastate trunk lines and any enhanced services it wished to provide, while the local telephone companies would collect the revenue from the calls within their geographic areas and remained responsible to their state public utility commissioners. The original settlement split AT&T along the lines of 'natural monopoly' versus 'competitive' services. Local network services were considered to be monopolistic but toll service and customer provided equipment were considered competitive. The intention was to stop AT&T frustrating competitors to its trunk services through its local operating companies.

This division between 'plain old telephone' and competitive services was however breached by Judge Harold Greene who modified the consent decree to forbid AT&T to enter electronic publishing for a seven year period and to allow the local operating companies both to compete against AT&T in the equipment market and to keep the Yellow Pages. However the Bell Operating Companies lost their embedded customer premises equipment which became the property of AT&T.[39] Eleven states challenged this decision and AT&T's ability to decide what assets to allow local telephone companies on break-up, but were unsuccessful in that challenge.

The initial consent decree left considerable numbers of questions to be worked out in the eighteen months allowed before the separation had to occur. Primary among them were the questions of what would happen to AT&T's existing separation payments to the local operating companies, payments which were banned under the consent decree; how many operating companies there would be; what area they would cover; and what assets and debts they would inherit from AT&T. Critics argued that the split gave AT&T one third of the assets with two thirds of the revenue, while the local operating companies received two thirds of the costs with one third of the revenue.[41] There was immediate Congressional concern about what would happen to the concept of 'universal telephone service' once the separation payments from AT&T had gone and hearings began within three weeks of the consent decree being made public. Under the consent decree the twenty-two previous operating companies have been grouped into seven regional companies and into 150 local access and transport areas—LATAS— for entry into which access charges are levied to replace the existing long-lines contributions to the costs of the local network. Debate continues as to who should pay these access charges.

Although AT&T had previously agreed with Congressional staff that long-lines should contribute to the upkeep of the local network through a sharing of joint costs, following the consent decree it began to argue that this access charge should be related to the cost of the hardware in the system—wires and switching equipment—not to usage, and that it should be borne wholly by the local consumer. In pressing for a return to the old 'board-to-board' system of payment, AT&T argued that to place any part of the charges on interstate toll would hamper innovation and increase the probability of bypass of the local network.[42] To cover the economic cost of the system as estimated by AT&T,

customer charges would have risen from the previous $10 per month to between $20 and $30 per month. However if long-distance carriers were also to pay access charges to each LATA, then the cost to residential consumers could be lessened.

AT&T and the other carriers seem to have been successful in convincing the FCC that any imposition of access charges on carriers would lead to bypass of the local network by large users making the most of new technological possibilities. In an acerbic exchange in Congress the FCC was accused of wishing to subsidise new technology.[43] In December 1982 the FCC proposed that there should be a five year transitional period, beginning in 1984, at the start of which consumers would pay half of the $8. 5bn non-traffic sensitive costs. The balance would be paid by the long-distance carriers, based on actual usage of the public switched network, thereby exempting private line and dedicated access route traffic. This charge would gradually decrease over the interim period until consumers bore all the costs of the local network. It also proposed a 'universal service fund' out of which long-distance carriers would cross-subsidise high-cost services in remote areas. Its original proposal was for a $4 access charge for all consumers.

Following an outcry from Congress, from State Commissioners and from Judge Harold Greene, in July 1983 the FCC announced modified access charges of $2 per month for residential consumers and $6 per month for business users, rising over a six year period. AT&T was to continue to meet the largest proportion of the remaining charges, but its eight major competitors faced sharply rising access costs. The proposal pleased no one, fifteen Bills were tabled in Congress and the FCC did an about face and postponed any increase until April 1984, three months after divestiture. This decision landed the local telephone companies (now grouped into seven regions) with the problem of making up the $1bn loss of revenue and faced AT&T with an inability to reduce its long-distance charges, a FCC decision which had been delayed pending the final access charge decision. In April 1984 in an election year the FCC once more decided that access charges on residential and single line business users should not be imposed until July 1985, although those to multi-line business were imposed in 1984. At this point AT&T petitioned the FCC for relief and eventually the question of the charges passed to Congress. It decided and the FCC eventually agreed to $1 per month increased charges to residential consumers, increasing to $2 in June 1986, with no further increases scheduled pending further study.[44]

This amount then left a shortfall which AT&T and its competitors have had to make up. Whereas AT&T has paid for access to LATAs on a usage basis its competitors have benefited from a 35 per cent discount, paying on a flat rate basis. While smaller companies were penalised by the flat-rate charge the larger ones complained in 1985 to Congress and the FCC that they needed a delay on the payment of usage charges, past the 1986 deadline imposed by the FCC. By 1985 only MCI with 5 per cent of the interstate market was making money.[45]

In fact the FCC rates for access to LATAs does not prevent states from charging more to long-distance carriers. AT&T complained in 1984 that in Texas for instance the access charges were so high that it lost revenue on long-distance calls in that state. But high access charges to carriers also have the disadvantage that they provide an incentive for long-distance carriers to bypass the local networks altogether, either by constructing their own network, by using those of cable companies, by using microwave transmission from satellite earth stations, or by using small dish receivers for point-to-point satellite transmission. State utility commissioners have attempted to ban these means of evading the local network, without success. Other schemes have based access charges on the channel capacity of carriers, scaling charges on the relative value each carrier gains from access. The intention of these schemes is that all the carrier's channels, whether switched, or private lines or other bypass installations should contribute to the local network costs.[46] The problem for the local companies is that a very small number of users contribute a large amount of revenue and they are therefore vulnerable to bypass by these users both by satellite and, in the large conurbations, by interactive broad-band cable. Inevitably they have begun to woo these large users with discriminatory tariffs.[47]

The problem of bypass seemed containable until the state commissioners and local operating companies were thrown into confusion in 1985 by the announcement that the FCC would allow AT&T to construct facilities to bypass the local networks. The regional companies argued that AT&T was into the business of reintegrating its monopoly by reconstructing a local network of its own. AT&T argued that it had no intention of doing so without first negotiating with the individual operating companies. Both it and the FCC contended that the way for the regional companies to meet the threat of bypass was to provide special low rates for large business users which did not include any element of contribution to the costs of the local network. Whereas these large business users were once the catalyst for the breaching of AT&T's

monopoly, together with AT&T they are now the catalyst for the breaching of the local monopoly of the regional companies.[48]

An interesting feature of the current regulatory environment in the United States is conflict of policy between the FCC and the Justice Department and Judge Harold Greene, who continues to oversee the consent decree. Whereas the FCC has moved to repeal its Computer II distinction between 'basic' and 'enhanced' services, and has allowed AT&T to amalgamate its separate companies, the Justice Department seems old-fashioned in its continuing concept of 'natural monopoly' based on both technological and geographical separations. Nor does the decision make sense in terms of consistency. GTE, which is an independent company with local monopolies, manufactures and provides both long-line and enhanced services.[49]

While AT&T is under the regulation of the FCC, which seems intent on deregulating it as soon as possible, the regional operating companies are subject to the Justice Department and the Judge. The regional companies have had to apply for permission to the Judge for instance for a definition of 'customer premises equipment' which would include high technology products such as computers with communications capabilities.[50] The process has been slow and piecemeal and their fundamental complaint that they cannot either provide enhanced services or long-distance services against AT&T will not be addressed until 1987. Nevertheless the companies made increased profits in 1985, the largest Bell South almost equalling the profits of AT&T which were $500m down from the $2.1bn forecast.[51] These profits have allowed the companies to diversify into high-street retailing of computers and office equipment and to upgrade the local network for the provision of ISDN. It seems highly likely that their ability to sell equipment for which they may not provide transmission lines will lead to pressure from users for end to end service. And it remains to be seen how prepared are local consumers to fund the upgrading of the network when they may not use it for many years.

Following the consent decree AT&T argued that costs to consumers would have risen in any case because of faster depreciation of equipment and that the consent decree was not to blame.[52] The FCC argued similarly. But in a Congressional investigation of the reason for local telephone companies demands for rate increases of anything up to 25 per cent, Congressional staff found that the consent decree and FCC actions were primarily responsible. Together the additional costs of separation, and of FCC decisions insisting on faster depreciation of local operating company equipment and that they should 'expense' customer premises equipment in the first year rather than add it to the rate base accounted for 50 per cent of additional rate demands. State commissioners no longer had a number of services over which to average the cost of the local network. The implication that state regulators are subject to the FCC has not gone unchallenged, but one of the remarkable aspects of AT&T's divestment is the extension of FCC decisions into intrastate matters.[53] The FCC decision to allow AT&T to construct bypass facilities is only the latest in this trend.

Almost two years after the divestment, the implications are more easily seen. For the 4 per cent of private companies which in 1975 provided 62 per cent of long-distance revenues from business and for the 4 per cent of residential subscribers who contributed 30 per cent of long-distance residential revenues telephone bills have decreased. Long-distance rates decreased by 5.1 per cent in 1984 and by 5.6 per cent in 1985 as the access charges first to multi-line business consumers and then to residential consumers were phased in. But local rates have increased by an average of 9 per cent and connection charges by an average 27 per cent. By 1985 the seven regional operating companies requested $10.9 billion from state commissioners for rate increases and received $5.1bn according to one set of figures. The Consumer Federation of America estimated that 5.5 million people might be driven off the phone network by the higher charges, although operating companies had introduced usage-based plans to help prevent disconnection.[54]

In terms of competition in the long-distance market little changed between 1981 and 1985. The adoption of equal access on an exchange by exchange basis gave a head-start to AT&T in signing up customers for long-distance service. With continuing close ties to AT&T, operating companies, although supposedly giving residential consumers a choice of long-distance carrier, gave to AT&T those who did not specify an alternative. In a fervour of marketing customers were wooed by competing telephone salesmen on the street. But the system was biassed in favour of AT&T, in that its competitors did not have access to the lists of customers in exchange areas.[55] Long distance rates are now lower than at any previous time, but the combination of AT&T's price cuts, coupled with increased access charges and continuing investment in their own optic fibre networks has meant that only AT&T, the independents and MCI have made money.

At the same time the FCC seems to have decided to release AT&T from many of its regulatory shackles, using the argument that market share does not equal market power. Although AT&T's long-line competitors argue that they need more time to establish a truly competitive market, the FCC seems more concerned to facilitate the battle between AT&T and IBM. Hence both have been released from separations of their businesses which hampered their competition in computer services and equipment.

The process began with IBM. Despite its appeal to the telephone user, SBS had considerable difficulty in making satellites pay. In 1984 Comsat withdrew and IBM increased its holdings in the company to 60 per cent. In addition the FCC, which had previously insisted on an arms' length relationship between IBM and SBS, reversed that decision. IBM's sales force is now allowed to sell SBS services, thereby tying together transmission and end-user equipment in head on competition with AT&T. In 1985 IBM bought Aetna's share of SBS and then sold SBS to MCI for a 16 per cent share in that company. The merger brought MCI an extra 1 per cent share in the business data networks market, bringing its share of the long-distance market to 6 per cent, more than twice that of GTE/Sprint the next largest company.[56] Taken together with IBM's takeover of Rolm, the telecommunications manufacturer the previous year, the combination is expected to compete hard against AT&T for government and large business contracts. It marks the beginning of concentration in the long-distance market among companies struggling to compete. Industry analysts expect no more than three companies to survive within the market.

In a similar recognition that equipment, data and voice communications are interdependent in 1985 the FCC voided its Computer II decision. AT&T was allowed to combine its two companies to provide integrated information networks with their associated equipment in competition with IBM. AT&T had argued that divestiture and competition in the long-distance market had made the separation between the two companies unnecessary, and backed its arguments to show that its share of the equipment market had fallen to 30 per cent. Although the FCC demanded accounting practices which it said would preclude cross-subsidisation, the Consumers Association and AT&T's competitors argued that they were totally inadequate. The result they said would be overcharging for residential and small business customers so as to provide discounts on equipment and to special business customers.[57]

Given that the FCC on the same day also struck down a proposed AT&T tariff on the grounds that it was predatory, perhaps the FCC felt that it was still in control of the company. Nevertheless the merger of IBM and MCI has provoked further pressure from AT&T for deregulation, pressure which several analysts believe has a good chance of success with the FCC. Many fear however that the result of deregulation would be that AT&T, still with 85 per cent of the long-distance market, would drop prices and drive out the competition.[58]

The losers by deregulation have been the telecommunications workforce and poorer residential consumers. AT&T's workforce of 117,000 has been reduced by 24,000 and what was previously considered a job for life has become highly insecure. With the entry of non-unionised companies into telecommunications and the establishment of non-unionised subsidiaries what used to be a 100 per cent union membership is now down to 35 per cent. In a growth industry the Union has lost 50,000 of its 650,000 members.[59] Meanwhile AT&T's profits, which dipped in 1984, rose in 1985 and the seven regional company shareholders enjoyed increased profits. Deregulation has effectively provided a transfer of wealth from individual residential customers to big business and is gradually sacrificing the concept of universal telephone service. As the battle between IBM and AT&T and between AT&T and the regional companies increases, the most obvious beneficiaries are large business users. Although the interests of these users have been the catalyst for deregulation from the first Hush-a-Phone conflict, the decision by the FCC to place all the costs of the local network onto local customers, foiled originally by Congress but *de facto* reinstated in 1985, places their interests above the rest of the community. And, as we shall see in Chapter Seven, coupled with moves to deregulate international telecommunications, the interests of these users, carriers and equipment companies are also now paramount in the international transmission market.

Notes and references

1. On the question of 'basic' and 'enhanced' services see: Michael Beesley, *Liberalisation of the Use of British Telecommunications Network*, London, HMSO, 1981, pp. 1–5.
2. Richard E. Wiley, 'Competition and Deregulation in Telecommunications: the American Experience', in Leonard L. Lewin, *Telecommunications in the United States: Trends and Policies*, Dedham MA., Artech House, 1981, pp. 37–42.
3. Harry M. Shooshan, III, 'The Bell Breakup: Putting it in Perspective', in Harry M. Shooshan III, (ed.), *Disconnecting Bell. The Impact of AT&T Divestiture*, New York, Pergamon Press, 1984, pp. 8–9.
4. Vail had previously been passed over for president and had left AT&T. On this period see: Richard Gabel, 'The Early Competitive Era in Telephone

Communication 1893–1920', *Law and Contemporary Problems*, **34**. 2, Spring 1969, pp. 340–359.

5. Ibid., p. 347.
6. Kurt Borchardt, *Structure and Performance of the US Communications Industry: Government Regulation and Company Planning*, Boston, Mass., Harvard University, 1970, pp. 24–5.
7. Gerald Brock, *The Telecommunications Industry: The Dynamics of Market Structure*, Cambridge, Mass. & London, Harvard University Press, 1981, p. 160.
8. Ibid., p. 172.
9. Harry M. Shooshan III, op. cit. p. 12.
10. Smith *v*. Illinois Bell Teleph. Co. PUR1931A 1 (1930) 282 US 133, quoted in Ben Johnson, 'Bypassing the FCC: an Alternative Approach to Access Charges', *Public Utilities Fortnightly*, 7 March 1985, pp. 19–20.
11. William Melody, 'Efficent Rate Regulation in the Competitive Era', for *Telecommunications Symposium*, Washington State Legislature, Seattle, 11–12 July, 1984, p. 3.
12. Gerald Brock, op. cit., pp. 179–80.
13. Interview with John de Butt, *US News and World Report*, 22 November 1976, p. 43.
14. Stephen Breyer, *Regulation and its Reform*, Cambridge, Mass., Harvard University Press, 1982, pp. 293–7. On 'stand-alone' costing of local networks see: William Melody, op. cit., pp. 12–13.
15. Charles Brown, Statement to Joint Hearings before the Senate Committee on Commerce, Science and Transportation and the House Committee on Energy and Commerce, *Universal Telephone Service Preservation Act of 1983*, 98th Congress, 1st Session, S 98-30, HR98-39, 28–9 July 1983, p. 279; William F. Baxter, in testimony to Joint Hearings before the Subcommittee on Telecommunications, Consumer Protection and Finance of the Committee on Energy and Commerce and the Subcommittee on Monopolies and Commercial Law of the Committee on the Judiciary, *Proposed Antitrust Settlement of US* v. *AT&T*, 98th Congress, 2nd Session, HR 97–116, 26 and 28 January 1982, pp. 100–101; Judge Harold H. Greene, address to the Consumer Federation of America, Washington D. C., 17 February 1984, quoted in William H. Melody, op. cit., p. 7.
16. Report to Congress by the Controller General, *Legislative and Regulatory Actions Needed to Deal with a Changing Domestic Telecommunications Industry*, CED-81-136, Washington D. C., US General Accounting Office, 1981, pp. 29–90.
17. Timothy Wirth, Chairman, Hearing before the Sub-committee on Telecommunications, Consumer Protection and Finance and the Subcommittee on Oversight and Investigations of the House Committee on Energy and Commerce, *FCC Regulation of Common Carriers*, 97th Congress, 1st Session, HR 97-78, 24 September 1981, Washington D. C., US Government Printing Office, 1982, p. 1.
18. Anne W. Branscomb, 'Communication Policy in the US: Diversity and Pluralism in a Competitive Market Place', in Patricia Edgar and Syed A. Rahim (eds.) *Communication Policy in Developed Countries*, London & Boston, Kegan Paul International, 1983, pp. 43–8.

19. Dan Schiller, 'Business Users and The Telecommunications Network', *Journal of Communication*, 32, 4, Autumn 1982, pp. 84–96.
20. Kurt Borchardt, op. cit., pp. 36–7.
21. Dan Schiller, op. cit., p. 90; Kurt Borchardt, op. cit., pp. 32–3.
22. Walter Karnopp, manager of Eastern Oregon Telephone Company, quoted in Borchardt, op. cit., p. 41.
23. Robert S. Magnant, *Domestic Satellite, an FCC Giant Step: Toward Competitive Telecommunications Policy*, Boulder, Colorado, Westview Press, 1977, p. 139.
24. Robert W. Crandall and Bruce M. Owen, 'The Marketplace Economic Implications of Divestiture' in Harry M. Shooshan III, op. cit. pp. 53–5; *Washington Post*, 19 January 1985.
25. Lawrence G. Roberts, 'Data by the Packet', *IEEE Spectrum*, February 1974, pp. 46–51.
26. Robert S. Magnant, op. cit., p. 174.
27. *The Economist*, 281, 21 November 1981, pp. 86–7.
28. For a history of American cable TV see: James W. Roman, *Cablemania: The Cable Television Sourcebook*, Englewood Cliffs, New Jersey, Prentice-Hall, 1983.
29. *The Economist*, op. cit., pp. 86–7.
30. Robert S. Magnant, op. cit. pp. 229–37.
31. Roger Noll, 'The Future of Telecommunications Regulation'in Eli M. Noam (ed.), *Telecommunications Regulation Today and Tomorrow*, New York, Law and Business Inc., p. 44.
32. Richard E. Wiley, 'The End of Monopoly. Regulatory Change and the Promotion of Competition', in Harry M. Shooshan III, (ed.), op. cit., pp. 35–6.
33. For a history of the introduction of long-lines competition see: *Telecommunications in Transition: The Status of Competition in the Telecommunications Industry*, report by the Majority Staff of the House Subcommittee on Telecommunications, Consumer Protection and Finance of the Committee of Energy and Commerce, 97th Congress, 1st Session, 97-V, Washington D. C., Government Printing Office, 1981, pp. 69–121.
34. Robert C. Hall, President and Chief Executive, SBS, 'Remarks on Business Communications: The Business of SBS', in Alfred A. Green and Richard E. Wiley, *The New Telecommunications Landscape*, New York, Law and Business, 1984, pp. 21–33.
35. Ben Johnson, 'By-passing the FCC: an Alternative Approach to Access Charges, *Public Utilities Fortnightly*, 7 March 1985, p. 19.
36. Henry Geller, 'The New Telecommunications Act as a Regulatory Framework' in Eli M. Noam, *Telecommunications Regulation Today and Tomorrow*, New York, Law and Business, 1983, pp. 205–55.
37. *Telecommunications in Transition: the Status of Competition in the Telecommunications Industry*, op. cit.
38. Steve Weinberg, 'The Politics of Rewriting the Federal Communications Act' in John D. Havick, (ed.) *Communications and the Political Process*, Westport, Connecticut, Greenwood Press, 1983. pp. 71–89. See also, Henry Geller, 'Regulation and Public Policy After

Divestiture: The FCC and Congress' in Harry M. Shooshan (ed.), op. cit., pp. 94–6.

39. In 1983 the FCC received 43,000 pages of tariff filings on access charges compared to 22,000 pages in 1982. More than 1,500 local telephone companies filed 76 access tariffs each plus 100 other tariffs: statement of J. Dexter Peach, Director Resources Community and Economic Development Division, General Accounting Office, Hearings of Subcommittee of the Committee on Government Operations, *The Impact of the FCC's Telephone Access Charge Decision*, 98th Congress, 1st Session, HR 98-88, Washington D. C., Government Printing Office 1984, pp. 607–40.

40. Charles Brown, Chairman AT&T, in testimony to Joint Hearings on *Proposed Antitrust Settlement of US v. AT&T*, op. cit., p. 46.

41. Rep. Ronald M. Mottl, ibid., p. 5.

42. *Universal Telephone Service Preservation Act of 1983*, Joint Hearings before the Senate Committee on Commerce, Science and Transportation and House Committee on Energy and Commerce, S1660; HR 3621, Washington D. C., Government Printing Office, 1983, pp. 321–2.

43. Ibid., p. 78.

44. Ben Johnson, op. cit., pp. 19–21.

45. *Washington Post*, 6 September 1985; 12 September 85.

46. Ben Johnson, op. cit., pp. 21–3.

47. On the likely post-divestiture strategy of local companies see: Harry M. Trebing, 'A Critique of Structural Regulation in Common Carrier Telecommunications', in Eli M. Noam (ed.), op. cit., pp. 154–75.

48. *Washington Post*, 31 October 1985.

49. *Washington Post*, 19 November 1985.

50. *Washington Post*, 11 November 1985.

51. *Washington Post*, 1 February 1985.

52. Charles Brown, Chairman of AT&T, testimony to Joint Hearings on *Proposed Antitrust Settlement of US v. AT&T*, op. cit., pp. 18–20.

53. *Local Telephone Rate Increases*, report by the Committee Staff for the House Committee on Energy and Commerce, 98th Congress, 2nd session, 98-U, Washington D. C., US Government Printing Office, 1984.

54. *Washington Post*, 19 May 1985.

55. *Washington Post*, 5 May 1985.

56. *Washington Post*, 1 February 1985.

57. *Washington Post*, 18 September 1985.

58. *Washington Post*, 27 June 1985.

59. *Washington Post*, 17 July 1985; 22 August 1985; 26 October 1985.

3 Britain: competition, public control and liberalisation

Introduction

Whereas telephone service in the United States developed under a dominant private entity, in Britain, after a period of formal competition, the monopoly rested with central government bureaucracy. The first thirty years of the telephone were however years of regulated private enterprise. These thirty years demonstrated the British liking for structural rather than behavioural regulation. Despite formal competition, the uneconomic realities of dual investment in local networks created *de facto* local unregulated monopolies. The geographical limitation of these local networks through structural regulation, coupled with recurring threats of nationalisation stimulated local monopoly exploitation, which in turn led to public pressure for nationalisation.

Once nationalised the extension of the network was consistently undermined first by Treasury desire to protect its existing investment in telegraphs and then by its use of the telephone monopoly as a revenue resource. Lack of investment precluded the necessary technological upgrading while lack of marketing kept usage rates low.

Only during the 1960s did governments come to understand that telecommunications were essential for economic development, but by then the effects of the Second World War, the lack of subsequent investment and the Post Office's dominant engineering culture had created an almost irreversible situation of decline. Poor service, long waiting lists and failing exports of equipment eventually gained political recognition, but political responsibility was off-loaded onto the domestic equipment supply industry. Despite being officially under public control, the Post Office retained more or less complete autonomy over technological decisions. Because of their small domestic base, equipment manufacturers depended on the Post Office to develop equipment suitable both for domestic supply and export, but such commercial considerations were alien to an organisation which set high store by gold-plated technology. Just as in the United States the costs of the British monopoly's R & D and its cost-plus method of contracting work were passed on directly to the consumer.

Both as a civil service department and later as a public corporation tariffs were subject to government intervention for the purposes of macroeconomic control. They were also used by the monopoly to dampen demand. Regulation of profits was on a rate of return basis, with almost no control over technological decisions or trade-offs. In general trunk calls were priced high, and both they and international calls contributed increasing amounts to the corporation's profits.

Frustrations with the poor service among politicians led from the 1930s onwards to demands for privatisation of the Post Office monopoly. Liberalisation eventually came about as the result of a number of converging pressures. The old technology of the national network proved unsuitable for fast data transmission at the same time as computer manufacturers, such as IBM, wanted to enter the equipment and transmission market. These demands for technological upgrading from large users, such as the City, and demands for equipment liberalisation from computer companies were echoed by the traditional telecommunications equipment suppliers, anxious to be rid of their semi-agency status. Liberalisation also fitted with the free market philosophy of the Thatcher government, elected in 1979, and with its desire to reduce the power of public sector trade unions.

At first the intention seems to have been only to liberalise the equipment monopoly. Almost inevitably, repeating experience in the United States, this liberalisation went hand in hand with demands for the liberalisation of transmission and with the concomitant problems of segmenting the total market in an attempt to protect the voice monopoly. Hence, as the FCC found in America, the introduction of competition actually increased rather than decreased the need for behavioural regulation. Liberalisation gave power to the civil service over both structural and behavioural regulation, but it was unequal to the task of controlling a liberalised British Telecom, aggressively defending its position. Hence although formal power shifted to the bureaucracy, it was the liberated entity which gained most from liberalisation.

The era of competition

Telephone service began in Britain run by private companies in competition with the telegraph and the mail. These latter services were both run by the British Post Office, then a department of the central government. The telegraph service, originally provided by private companies, had been nationalised in 1869 when the Post Office was given a legal monopoly.

Telephone development was based on the American inventions of Bell and Edison. In 1878 an agent of the Bell company attempted to sell its patent rights to the Post Office, but the Post Office could not get the authorisation it needed from the Treasury. Bell then formed a British company and began to build telephone exchanges. One year later, 1879, the Edison Telephone Company followed.[1]

Because only nine years previously the Post Office had paid rather too much for its nationalisation of the telegraph service it was not about to see its telegraph business undercut by the telephone. In 1878 the Postmaster General (the minister responsible for the Post Office) proposed the insertion of a clause in the 1878 Telegraph Bill in which: 'The term telegraph in addition to the meaning assigned to it by that Act [the Act of 1869] shall include any apparatus for transmitting messages or other communications with the aid of electricity, magnetism or any other agency.' This clause, intended to bring the new telephone under the Post Office monopoly of telegraph, was rejected by the House of Commons. The Post Office then took the matter to the courts and won. The 1880 court ruling produced an interpretation of the telegraph monopoly which included existing and future methods of communicating by electricity. Thereby the Post Office held the legal monopoly, but the companies held the patents.[2]

The Post Office then wanted to set up its own telephone service, but, because it was already losing money heavily on the telegraph service, the Treasury opposed the idea. It was forced to license the United Telephone Company (the two companies had merged) to provide the service, but was given permission by the Treasury to establish a limited system of its own in order to improve its bargaining position. In 1881 UTC agreed not to appeal the court ruling and to grant the Post Office a patent licence so that it also could enter the telephone business.

In return UTC was granted licences by the Postmaster General, but these did not allow the company to erect poles or wires on other people's property. They also limited its operations to within a radius of four or five miles of an exchange in London or within a radius of one or two miles elsewhere and provided the Post Office with 10 per cent of company receipts. In a similar strategy to AT&T, the Post Office assured its own position by keeping all long-distance lines. However, in the British case the intention was to protect the telegraph from the telephone. Making private investment less attractive and monopoly prices inevitable (tariffs were uncontrolled) all licences were to expire on the 31st January 1912. Again there was no certainty as to what would happen to the licensee's property after that date.[3]

Although the Postmaster General stated that 'it would not be in the interest of the public to create a monopoly in regard to the supply of telephonic communication', the era of competition between the UTC and the Post Office suffered from the defects of a legally dominant publicly controlled entity acting as regulator of its own competition. High costs, low penetration, a fixed period for the franchises and local monopolies combined to create high tariffs.[4]

Although the Post Office began to establish its own exchanges in certain towns the Treasury objected to it marketing the telephone, arguing that 'the State should not be a competitor in trade' and should not 'act in anticipation of possible demand'.[5] And, because the Post Office was not prepared to undercut its telegraph returns, trunk lines also failed to materialise. The result was that whereas in the United States, with a lower rate of urbanisation than Britain, by 1885 there were 135,000 telephones, in Britain there were only 12,800 in the whole country, 3,800 of which were in London.[6]

General public dissatisfaction resulted in the relaxation of the regulation of the Telephone Company in 1884. Its geographical limitations were removed, and it was allowed to provide trunk wires. However the Government reserved the right to purchase the licensee's plant in 1890, 1897 or 1904 and all outstanding licences were to expire on 31 December 1911. The question of what would happen to the licensees' property on the expiry of their rights was again left untouched. Although the UTC and its subsidiaries amalgamated into one company, the National Telephone Company, thereby threatening a private national monopoly, the government refused to license other than the one company, arguing that further competition should only be allowed if the Company abused its position.

Having liberalised the trunk lines the Post Office then reduced the prices of its long-distance telegraph service by 50 per cent, putting its revenue below its operating expenses. This predatory pricing did not prevent expansion of the lines. In turn, that expansion led to further fears of a national private monopoly and further losses of telegraph revenue. In 1892 the Post Office decided that it would purchase the whole of the trunk lines, a decision taken on the explicit reasoning that the telephone was a direct substitute for the telegraph.[7]

Sir Evelyn Murray, who was secretary to the Post Office from 1914, suggests that the Post Office actions had a direct political intent. He argues that the government was aware that it would be forced to provide a national telephone service eventually and wished to forestall another expensive nationalisation of a profitable service, as had happened in the case of the telegraph. 'Ministers foresaw that sooner or later a State system was a probable, if not the inevitable, solution, and with the precedent of the telegraphs before them, they were bent on preventing the consolidation of a lucrative business which would ultimately have to be purchased at exorbitant cost.'[8] He points out that the trunk lines were purchased in 1895 at cost price.

Having nationalised the trunk lines the Treasury then refused to allow them to be extended unless the Post Office could guarantee that the revenue from them would cover the capital cost. The Post Office was placed in the position of asking the NTC to guarantee an annual revenue before it could construct a line.

Nor did the NTC's problems end with those guarantees. Although the 1892 Telegraphs Act had given the company power of way-leave, it had also laid down the condition that the relevant local authority had to agree to the laying of wires. Because of its monopoly tariffs, until 1894 the company was unable to persuade any local authority to give its agreement. The main opposition to the company came from the urban local authority association—the Association of Municipal Corporations—which wanted statutory regulation of the company's charges. Unsuccessful in its pressure on the government to regulate the company's behaviour, the Association recommended that its members not co-operate with the company. At the same time the Post Office refused either to license the local authorities to provide their own services or to expand its own services. By 1898 it had only forty-nine exchanges of which forty-one had fewer than nineteen subscribers and thirty-three had fewer than eight.

These various issues were explored by a Select Committee of the House of Commons in 1898. Post Office witnesses were of the opinion that while full-blown competition would promote confusion a powerful private monopoly was undesirable and that eventually the state would take over the NTC's service. In the event the Committee recommended that both the Post Office and the local authorities should compete with the NTC. The 1899 Telegraph Act allowed such competition, although, by prohibiting it from opening any more exchanges without the Post Office's consent, it also increased structural regulation of the NTC.

Following this Act sixty local authorities sought licences to operate their own telephone service of which thirteen were granted by the Post Office and only six eventually taken up. All of these, with the exception of Hull, failed (Hull continues to provide its own service). They were sold either to the NTC or to the Post Office. By 1905 therefore, when Parliament responded to public pressure and eventually agreed that the state should buy out the NTC in 1911, the position was as follows. The bulk of the local exchanges were owned and operated by the NTC under its licence expiring in 1911, but in London and some provincial cities there were also Post Office exchanges with about 10 per cent of the total subscribers. There were also a number of local authorities with their own exchanges and the Post Office owned the trunk lines. In 1911 the Post Office bought the remaining assets of the NTC. The so-called first competitive era in British telecommunications had been ended with public ownership replacing the existing limited competition.[9]

The framework of public control

The 1911 purchase of the telephone network did not alter the existing relationship of the Post Office and Treasury. As a government department all expenditure had to be approved by the Treasury. Appropriation accounts had to be submitted to and voted on by Parliament each year. All the surplus revenue generated by the Post Office had to be repaid to the Treasury and its day-to-day running was completely under Treasury control, but Parliament was unable to see what costs and profits accrued separately to the telephone or telegraph or postal services. Bureaucratic procedure dominated the organisation and ministers overseeing the department came and went with unusual rapidity.[10]

By 1928 both Conservative and Liberal MPs were calling for the privatisation of telecommunications on the grounds that it would be more efficient. As Gerald Brock points out one major problem of this time was the need for capital investment for expansion—investment depended on political approval and was met out of revenue, rather than borrowing.[11] Customers had therefore to pay for expansion via higher tariffs and rentals. Neither was the cost of investment in plant under Post Office control. Building of exchanges was undertaken by the Ministry of Public Works, which was more concerned with building marble edifices for posterity than with providing commercial premises at reasonable cost. Whereas in 1927 it cost AT&T £47 per line for construction, it cost the Post Office £77.[12] High costs and limited revenue in turn placed a limit on the expansion which was possible.

Reflecting this high cost of usage, telephones in Britain were considerably less used than those either in the United States or Japan.

Whereas in the America in 1929 there were 257.7 conversations per head of population, and in Japan 48.8, in Britain the number was 32.1. In 1927 local calls in Britain were twice as expensive as in the United States and almost three times the price of those in Norway and Sweden, while trunk calls of hundred miles were five times as expensive as those in Sweden.[13]

The slow development of the telephone in Britain can be seen from a comparison of American and British figures. In 1906 the United States had one phone per fifteen people. Almost thirty years later (1930) Britain had less than one phone to twenty-five people—less than Germany, Switzerland, Norway, Australia, Sweden, Denmark, New Zealand, Canada and the United States. By then America had one phone per six people and Canada one per seven. High cost and low penetration both acted to reduce the utility of the telephone to the whole community.[14]

In one of the first references to the income elasticity of telephone usage, Murray suggests that the differences in penetration in the United States and Britain were not only due to cultural differences but also to the higher income of North American working class people. He argues that:

the annual cost of a telephone in the United States, though instrinsically greater than in England, bears a much smaller ratio to the average wage earner's income. In consequence the telephone has secured a firm footing among the working classes in America, while in this country residential lines are practically confined to the higher paid strata of the population.[15]

By the 1930s letters and telegraph were still the major methods of communication. Between 1911 and 1981 three changes were made in the formal organisation of the Post Office, but none in its legal monopoly. In 1932 it was decided that the Post Office might keep a proportion of its profits for reinvestment, a decision which was rescinded as soon as war broke out and not implemented until 1961. It remained a department of central government until 1969, when in seeming desperation that it could not improve the quality of the telephone service the Labour government made it into a public corporation. Reacting to trade union pressure from the mail workers, although within the new public corporation the two became separately run, the Post Office's joint responsibility for mail and telecommunications was retained, Joint responsibility for posts and telecommunications also had the advantage that while protecting the jobs of postal workers via cross-subsidisation, the arrangement was also likely to protect telecommunications from privatisation by a future Conservative government.[16] In the debate on the transfer to public corporation status right-wing Conservative politicians had raised once more the possibility of privatisation.[17]

Public corporations in Britain are based on a model first initiated by Herbert Morrison in the post-war Labour government. The intention originally was that utilities should remain under public control but should be allowed to operate at arms' length from government. Public corporation status released the Post Office from day-to-day questioning of its actions within Parliament. It also released it from having its budget approved annually by Parliament and allowed it to operate normal profit and loss accounts. But the new status did not release it from overall control by the Treasury. Its investment programme and borrowing were still strictly controlled, although it was under an obligation to provide an overall return on capital for both telephones and mail of about 8 per cent. Tariffs were set to gain that return on capital but the government often interfered in the tariff setting for its own macroeconomic ends. Hence the Conservative government of 1970 froze telephone tariffs in its desire to keep down inflation, with the result that the telephone service made a loss during the 1970s which was then met out of public taxation.[18]

In common with other public corporations, such as British Rail, relations with government were a source of perpetual friction exacerbated by the poor quality of service and unsatisfied demand during the 1950s and 1960s. During the 1960s, when the telephone became relatively cheaper than other commodities and particularly after the introduction of direct dialling in 1958, the Post Office consistently underestimated demand. The waiting list of 450,000 in 1950 was gradually reduced by the institution of shared service, but rose again during the 1960s and early 1970s to reach 250,000 in 1973. Tariffs, rentals and connection charges were manipulated throughout this period in order to dampen demand. Connection charges were increased by 400 per cent between 1955 and 1965.

After 1960, the major bottleneck to supply arose in exchange rather than line equipment. Governments were forever changing their minds about the investment programme. These problems of short-term expansion and cuts fed back into the equipment suppliers who were unprepared to risk long-term expansion of manufacturing capability, especially when the technology required was the out-dated Strowger.

Although, as Douglas Pitt demonstrates, once the Post Office became a public corporation it attempted to alter its internal organisation from the bureaucratic, top-down approach to that of a more commercially aware organisation, certain of its behaviour patterns continued to be moulded by its origins.[19] Following its buy-out of the NTC in 1911 the Post Office had entered into a series of bulk-purchase agreements with a number of suppliers. These agreements were a form of cartel in which purchases of particular products were shared between manufacturers.

In 1925 it also decided to standardise its exchange system and settled on the Strowger electro-mechanical exchange. A number of committees then shared out exchange production and had to approve any alterations to the technology. When a new range of exchange equipment was planned after the Second World War a research committee became responsible for co-operative R & D between manufacturers and the Post Office. At this point there were five manufacturers involved—General Electric Co. (GEC), Associated Electrical Industries (AEI), English Electric, Plessey and Standard Telephone Cable (STC, a wholly owned subsidiary of ITT). The research and manufacture was based on a semi-electronic technology specific to Britain, termed reed-relays. The possibility of using the alternative cross-bar technology, then in use almost everywhere else, was rejected several times, (although Plessey developed its own small exchange system for export) because of the high cost of capital investment.

The Labour government of the 1960s decided first that there were too many telecommunications equipment manufacturers and brought about a merger of GEC, AEI and English Electric. It further decided that the cartel arrangement between the manufacturers and the Post Office was responsible for their failure to provide exchange equipment. It introduced competitive tendering. In turn, given the fact that the Post Office was still installing electro-mechanical or semi-electronic equipment requiring heavy maintenance, competitive tendering had the effect of increasing training and maintenance costs.

When the decision was taken to move to fully electronic exchanges, once more the old cartel re-established itself for the purposes of both R & D and manufacture. Hence System X, the electronic exchange, was developed in the 1970s by the Post Office in conjunction with GEC, Plessey and STC. Pye TMC, a Philips (The Netherlands) subsidiary, despite wishing to enter the cartel, was kept out until the others had gained a lead in manufacture. The Post Office was half-hearted about developing the technology because, as in the days of the telegraph, it wanted to exploit fully its recent capital investment—although that was still mainly the old Strowger equipment. The committee system, the Post Office's lack of urgency in developing the electronic system and the separate locations adopted for development of separate parts of System X made for an inefficient development process. Hence by the end of the 1970s the British network was in poor technological shape, with 75 per cent Strowger equipment coupled with the 15 per cent semi-electronic reed relay based TXE4 and some cross-bar. Even manual exchanges were only finally phased out in the mid-1970s.[20]

During the twenty year period before 1981 the rapid increase needed in exchange capacity coupled with the scrapping of manual exchanges had resulted in a very rapid growth in purchases from the equipment manufacturers. Although the Post Office had ordered an international exchange in the 1960s from Ericsson of Sweden, the vast majority of its supply of public exchanges had been taken from STC, Plessey and GEC. This growth was suddenly halted in 1975 when the Post office found that it had 15 per cent spare capacity and equipment orders were cut back. However by that time approximately 50 per cent of the sales of manufacturers were in public exchanges to the Post Office while only 5 per cent of total sales were public exchanges sold abroad. In all by 1975 the Post Office took 67 per cent of total sales, while sales to other British customers totalled only 20 per cent.[21] By 1981 the dependence of the manufacturers had increased further with BT responsible for taking 75 per cent of manufacturers' sales.

In the private exchange market the indigenous manufacturers had consistently lost market share to foreign enterprises—IBM, Ericsson and ITT (United States)—all of whom could offer electronic PABX in competition with the electro-mechanical offerings of GEC and Plessey. In exports the industry had gradually weakened from a leading position in the immediate post-war world when Strowger equipment had been exported to the sterling area. By 1978 the Third World market had expanded to $4 billion a year but British companies had lost market share to West Germany, Sweden, Japan and the United States. Exports were only 14 per cent of total production (down from 23 per cent in 1967), but there was still a balance of trade surplus.[22]

Despite a protected home market the British companies had made little impact on the export market. The manufacturers blamed the technical specifications of the Post Office, while the Post Office and its trade union blamed the manufacturers lack of adventurousness. As Francis Cripps and Wynne Godley point out, although major responsibility rested on the various governments for not understanding the interdependence of home supply and exports and not making the Post Office responsible for equipment exports, the manufacturers also bore some responsibility. Without any home market at all Ericsson of Sweden had managed to build up exports.[23]

Throughout this period the growth of the British network was slow, ranging from the average annual 5 per cent growth rate in the period 1960–65 to 8 per cent between 1970 and 1975, and below 6 per cent in the years between 1976 and 1981.[24] The major growth came in residential telephones—an increase of 50 per cent between 1975–81 compared to a 14 per cent increase in business demand.[25] During the period from 1955 to 1975 local calls had decreased marginally in price while trunk call charges had decreased in real terms by nearly two thirds, most of the decrease taking place from 1965. Hence the cost advantage of new technology had been felt mainly in the trunk call traffic, where STD had helped to increase trunk demand to 15 per cent of total calls. Similarly STD had increased demand for international calls and by 1981, international telephone and telegraph produced 18 per cent of its revenue, and, within Europe Britain had the cheapest transatlantic rates and leased circuits.[26] But only 14.5m households had a telephone in 1981, leaving 5m (25 per cent) of households without access.[27]

When the Thatcher government of 1979 was elected the Post Office still had the monopoly it acquired in 1911. It was responsible for the whole telephone service, for providing customers with equipment, for approving and maintaining that equipment, for providing the transmission lines, for purchasing exchange equipment and for R & D. The monopoly had in fact been so worded by the Labour government in 1969 that while the Conservative opposition wanted to include within the monopoly only existing services the actual wording included all possible future services. Despite their disapproval of the definition it was repeated with almost exact wording in the 1981 Act. In fact BT did not actually provide a monopoly of services. It was prepared to allow general licences to certain services over which it had a formal monopoly provided that those services did not involve private switching between independent parties and provided that it had no commercial interest in the service—for instance cable TV and private radio systems. But it had also refused licences to radio-paging services in London and to services which involved switching to third parties which were unrelated organisations. In effect services which would allow sharing of leased lines were precluded. On the equipment side although it had the monopoly of telephones and PABX under 100 lines it was excluded from those of over 100 lines, where the British manufacturers had consistently lost market share to IBM and Ericsson.

Although it was subject to macroeconomic control by the Department of Trade and Industry, in many respects the Post Office was free of restraint. To a large extent public ownership was seen as a substitute for regulation. The consumer was represented by the Post Office Users' Committee but that organisation had little influence, except possibly in delaying proposed tariff increases. Stephen Littlechild gives an example of the introduction of higher daytime telephone charges with very little publicity.[28] The balance between the costs of various services and tariffs were not matters of public debate. A form of social regulation was included in its monopoly in that it had to to provide telephone service to rural communities, and had to maintain public call boxes and emergency calls. In fact during the 1970s the form of social regulation which allowed the Conservative government to compensate the Post Office for holding down tariffs may well have helped to ensure increased costs because these could be recouped via the subsidy. Even the various Select Committees on the Post Office paid little attention to costing or pricing mechanisms.[29] And the government itself did not receive the information necessary from the Post Office to make decisions on trade-offs between investment strategies, quality of service, operating costs and prices.[30] Although the Post Office was publicly controlled it is difficult to argue that it was a regulated monopoly in the sense in which the term is used in the United States. The Beesley Report in 1981 commented: 'It is also perhaps fair to say that the Post Office has operated in the past with relatively little pressure to explain and justify its commercial conduct.'[31] There was also little pressure on the corporation to hold down its costs and considerable pressure for it to become self-financing in order to reduce calls on the Public Sector Borrowing Requirement.[32]

Liberalisation

In its manifesto of 1979 the Conservative party, led by Mrs Thatcher gave notice that it would reduce the size of the public sector. Several factors seem to have contributed to the decision on liberalisation. The Thatcher government's general concern about the size of the PSBR and at the loss of ground in exports of the British telecommunications equipment manufacturers were background factors to liberalisation, as was the appointment of one of the most liberal of the then Conservative ministers, Sir Keith Joseph, to be Minister of Industry.

More specifically the technical efficiency of the network was low. Two years before the election the Carter report had cast doubt on the Post Office's desire to digitalise its network. Data tranmission was slow although at 17,000 the number of computers with data tranmission capacity was the largest in Europe.[33] By 1979, the City, already involved in the internationalisation of banking and fast international data communications complained about the poor national service. IBM, already successful in the private PABX market pressed for entry into that for public exchanges. A further impetus to the concept of liberalisation seems also to have come from the government's antipathy to powerful public sector trade unions. The idea of a competitor to the Post Office in transmission may even have originated in the 1978 industrial action of the Post Office engineering union when it demonstrated the disruption it could cause.[34]

Attention was first concentrated on the separation of the mail and telecommunications sides of the Post Office and on liberalisation. The announcement of the proposed split, made in September 1979, precluded the privatisation of telecommunications on the basis that privatisation 'was inappropriate to telecommunications which could raise its finance without call on the Exchequer'.[35] Nor was there much urgency given to the decision. The timetable envisaged an act to split the corporation in 1981 and then a period of adjustment of two to five years while British manufacturers geared themselves up to a liberalised equipment market.

However, by mid-1980 the Chancellor of the Exchequer was already floating the idea of the privatisation of telecommunications. A merchant bank which conducted a feasibility study at this time concluded that the project was possible and put a value of £8m on BT's assets, which proved to be accurate. It was about this time that the idea of a competitor to BT also seems to have been first floated, although it was a year before the public announcement of the Mercury consortium.

Towards the end of 1980 the government announced the appointment of a Minister for Information Technology whose responsibilities would include steering the bill through Parliament. The Bill envisaged that telecommunications would stay under public control as a public corporation but would be split from the postal service. Its monopoly was to be liberalised, the original memorandum concentrating primarily upon equipment. The idea that the equipment monopoly was suitable for liberalisation was not new. It had been put forward by the Carter Committee investigation into the Post Office in 1976 which had also recommended the divorce of telecommunications from posts. The arguments were based then as they were in 1981 on the existing liberalisation of equipment in the United States.[36]

The original memorandum on which the Bill was based specified that customers would be able to provide their own attachments subject to the exception that BT would supply the first telephone instrument. Technical standards for the equipment were to be determined by an independent body later named as the British Standards Institution and were in general to be limited to safety standards. Under this provision BT lost its monopoly of supply over PABX of under 100 lines. BT was however to remain responsible for maintenance of all PABX and for the first telephone and was to be the only organisation permitted to carry out on-line testing.

The provision that BT should be responsible for maintaining PABX provoked a storm of protest from both manufacturers and customers. The manufacturers argued that BT would be unable to maintain the numbers of PABX which would come onto the market and, in particular would be unable to maintain the new generation incorporating word processing and communications facilities—at the time of the memorandum's publication there were already twenty different types.[37] The proposal that BT should maintain these PABX suggested that its maintenance engineers would be developing a software capability, and in turn this development was viewed as a possible future threat when digital equipment in the public exchanges might be able to replace some of the functions of PABX. In the final bill the proposal was altered to give BT maintenance responsibility only for analogue, not digital, PABX.

BT retained the monopoly over the main trunk and local network and retained responsibility for the supply, installation and maintenance of the wiring on subscribers' premises up to the first direct connection with the network. Internal wiring could be open to competition but had to be accepted by BT and approved by BT for maintenance purposes, a provision which later led to complaints of anti-competitive behaviour.

BT was also to be allowed to compete 'in the supply, installation and maintenance of all terminal equipment and in the provision of specialised services to third parties'. It was to do so however through appropriate arms' length financial arrangements and powers would be available to require BT to set up a self-accounting subsidiary or subsidiaries.[38]

Liberalisation of transmission awaited a report commissioned by the government. The Beesley Report, conducted by an academic economist, Professor Michael Beesley, was published in April 1981. The original government memorandum based on BT's position stated that a distinction could be made between 'genuine' VANs and those which would infringe on BT's commercial viability. In other words it adopted a distinction between 'basic' and 'enhanced' services.[39] Beesley demolished that distinction and extended the study to consider the benefits and costs of resale of leased lines. He concluded that to equal the American development of non-voice services, they would need to include voice services. He argued that if BT moved to a cost-based structure for each service or to equalising returns on charges then the loss to BT's revenue could be accommodated by a 'balancing' of its return on charges. At the maximum he estimated that resale would entail an increase of £6.4 in rental prices to residential consumers. He also concluded that encouraging resale at home would have strategic importance in the international market: 'the longer term strategic point about admitting resale as a principle is whether it will hasten the day when resale emerges on the international scene'.[40] By allowing resale in the domestic market while it was still forbidden in the international market Britain could become the centre for the: 'accrual of internationally mobile service companies.. presenting a favourable home for company headquarters with associated research and development'. It would increase pressure for the liberalisation of the relevant international agreements. The intention of this advocate of liberalisation was to make Britain the centre for American multinationals.[41]

Beesley did not advocate that a direct competitor to BT should be licensed, although he anticipated that resale would itself lead to full liberalisation. He also argued that in America AT&T and local companies were being encouraged by regulators to raise short-distance charges by making them usage-dependent and to lower long-distance charges. 'This would have the effect of increasing the chances of direct entry to local distribution of telephone services, by existing or new devices, hence introducing competition to the most entrenched monopoly position: that in local competition.'[42] The implication was that BT should be encouraged to charge above marginal costs for residential service so that competition in local network services would enter.

The government's response was broad agreement with the recommendations for increased competition but an implicit rejection of Beesley's arguments that open resale should be allowed. Instead it announced that from the beginning of 1982 there would be freedom for the private sector to use BT circuits to compete with BT in a variety of services, provided that those services would 'involve substantial elements additional to the basic network facilities'. In other words it accepted BT's rather than Beesley's arguments. Further liberalisation in international services was also rejected for the moment.

The Industry Minister argued that these new competitive services would reduce BT's revenue only by an amount which could be met by an additional 10 per cent increase in telephone rentals by 1990. He did not mention that BT had estimated for the Beesley Report that for each 10 per cent increase in rentals a further 2.5 per cent of customers would be lost, or that 25 per cent (5m) households already had no telephone.[43]

BT's response to the report was to point to the quid pro quo which it recommended. In return for open competition on resale of leased lines it argued that BT should be allowed to raise money on the open market. Faced with a capital investment programme of £2.2 billion for 1981–2 and a government borrowing limit of £180 million, later raised by an extra £145 million, BT faced a shortfall in its capital requirements of £300 million.[44]

In the summer of 1981, the government also announced that it had received a detailed proposal for a business transmission system to compete with BT and that it was in principle in favour of such a proposal. It seems that the idea of a specific competitor to BT's domestic network came about during the plans for liberalisation in the summer of 1980 in and around the Ministry, an idea provoked it seems by the 'dreadful service' which the Post Office was then providing to the City. The Mercury consortium consisted of Cable and Wireless, a company with telecommunications experience in Hong Kong, Barclays Bank and British Petroleum. The consortium's presentation was made to the Ministry in the summer of 1981. Mercury planned to link up the twenty-six major cities in Britain by optic fibre cable laid along railway tracks, and to provide trunk and international services to business. The consortium was anxious to establish a service by 1983 and wanted its licence issued by the autumn of 1981. The hurry was caused by the imminence of a general election in 1983–4 and the possibility that a Labour government might revoke the liberalisation of BT's monopoly.[45]

Liberalisation was fought by the trade unions within the Post Office, by the Post Office itself and by the Labour opposition. Although an extensive consultation exercise was undertaken by the Ministry with the Post Office, manufacturers and major customers' organisations, trade unions were excluded from the exercise. It could be that the minister hoped to buy off trade union opposition with the original provisions for maintenance which would have safeguarded the jobs of the Post Office Engineering Union (now the National Communications Union). In this he was unsuccessful. Through their sponsored MPs in Parliament and through the Labour party in particular the trade unions fought against the passage of the Bill. They were particularly successful in gaining the support of Conservative Politicians concerned at the possibility of increased charges in rural areas.[46]

Despite the fact that BT was itself against the liberalisation, the threat of competition made it less than sympathetic to the trade unions. A new chairman, Sir George Jefferson, from aerospace, appointed in 1980, had already set about altering the ethos of the corporation to a customer-orientated commercial company. Within BT the creation of four profit-orientated divisions was itself a profound change from the previous centralised bureaucracy.[47]

Despite the opposition of the Labour party, the liberalisation bill passed easily through Parliament with much self-congratulation from the government. Kenneth Baker, the Minister for Information Technology, saw the new regulatory framework as a half-way house between pure monopoly and the free market. He is quoted as saying:

The new framework we have created is unique. It is a halfway house between the US free market controlled by a regulatory authority and a host of litigation, and the corporatist solution or national monopoly prevailing in Europe. It has already attracted the attention of the Japanese and the EEC Commission who are looking for new regulatory models.[48]

The new legislation increased the power of the Minister, who now had the authority to license either directly or through delegation to BT both equipment and transmission. Licenses were to be used to specify the standards for certification of equipment; to authorise the attachment to the network of items or categories of equipment; to sanction the development of complete 'systems' and modes of use of the network and to permit the introduction of alternative services in competition with BT. The act also gave the Minister power to insist on some action by BT or to remedy some action and directly increased his discretionary power. This increased central power, a feature also of other legislation from the Thatcher government, was justified on the grounds that it would allow flexibility in the implementation of the liberalisation. Despite intensive lobbying which took place during the passage of the bill, many within the industry arguing that there should be an independent statutory body to manage the liberalised regime, the proposal was rejected by the government in favour of control by the Ministry.[49]

The way in which the powers were actually used or delegated

obviously had an impact on the real extent of liberalisation which ensued. The immediate post-liberalisation period was primarily concerned with the liberalisation of the equipment monopoly and also with the issuing of a licence to Mercury, which received a letter of intent from the government in October of 1981.

In the equipment market the practical necessity to phase liberalisation over a number of years and dependence on BT for technical expertise limited the liberalisation programme. Formally the British Standards Institution became responsible for setting the standards for equipment but because of the time needed to formulate standards, and because the equipment certifying body, a subsidiary of the British Electrical Equipment board was inadequately financed and staffed, BT continued to wield power over equipment certification. The timetable agreed for liberalisation of equipment envisaged that telephones and modems should be liberalised first, by November 1981, and that the final liberalisation in July 1983 would be of PABX.[50] The order of this liberalisation was agreed between BT, the manufacturers and the Ministry. Although it was presented as a means of allowing British manufacturers to introduce new PABX it can also be assumed to have been in BT's interests in that the small PABX market was expected to have the strongest growth potential. In other words the market in which BT's supply would be most subject to external competition was kept under BT's control for the longest period.

By the winter of 1981 when it had become embarassingly obvious that despite the hype on liberalisation almost no new products had reached the consumer, and BT was handling certification in a leisurely manner, the Ministry introduced new certification arrangements.[51] It stepped in to take control of certification of equipment to be sold on the open market, first certifying telephones already available through BT and then inviting applications for certification from suppliers. Three months later the Ministry complained that of ninety-six telephones submitted for certification only one was wholly British. And, by mid-June only one new telephone design had been approved for competitive supply while none of the six types of PABX selected by the Ministry for testing had won approval.[52]

In some cases the Ministry was more anxious for direct sales in competition with BT than were the firms themselves—partly because they had no retail outlets and no mechanisms for providing information to customers and partly because they had no wish to offend BT, their largest customer. In other areas, such as telex equipment, even though the firms wanted private sales BT was reluctant to allow them because it had only just started to replace the 120,000 old telex terminals in use in Britain. In November 1981 BT announced that it would sell telephones as well as rent them and then announced that it would manufacture its own cheap push-button telephone.[53]

On the transmission side operators could apply to use BT circuits during the interim period (until April 1982) to supply any VAN services which BT was not supplying. After that date the private sector would be able to use BT circuits to compete with BT in the supply of all kinds of services provided these services involved substantial elements additional to the basic network service. Resale of network capacity or international transmission by dedicated circuits were excluded from the VAN, which would be licensed. VANS which were purely in-house would also be licensed. Licenses were to be issued by BT in conjunction with the Ministry, although a right of appeal existed to the Secretary of State and an informal advisory panel.[54] Hence BT became the judge of its competitors, a situation which led to complaints and to the Ministry taking over the licencing function in the Spring of 1982.

There were further problems with the issue of Mercury's licence. Despite the initial rush it was not issued until February 1982, four months after the split between BT and the Post Office had taken place and the new liberalised regime had begun. The delay was caused by two factors. First Mercury wished to be interconnected to international public switched networks, meaning that once Mercury had reached agreement with another carrier in another country then a Mercury customer could dial anyone in that country. The proposal threatened BT's revenue more than any other, since its growth market was in international calls, and it was these which subsidised domestic calls.[55] The government insisted that under the current legislation Mercury had to act as an agent of BT. The second problem was the technical and commercial basis of the interconnection that would take place between Mercury and the BT network. While Mercury's interests were in establishing as much interconnection as possible, BT's interests were obviously in limiting that interconnection. By the time the licence for Mercury was issued in February 1982 the two had agreed technically on three levels of interconnection—that Mercury's network could be connected to a switchboard maintained by BT; that private circuits leased from BT outside the trunk network of Mercury could be linked in to it; that there would be dialled connection between the two networks. Commercial terms and a fourth layer of interconnection, allowing the two networks to be 'transparent' were left in abeyance for several months.[56]

In general this post-'liberalisation' period can be characterised as a period in which BT managed to run rings around the Department of Industry. The Department made no secret of the fact that it was displeased with the way in which BT had responded to liberalisation. But the Ministry itself was criticised by the manufacturers for underestimating the tenacity of BT and underestimating the complexity of liberalisation. The lesson which seems to have been learned in this period was that BT was capable of overwhelming civil servants with lengthy technical arguments, that civil servants were not trained for the detailed regulation necessary and that some kind of regulatory body besides the Office of Fair Trading was necessary to act as a focus for complaints against BT's unfair competitive behaviour.

It was at this point that the possibility of privatisation of BT seems to have arisen again and we shall discuss the process of privatisation in Chapter Five. There were obvious gainers and losers however even in the few months of the liberalisation of BT's monopoly. The gainer in liberalisation was BT especially, which was able to use the power given it by government to delay its competitors, and to delay the approval of apparatus. The very fact that BT would test equipment was itself enough to deter competitors from submitting equipment for approval for sale on the open market. Even that equipment already supplied through BT had to go through this process of testing and approval. Another gainer initially was the City, which both received special treatment from BT, and benefited from the reductions in cost of international and trunk calls. Large business customers in general benefited from new services initiated by BT soon after its liberalisation such as Sat-stream to Canada and a new data communications service between large cities in Britain. A further gain accrued to the Ministry, which received increased regulatory power over BT and to the politicians who steered through the liberalisation measure. Kenneth Baker, the Minister of Information Technology, eventually received his reward in a Cabinet post. Losers were the equipment manufacturers who could not get approval for equipment and other businesses who could not get licences for VANs. In general liberalisation channelled wealth away from British manufacturers to those overseas and away from manufacturing to heavy users of long-distance and international communications—financial services and information companies. And in all the hiatus about equipment liberalisation, there was almost no public debate on the question of BT's transmission monopoly of local networks or what local network costs its competitors should contribute towards, or what rate of depreciation it should adopt, or what its investment strategy should be, or how it should cost its services, or how it should be prevented from cross-subsidisation. These behavioural 'regulatory' questions were ignored by virtually everyone.

Notes and references

1. Jeffrey Kieve, *The Electric Telegraph. A Social and Economic History*, Newton Abbott, David Charles, 1973, pp .154–75.
2. Viscount Wolmer, *Post Office Reform, its Importance and Practicability*, London, Ivor Nicholson, 1932, p. 94.
3. Ibid., p. 96.
4. Ibid., p. 96.
5. Ibid., p. 98.
6. Ibid., p. 97.
7. Sir James Ferguson, Postmaster General, quoted in Viscount Wolmer, op. cit., p. 100.
8. Sir Evelyn Murray, *The Post Office*, London and New York, G. P. Putnam's Sons, 1927, p. 126.
9. Sir Evelyn Murray, op. cit., pp .125–8; Viscount Wolmer, op. cit. p. 108. A further historical account is to be found in Douglas Pitt, *The Telecommunications Function in the British Post Office*, Farnborough, Saxon House, 1978, pp .23–37.
10. Viscount Wolmer, op. cit., p. 14.
11. Gerald Brock, *The Telecommunications Industry: The Dynamics of Market Structure*, Cambridge Mass. and London, Harvard University Press, 1981, p. 147.
12. Viscount Wolmer, op. cit., p. 155.
13. Ibid., pp .148–9.
14. Comparative figures are given by Gerald Brock, op. cit., p. 144; Viscount Wolmer, op. cit., p. 119.
15. Sir Evelyn Murray, op. cit., pp .149–50.
16. Jill Hills, *Information Technology and Industrial Policy* Beckenham, Croom Helm, 1984, pp .117–8.
17. For an exposition of these pro-privatisation views of the time see: Michael Canes, *Telephones-Public or Private?*, London, Institute of Economic Affairs, 1966.
18. Jill Hills, op. cit., p .119.
19. Douglas Pitt, op. cit.
20. Francis Cripps and Wynne Godley, *The Planning of Telecommunications in the United Kingdom*, Cambridge, Dept. of Applied Economics, 1978, p. 14.
21. Ibid., pp. 9-19.
22. Ibid., pp. 19-22.
23. Ibid., p. 72.
24. British Telecom, *Statistics 1981*, London, British Telecom, 1981, p. 6
25. Ibid., p. 7.
26. Francis Cripps and Wynne Godley, op. cit., pp. 11–12.
27. British Telecom, op. cit., p. 13; HMSO, *Social Trends*, London, HMSO, 1984, p. 33.

28. Stephen C. Littlechild, *Elements of Telecommunications Economics* London, Institute of Electrical Engineers, 1979, pp. 38–9.
29. House of Commons Select Committee on the Nationalised Industries, *First Report on the Post Office*, London, HMSO, 1967, hardly considers costing. *Report of the Post Office Review Committee*, London, HMSO, 1977, pp. 31–2. (Carter Report) touches on costing, but only to complain about the lack of adequate measures.
30. *Carter Report*, op. cit., p. 39.
31. Michael Beesley, *Liberalisation of the Use of British Telecom's Network*, London, HMSO, 1981, p. 3. (Beesley Report)
32. *Carter Report*, op. cit., p. 134.
33. Ibid., pp. 101–2; *Beesley Report*, op. cit., p. 9.
34. John Kay, 'The Privatization of British Telecommunications', in David Steel and David Heald (eds.), *Privatizing Public Enterprises*, London, RIPA, 1984, pp. 77–86.
35. *Sunday Times*, 16 September 1979.
36. *Carter Report*, op. cit., pp. 107–8.
37. G. B. Bleazard, *Telecommunications in Transition—a Position Paper*, London, National Computing Centre, 1982, p. 24.
38. Memorandum accompanying a statement by Sir Keith Joseph to the House of Commons, 21 July 1980.
39. Ibid.
40. *Beesley Report*, op. cit., p. 27.
41. Ibid., p. X; see also report of World Telecommunications Conference, *Financial Times*, 12 December 1984.
42. *Beesley Report*, op. cit., p. 30.
43. *Beesley Report*, op. cit., p. 15; *Guardian*, 16 April 1981.
44. *Guardian*, 16 November 1981.
45. *Financial Times*, 24 February 1982.
46. David Thomas, 'The Union Response to Denationalisation', in David Steel and David Heald, *Privatising Public Enterprises*, op. cit., pp. 59–76;
47. POEU, *Making the Future Work. The Broad Strategy*, London, POEU, November 1984, pp. 24–8.
48. G. B. Bleazard, op. cit., p. 46.
49. Ibid., p. 65.
50. Ibid., p. 57.
51. *Financial Times*, 17 November 1981; 30 April 1982.
52. *Financial Times*, 28 July 1982
53. *The Guardian*, 20 November 1981.
54. *Financial Times*, 24 February 1982
55. *Beesley Report*, op. cit., p. 25.
56. *Financial Times*, 24 February 1982.

4 Japan: liberalisation under public-control

Introduction

The study of Japanese policy-making has primarily been the province of American scholars, rather than European. Perhaps because they are used to a more pluralistic framework, the main lines of emphasis have been on the corporatist aspects of links between the Japanese state and industry. In particular, during the 1950s and 1960s the country became known as 'Japan Inc'.

Those who examined Japanese industrial policymaking came to the conclusion that there were two patterns to be seen. First policymaking could be viewed as stemming primarily from the bureaucracy, as it had done in pre-war Japan. In this analysis MITI, the Ministry for International Trade and Industry, by a variety of mechanisms such as import controls, export controls and low-cost bank loans controlled the expansion of Japanese industry. A second analysis portrayed MITI, the Liberal Democratic party and Keidanren (the Federation of Economic organisations) as the triple pillars of 'Japan Inc'. Both models emphasised the consensual nature of Japanese policymaking and industrial planning.

It was not until the 1970s that cracks were perceived in this consensual process and the conflicts between established and non-established companies and between Ministries were brought to light.[1] Now, in the 1980s the highly competitive element in Japanese society is accepted by academics and the structural changes within the Japanese economy—the internationalisation of companies and the liberalisation of both trade and financial markets—are seen as a limitation on MITI's traditional influence.[2]

The history of telecommunications in Japan illuminates these different trends in policymaking. Telephone service developed under the monopoly of central government, first vested in the Ministry of Communication, and then in NTT, a public corporation. Even as a public corporation, NTT was still very much under central government control. Given the task of providing a universal telephone service, NTT's extension of the network between 1950 and 1980 was remarkable. Limited by legislation which kept local call rates stable for twenty years, it was able only to keep up its expansion by making access charges high. That, despite these heavy access charges, it expanded at the rate of more than 20 per cent per annum is evidence both of the rising living standards of the time and the increasing value of the telephone to individuals and business as the network expanded. Limitation of local call revenue coupled with the post-war model it took from AT&T and Bell Labs, pushed NTT into perpetual upgrading of the technological efficiency of the network, leading eventually to a lowering of the very high trunk call charges.

It was however the actions of MITI which prevented NTT from concentrating solely on the telephone network, and forced it into providing a public data communications network. Bureaucratic competition acted to liberalise data communications and with it all customer premises' equipment with the exception of the first telephone. Hence, by 1981, data communications, including resale and interconnection of leased lines with the public network was almost fully liberalised, the exception being value added networks by large companies. International leased circuits were also heavily controlled by the private, government-regulated company, KDD, which both had the monopoly of international communications and kept its charges high.

This system of regulation and liberalisation benefited the residential consumer and domestic manufacturer to the detriment of large service companies and trunk and international callers in general. It was also to the detriment of American telecommunications manufacturers who wished to enter the Japanese market.

American pressure began in the late 1970s, at a time when it seemed that the American economy was sliding into recession and when the Japanese progress in microelectronics had begun to threaten the United States's world technological lead. It was focused against NTT's traditional relationship with its suppliers, which unlike manufacturers in the United States or Britain, manufactured integrated tele/computing equipment. These suppliers, both vertically integrated into microchip manufacture and horizontally integrated across both telecommunications and computing represented the greatest world challenge to the American computing industry.

The history of NTT's liberalisation and subsequent privatisation illustrates however the necessity for external pressure to be allied with domestic interests who will gain from a redistribution of resources. These interests were to be found in the bureaucratic fight for turf between the low-status Ministry of Posts and Telecommunications and the high-status Ministry of International Trade and Industry.

Historical background

Unlike Britain, Japan never suffered a period of semi-competition in telecommunications. The telegraph was introduced to Japan in 1871 and a national network had been established by 1880 under government control. Two telephones were tested by the Japanese bureaucracy in 1877, but presumably in order to protect telegraph revenues, the telephone was not introduced until 1890, rather later than in Britain. The first telephone was British made.

From its first introduction the telephone was controlled by the central bureaucracy together with posts and telegraph under the Ministry of Communication. Growth of the telephone network was as slow as in Britain. There were about 12000 subscribers in 1910.[3] These were mainly business subscribers and until some time after the Second World War the telephone remained a status symbol for residential subscribers. Unlike Britain, in 1902 subscribers were allowed to provide their own PABX which they then had to maintain themselves.[4] Until the 1920s the system remained that of manual exchanges, and as equipment clogged up with traffic a waiting list developed. As in Britain, investment was limited by central government.

Automatic exchanges began to be introduced after the Great Earthquake of 1923 which destroyed much of the telephone system. But unlike Britain where standardisation took place at this time, the Japanese used two competing systems, one German and one British, which, from 1930, were both manufactured under licence in Japan. However, the two systems produced problems in compatibility which had not been sorted out by the time of the outbreak of war.

The first international telephone line was opened in 1932, one year after the establishment of the International Telephone Company. But, during the war, the Ministry of Communications took over all international communications. By 1945 there were approximately one half the number of telephone subscribers in Japan 1.1 million, as there were in Britain (2.1m), and similarly the majority of people communicated by letter or telegraph. In fact domestic telegraph traffic in Japan did not peak until 1963.

Much of the telephone system was destroyed at the end of the war, about half a million connections being lost, and the number of subscribers only passed the one million mark again in 1950. During the American occupation, in order to speed Japan's economic recovery, the occupying forces issued a memorandum to the government of Japan requiring the reorganisation of the telecommunications service.

In 1949, the original Ministry of Communications was split into two, one Ministry responsible for posts and the other for telecommunications. Following the example of AT&T and its Bell Labs., the new Ministry emphasised research and development. The Electrical Communications Laboratory was created as part of this Ministry and it was decided that all new equipment should be designed by ECL so that leadership in the technology would reside with the government administration.[5]

At the end of the occupation there was a movement, backed by the then Prime Minister Ushida, to have a privately owned telecommunications carrier and to use American technology. The Minister of Telecommunications, Eisaku Sato (later to be Prime Minister) opposed him, with the result that a compromise was reached. In 1952 the Ministry of Communication became NTT, which was inaugurated as a public corporation with a monopoly of domestic telecommunications. The Ministry of Posts gained responsibility for communications policy and became the Ministry of Posts and Telecommunications (MPT). International telecommunications were designated the monopoly of Kokusai Denshin Denwa (KDD), a government regulated company, in which NTT holds 10 per cent of the equity. The ECL became part of NTT.[6]

At that time there were just 1.5 million telephone customers of whom only 6 per cent were residential and there was a waiting list of 360,000.[7] The legislation which created NTT set its task as: '... to establish a system for effective and efficient operation of public telecommunications and to expedite the consolidation and expansion of the public telecommunications facilities and thereby promote the welfare of the public'.[8] The major focus in Japan, just as in the United States and Britain, was to achieve a system of universal service, but the task was greater since there were fewer telephones already in the network.

Although both NTT and BT were public corporations before privatisation, the term actually means different things in the two countries. NTT's status was akin to that of the Post Office as a civil service department but with greater Parliamentary control. Whereas a public corporation in Britain provides an annual report to Parliament and is shielded from day-to-day interference by Parliament in the running of its affairs, NTT's budget was submitted to the Parliament on an annual basis, and staff could be called before Parliament for questioning. (Such questioning is unusual in Britain, but customary in the United States.) In addition NTT's staff came under civil service conditions of service, being unable to strike and with wages held down to match those within non-profit making corporations such as the Japanese National Railways. Just as the Post Office, even after being given public corporation status, had to pay the government a proportion of its profits as a levy, so NTT had to make payments each year. Investment decisions had to to be made on an annual basis, subject to Parliamentary approval.

At its inception NTT was given a monopoly over domestic telephone and telegraph transmission and over the supply of telephones. Equipment was originally for rental rather than sale and NTT had no power to manufacture. The equipment market was liberalised further in 1957 when customers were allowed to provide their own extension telephones, and again in 1970 when they were allowed to provide other attachments. The Japanese equipment market was therefore liberalised at about the same time as the Carter-phone decision had begun liberalisation in the United States. NTT retained only its monopoly over the first phone, on the grounds that the primary phone originally operated as a sub-system in its own right and in the event of a local power failure the customer could still be contacted through power supplied by the exchange. Once new types of phones were introduced the reason for NTT's monopoly ended. From 1983 NTT began to sell telephones on an experimental basis.[9]

The growth of the Japanese network came earlier than the British, reflecting the British policy of holding back demand and NTT's policy of five year plans to expand supply as quickly as possible. Between the inception of NTT and 1981 the number of telephone customers increased annually by about 13 per cent to reach 40 million by the end of 1981. This average conceals the 21 per cent annual growth between 1965 and 1975. The backlog of demand peaked at 2.91 million in 1970 when NTT upped its installation rate from 1.5 million lines to 3 million per year. Nevertheless, it took until 1979 for the waiting list to be finally cleared. From 1978 onwards the market matured, with growth in the 1980s of only 3 per cent per annum.[10]

Nationwide Subscriber Trunk Dialling was introduced in 1979 at the same time as in Britain, but the newer technology of the Japanese system was reflected in its costs and productivity. Whereas in 1975 the British Post Office had 19.1 million telephones with 247,205 employees or eighty-three phones per employee, in comparison Japan had 39.4 million telephones with 310,000 employees or 127 telephones per employee. In the United States, AT&T with 118.5 million telephones had 770,250 employees or 154 telephones per employee.[11] In other words NTT was 18 per cent less productive than AT&T but 35 per cent more productive than the British Post Office. By 1984 NTT had 201 telephones per employee, a productivity increase of 60 per cent compared to a 30 per cent increase in British Telecom's productivity.[12]

Unlike Britain the local call charge and access charge could not be manipulated to restrict demand or meet costs. Fixed by legislation local call tariffs stayed at ¥7 for twenty years, although the original base of pricing which allowed any length of time for that amount within a 5–7km radius was modified in 1972. In 1976 the unit was changed to ¥10 (4.5 cents; 3.4 pence) which it remains, providing the cheapest local call rate in any country.[13]

The effect of legislative control of local call tariffs was similar to that in the United States, where public utility commissioners kept local rates low—trunk call rates were probably kept high to compensate. Between 1951 and 1981 the cost of trunk calls was reduced by almost 75 per cent. Even so, by 1981 the price differential between trunk and local calls was sixty compared to twelve in Britain. For calls up to 60km the two systems were more or less comparable (the ratio in Japan was eight from a lower base price compared to Britain's four) but over very long distances inland trunk calls were as expensive in 1984 as a phone call to the Continent from Britain.[14] In 1983 NTT responded to domestic business pressure with a reduction in long-distance tariffs, arguing that this reduction reflected savings produced by new digital technology, but further tariff reductions in the price of these services which it wanted to institute in 1984 were not allowed by the MPT.[15]

Access to the network in Japan was also expensive. In 1984 the connection fee was ¥80,000 (about $400). Prior to 1983 subscribers also had to purchase a bond from NTT which was priced differentially between Tokyo and outside, costing between £150 and £500. The bond could be resold but the subscriber sustained a loss on the transaction. Thirty per cent of NTT's finance came from this source. Similarly to BT, over half of its funds for investment were generated internally, helping also to generate its imbalanced charges. In 1959 there were only 350,000 residential subscribers to the telephone service (less than 12 per cent of the total number of subscribers). By 1982 residential subscribers formed 70 per cent of the network.[16] Residential penetration is almost as high as American standards of 98 per cent—in 1984 NTT's network reached 96 per cent of households compared to BT's 77 per cent in Britain. In addition rural areas were served by a local cable system. Producing a form of competition with NTT, the numbers of telephones on this system dropped from 3 million in 1969 to 1.5 million in 1984 as NTT expanded its network.[17] The Japanese also use public telephones a great deal. Unlike the Post Office or BT, NTT has continually expanded their number so that with 1 million public telephones in 1984 access for those without a private telephone was easy—and cheap.

Turning to technology and equipment manufacture, NTT's purchasing power and R & D has had a major impact on the telecommunications industry in Japan. By 1980 it was responsible for a $3.5 million procurement budget. Until 1981 procurement was from Japanese manufacturers alone. Procurement provided the domestic basis for the export sales which began as the domestic market matured. In view of American complaints in the late 1970s about NTT's procurement policy and its relationship with its family of manufacturers, which provided the spur to privatisation, it is interesting to look for a moment at the way in which ECL, the Engineering Bureau of NTT and the manufacturers worked.[18] The process indicates the close relationship between the various actors which presents considerable difficulties for foreign manufacturers to emulate. Despite pressure to open this part of NTT's procurement to American companies, these traditional relationships militated against American success.

After NTT's inauguration in 1952, at first it used Western Electric's technology manufactured locally. Then, in order to help speed up the introduction of subscriber trunk dialling, NTT decided in the 1950s to develop its own cross-bar system. After the problems of the pre-war competitive systems NTT decided that there should be a unified system which was developed in a joint exercise between the four manufacturers: Fujitsu, Hitachi, NEC, Oki and the ECL.

In developing the cross-bar system in the 1950s three stages were involved. First there was co-operative investigation of possible systems. Then followed a stage in which the ECL and manufacturers shared both the design and the manufacture of the chosen systems and then came co-operative testing by all the parties concerned. The ECL was involved in all these stages: it put forward the fundamental concepts, led discussions and formulated conclusions. The relationship between manufacturers and NTT was closer and involved a greater leadership role on the part of the research laboratories than was the case in Britain. While the manufacturers were co-operating on the cross-bar public exchange they were also developing their own PBXs for sale overseas. In contrast British manufacturers were content at this time to export Strowger equipment to the Commonwealth.

In 1963 Bell Labs in the United States announced its first fully electronic exchange, No. 1 ESS, and as on other occasions an American innovation acted as a spur to Japanese development. In 1964 NTT decided on a ten year plan to develop stored program control (computer control) for the Japanese system and a new agreement covering the exchange of information, the ownership of patents from future work, the ownership of the software to be produced and the regulation of the publication of the results was drawn up. The manufacturers had to pay for their own trial manufacture and their own test models.

The organisation of the work took place through a number of committees and sub-committees each chaired by an ECL engineer but with the four manufacturers represented on each committee. First detailed designs were drawn up with all members of the committees sharing the work, with design work reviewed at weekly intervals by a working party meeting at ECL. Then, once the design work was completed construction was allocated to the manufacturers, under ECL control. Research costs were split between the five companies. When it became obvious that the first designs were not adequate for the task required by NTT, digital development work was stopped in the 1960s. Another set of committees were inaugurated and new designs begun. This time each manufacturer kept an engineer permanently at ECL. The ensuing system was put into service in December 1971 and then adopted as a standard system by NTT for new large offices. It became referred to as D-10. In comparison Britain had no stored program control system during the 1970s.

Whereas manufacture in Britain took place on a cost plus basis, NTT determined a fixed price with yearly revision dates to take account of economies of production. Both NTT engineers and manufacturers emphasise the overwhelming importance of providing manufacturing costs against R & D costs.[19] Because at least two models of a system were usually made it was possible to compare the accuracy of production between the manufacturers. The process of development was therefore a combination of co-operation and competition, with incentives to complete R & D as quickly as cheaply as possible and to achieve lower unit costs on the fixed price.

The Japanese manufacturers differ historically from the British and American. In both Britain and the United States telecommunications manufacturers have traditionally been separate from computer manufacturers, AT&T from IBM, GEC and Plessey separate from International Computers Limited (ICL). In Japan the major manufacturers of computers were already manufacturers of telecommunications equipment before diversifying into computers once the telecommunications market matured during the latter 1970s. During the 1970s they also became major manufacturers of integrated circuits.

Whereas in both Britain and the United States the convergence of telecommunications has resulted in competition for the same telecommunications/computing market from separate sets of companies and therefore for deregulation of the telecommunications market, not only did technological convergence come earlier to Japan but this conflict between different sets of manufacturers for the equipment market was not evident. However, conflict between traditional telecommunications and computing arose in the jockeying which took place between the Ministry of Posts and Telecommunications and MITI. MITI argued that the convergence of computers and telecommunications brought the new data communications services into its sphere of responsibility, while MPT argued that it fell within its aegis of telecommunications. MPT's argument was bolstered by the digitalisation of traditional switching and transmission systems. Since the 1960s competition and conflict between the two Ministries has been endemic.

The spur to computer development in Japan came in 1954 with the first import of an American computer into Japan, the same year that the five major Japanese manufacturers began production under licence of the transistor. Worried that the Japanese computer industry would be dominated by foreign competition MITI began to encourage the indigenous computer manufacturing industry. In 1955 it organised a Computer Research Project, which was followed by the 1957 Electronics Industry Development Provisional Act establishing MITI's position as responsible for overall policy towards the industry. Subsequently MITI targeted the computer industry to receive priority low interest bank loans. To gain technological know-how in a short space of time the Japanese companies entered into licensing agreements with American manufacturers, but the Japanese were forced to admit IBM into local manufacture in exchange for the licensing of basic patents. The domestic computer industry was heavily protected by foreign exchange laws and heavy tariff duties, but as a local manufacturer IBM was quickly able to take 50 per cent of the domestic market.

IBM's introduction of the system 360 machine in 1964 stimulated the local industry into outright competition and galvanised both MITI and the industry to produce a computer plan, after which the scale of support for the industry increased substantially. In 1968 an informal recommendation encouraged the development of the usage of computers within government agencies, so that public procurement became part of the strategy of strengthening the industry. This use of public procurement was hardly new—in 1963 a 'Buy Japan' Cabinet order had been issued which was not rescinded until 1973—but further impetus was given to public sector computerisation and the domestic manufacturers in general. As growth markets diversified from large mainframes to mini and microcomputers so IBM's share of the local market decreased from the 50 per cent of the 1960s to 30 per cent in 1970. MITI kept a watchful eye on IBM in particular, stepping in when it felt IBM was guilty of over-aggressive marketing.[20]

During the 1960s software was predominantly provided by the manufacturers. In an effort to unbundle and stimulate an independent software industry MITI issued a report in 1969 which accorded priority to the development of the industry and the training of personnel. The report led directly to a joint software venture between the Ministry and the five manufacturers. At the same time as it was attempting to liberalise the software market MITI also attempted to liberalise the data communications market. In 1967 it attempted to initiate a timesharing service but failed due to the opposition of the MPT to the sale of telephone lines to third parties.[21]

NTT had begun to provide data communications services for private companies in 1968 with the inauguration of an on-line service linking local banks. NTT's president compared the inauguration of this service to that of the telephone in 1890 and ten years ahead of his time talked of the coming information revolution using computers and communications.[22] Nevertheless NTT was still facing a waiting list for basic telephone service of almost 2.5 million people and clearly the provision of value added networks was not a primary objective.

Following its defeat MITI enlisted the support of Keidanren (the business trade association) and the Liberal Democratic party, whose members may have seen in the issue the possibility of campaign donations. MPT's offer of a case-by-case liberalisation was considered to be inadequate and eventually the LDP's Policy Deliberation Council (the highest policy-making organ in the party) suggested a compromise. From September 1971 leased data processing circuits were introduced. Companies were allowed to share circuits for interconnection to their own computers but interconnection with third parties and with the public network were still subject to the MPT's discretion.

In the trade-offs which took place NTT was allowed to increase its charges for the first time since 1952. The installation charge was increased to ¥50,000. At the same time a system of charging dependent on time and distance was introduced for the first time so as to permit the connection of computers to the network, and the customer premises' equipment monopoly of NTT was further liberalised. Resulting from this liberalisation MPT, NTT and the manufacturers later developed joint standards which allowed different makes of computers to communicate.[23]

Responding to demand, in 1972 NTT introduced its public data communication service which used a separate network for voice traffic. Numbers of leased data circuits and public circuits had grown by almost 900 per cent by 1981. In addition there were about 4000 VAN which were privately run, the major users being construction and manufacturing companies, banks and retailers.[24]

In other words at about the same time as the FCC was allowing specialised common carriers entry into AT&T's market with leased data circuits, the same process of liberalisation beginning with the sharing of leased circuits had begun in Japan. But unlike the United States where AT&T at this time was excluded from data communications, or in Britain where the Post Office was still experimenting with data communications, in Japan, at an early stage, NTT was one of the primary providers both of customised data networks and of a public data communications network which was seperate from the voice network. As data communications grew so pressure for further liberalisation came from MITI aided in particular by American companies, such as IBM, and despite the opposition of the MPT, concerned that IBM and AT&T might swamp the domestic data network market. From 1982 shared use of leased circuits or shared use of equipment attached to the public data network no longer had to have the approval of the MPT, third-party use of leased circuits was allowed and, provided certain standards were met, interconnection between leased circuit and the public data network was allowed. NTT retained the right of refusal of VANs only in the case of large companies.[25]

NTT's computer services section provided a turn-key facility to companies who wished to establish their own nation-wide VAN. By 1983 NTT was operating seventy-three different national private data communication systems, including a system introduced in 1979 linking all national banks. In addition by then it provided two public data communication services.[26]

Technological developments also brought a series of new services to both the business user and the residential consumer. Facsimile transmission is probably the most important of these in Japan. Because of the structure of the language most documents in Japanese are hand-

written rather than typed and facsimile is the easiest method of transmittal. Public facsimile service was introduced as early as 1930 with
phototelegrams (a form of electronic mail) transmitted by telephone
lines but died for lack of demand. Facsimile remained a technology
used for communications within NTT and other companies. In 1974
there were already 20,000 facsimile machines operating in Japan, way
ahead of developments elsewhere. Public facsimile network service
began in Tokyo in 1981 with the intention of having a nation-wide
service by 1986. Facsimile equipment production rose by 55 per cent a
year to 600,000 units in 1984, whilst costs of facsimile equipment fell
by 50 per cent.[27] NTT reported that the use of its facsimile transmission
service more than quadrupled in 1983 and facsimile subscriptions
increased by almost two thirds [28]

The concept of ISDN arose out of NTT's provision of these various
services, each with its own network. Inevitably customers wanted to
interface one service with another, but the costs for NTT of providing
such interfaces was prohibitively expensive. ISDN arose originally as a
form of cost-saving. It was proposed by Dr Yasasuda Kitahara, the then
executive vice-president of NTT, first in 1978 in Tokyo and then at the
third World Telecommunication Forum in 1979 under the title Information Network System. The goal of INS was to provide an: 'integrated
information system which can economically and efficiently handle
transmission, storage, conversion and processing of information
through the marriage of telecommunications and computers'.[29] This
public network, incorporating telephone, facsimile, data and video, was
to be completed by the year 2000. The network depended on the
development of four technologies, digital switching, optic fibre, satellite
communications and a new fifth generation of high speed intelligent
computers. It also involved charging by 'bit' rates of information transmitted, rather than by time or distance usage, as had become the norm
for telephone traffic.

The four networks—telegraph, telephone, data and facsimile, which
NTT ran separately—were to be integrated into one network combined
with video and telex services. In addition to two demonstration projects
in Tokyo and Tskuba Science City NTT intended that the system
should be publicly available in ten cities by 1986. To some extent
MPT's demonstration projects have overlapped with others sponsored
by MITI on the new media society—one of the features of INS is that it
considerably extends MPT turf—and competition between the two
continues.[30]

It was MITI's interest in 1970s in cable TV which was responsible for

MPT's sudden concern for the medium, which it had more or less dismissed as an alternative to traditional telecommunications transmission. In 1971 the MPT began to licence one-way cable and both Ministries have supported local experiments with interactive cable services. To some extent cable TV has been seen as an interim service for hard to reach localities in Japan's mountainous countryside, to be replaced by DBS using Japan's own satellites. In 1983 it had a penetration of about 12 per cent which was slightly more than in Britain. Experience has shown in both the United States and Britain that cable TV can take off in conjunction with satellite transmission and that once there is satellite transmission a market develops in SAMTV receiveonly dishes. Japanese companies, in particular NEC, are strong in the manufacture of these dishes, while the satellite and electronics industry are working towards a unified market. In 1983 MPT began to licence two-way cable systems. In terms of competition officials thought that the traditional telephone service would not be threatened by cable interactive services for another ten years.

From the point of view of foreign computer companies and for those running VANs the proposed ISN system was threatening. In the words of Kitahara: 'In digital networks service rates will be expressed in terms of bits. Moreover it will no longer be necessary for carriers other than the common carrier to create their own computer communications network. There will be no need to duplicate or triplicate investments.'[31] Not only would there no longer be any need for private VANs but the tariff rate for INS would measure the amount of information transmitted. Large private companies in particular were likely to be heavily hit by the new tariff rate and by the redundancy of their existing investment. A domestic constituency existed therefore which would benefit from the privatisation of NTT and the abandonment of a full INS system.

Turning to the pressures which built up towards NTT's privatisation it is necessary to look at the international context in which it developed. Japan's continued dependence on exports for a high proportion of GNP is of crucial importance in considering how its domestic policy developed. From 1977, when the United States first registered a trade deficit with Japan the question of the Japanese balance of trade with America has provoked tension in the two countries' relations. This tension has tended to focus at different times on specific commodities. In the period 1978–80 the commodities in question were integrated circuits and telecommunications equipment.

Between 1975 and 1978 the American overall share of Japanese imports reduced from 35 per cent to less than 29 per cent. It lost market share to Europe and the newly industrialising countries. In 1968, although Japan imported only $34 million of telecommunications equipment 81 per cent of that was American. By 1978 the amount imported had risen to $282 million, but the American share of those imports had reduced to 59 per cent. In semi-conductors there was the same story—a reduction from 85 per cent to 57 per cent in the American share of Japanese imports. Only in computer equipment and peripherals had its share increased from 55 per cent to 64 per cent.[32]

American concern was fuelled by the perception on the part of businessmen that the American economy was sliding into recession. NTT's purchasing programme became the centre of attention. Efforts by the Americans to persuade NTT to liberalise its procurement policies met with little success. By 1978 NTT was procuring $3.2 billion annually, a goodly proportion of which was for advanced telecommunications systems of which the Americans wanted a share, but NTT itself was none too obliging. It claimed that technical standards demanded domestic procurement. American businessmen and Congressional officials discussing with NTT executives the possibility of modifying NTT's procurement practices during the autumn of 1978 found NTT obdurate. In the words of one participant: 'NTT executives virtually stonewalled our requests and the meeting turned into a confrontation.'[33] This period led in the words of one employee to NTT being perceived as a 'symbolic devil of the closed market'.[34] Not long afterwards the NTT president made a public remark to the effect that NTT could buy buckets and mops from the Americans, but not much else. As the accusations hotted up he was quietly replaced, following a scandal which some say was blown up for that purpose.

By Western standards very marginal in the scale of corruption—some employees of NTT in the South had been found to have been fiddling expenses—the scandal precipitated the resignation of President Tokusi Akikusa, an NTT man, and brought in an outsider, Hisashi Shinto, previously head of Ishikawajima Harima Heavy Industries (IHI), with close links to Keidanren. As a pro-competition head of NTT he has proved to be a lynch-pin in the whole liberalisation and privatisation process.[35]

In 1980, following the replacement of its head, NTT agreed to revised procurement rules on a three-track basis. It agreed to go to open tender for most of its requirements and in the third track which involves the R & D previously done by its family of suppliers to invite proposals for co-operation on the development of new technology. For the first time information in English became available on NTT's procurement.

The divestiture of AT&T and the liberalisation of the American telecommunications market dramatically affected Japan's domestic industry. When the liberalisation of the American market began in 1968, the Japanese telecommunications network was also growing fast. The number of telephones in Japan grew from 1971 to 1982 by 129 per cent compared to the 46 per cent growth in the United States. Output increased by over 500 per cent between 1970 and 1980, yet in 1979 exports took less than 20 per cent of total production.

From about 1980, when growth in Japan slowed, exports became of increased importance to the manufacturers. During the following four years exports of telecommunications equipment increased by 40 per cent per year. More than half the total exports in 1984 were taken by the United States. In fact America took 14 per cent of the total output of the Japanese industry compared to 7 per cent for the whole of Europe.[36]

Whereas prior to AT&T's divestiture its local operating companies bought equipment from its manufacturing arm Western Electric, after divestiture the operating companies began to purchase on a competitive basis opening the market in private branch exchanges (PBX) to Japanese companies. Because of the fast changing technology in this market Japanese companies supplied it from equipment manufactured locally. However, in the consumer equipment market where Japanese companies are strongest they supplied the American market predominantly by exports from Japan. It is against this background that the Americans argued for further liberalisation of the Japanese market and for increased American purchasing by NTT.[37]

The purchasing policy of NTT is of importance to the Americans because of the relative strengths of the American and Japanese industries. Whereas Japanese manufacturers are particularly strong in consumer related-equipment, American strength lies in switching equipment, in satellite production and in data processing. Japan's communications satellite industry on the other hand is underdeveloped. The Americans seem to have thought that satellites were included in the original NTT agreement and only became aware that they were not when, in 1983, NTT attempted to buy necessary know-how from an Americans company. Japan has concentrated on developing its own satellite technology, buying in what it could not develop itself. In February 1983, Japan's first operative communications satellite was launched to provide direct dialling between the mainland and the southern islands of Ogasawara. In 1984 another satellite was launched to carry direct broadcast television, but there have recently been problems with the French made transponders which the Japanese are now planning to manufacture themselves for another satellite to be launched in 1989.[38]

One possible reason for the poor development of satellite technology in Japan is that the optic fibre industry and research in optic fibres is very strong. Nevertheless the development of a domestic satellite capability is enshrined in legislation and satellite technology is seen as a symbol of national prestige, The Japanese have been concentrating on developing satellites to broadcast in the Ka band—the highest available band, which is unused for broadcasts at the present time. In contrast Americans have primarily developed technology for broadcasting in the lower frequency bands and in the Ku band. In the Ka band they have been slow off the mark, research funded by the American government at NASA began only in the late-1970s. The Americans foresee the possibility that the Japanese may overtake them in satellite research and may build up an integrated system of high definition TV and consumer-related digitalised products to compete in the future. The Japanese expect to place Ka satellites in orbit by 1995. American interest therefore is in stopping the development of Japanese technology.[39]

American pressure on NTT was first in terms of the purchase of switching equipment and then later in terms of the purchase of satellites, and the opening of VAN to foreign companies. The pressure on procurement, exerted over a number of years was not overly successful. Procurement from foreign firms gradually increased from $20 million in 1981 to more than $120 million in 1983 but out of a budget of $2000 million in telecommunications equipment alone it still represented a small proportion of NTT's purchases.[40] Despite the more open procurement procedure and specifications in English, in 1984 NTT purchased about 6 per cent of its total budget from the United States. NTT has complained about the poor quality of American products. It also points to the fact that the fastest growth section of the market in Japan is that of customers premises' equipment and that, because of the differential growth between the capital and consumer sections of the market, NTT now procures less than 50 per cent of the total market. It is fair to assume, however, that the Americans envisaged that liberalisation of the telecommunications monopoly in Japan would act as a similar stimulus to imports as had deregulation in the United States.

Although traditionally MITI has been an agency concerned with protection of fledgling Japanese industries, its perspective in the case of telecommunications may well have been affected by the strength of the Japanese manufacturing industry and the problems posed by its exports to the United States, as well as its domestic bureaucratic interests in fighting the MPT. The telecommunications manufacturing industry grew between 1979 and 1984 at a faster rate than automobiles. Some of those within the telecommunications industry interviewed in Japan believed that MITI was prepared to buy off American pressure on automobiles with concessions on telecommunications.

Changes in markets have also had an impact on the attitude of manufacturers. Because of the growth differential between the NTT market and those for exports and for the Japanese private market, in 1983 NTT took less than 30 per cent of the total production of the industry. Although NTT is still the largest, most important, customer of companies such as Fujitsu and NEC, it takes only 10 per cent or less of their production. Their dependence on NTT and their desire for the 'closed family of NTT' may still be evident but that dependency relationship is not crucial to their survival.

Overall by the 1980s NTT had created a network which offered a variety of public services of a high technological standard. Because NTT had managed to satisfy demand and upgrade the network to a very low fault rate, in 1984 the primary criticism of NTT as a public corporation was its pricing of long-distance calls and its failure to allow all large companies to provide inter- or intra-company VANs. Like BT it was also accused of being overmanned.

KDD's monopoly of international services also came in for criticism. Regulated on a rate of return basis it held charges very high. Without an incentive to decrease costs it was more overmanned than NTT, and had also invested in high-cost property. Under pressure from business it reduced its tariffs several times during the 1970s and early 1980s, but, even so, in 1984, KDD's tariff of about £15 for three minutes to Britain was about five times that of BT's. And, whereas BT employed one person per 29.2 thousand international calls, KDD employed one person per 6.3 thousand such calls. Nor was direct dialling overseas available from many parts of the country, including even parts of Tokyo. In 1984, only 45 per cent of international calls were direct dialled. KDD blames the technology of NTT from which it leases domestic lines.

Although in 1984 70 per cent of KDD's was non-voice traffic—the majority being facsimile—it produced only 40 per cent of its revenue, suggesting that KDD may have been using its monopoly on telephone calls to cross-subsidise its telex, leased circuits and facsimile services for business. It is also noticeable that whereas KDD's operating expenses took 78 per cent of its revenue in 1984, NTT's took only 47 per cent. KDD bore all the hall-marks of a rate-of-return regulated monopoly, yet, presumably because its charges for business services were lower than its charges for public telephone calls, seemed to evade the criticism levelled at NTT.[42]

In conclusion, the state of liberalisation of the market in Japan was therefore closer to the situation in the United States where resale of leased lines was allowed from 1981, firstly for data communications but rapidly incorporating voice traffic as well, than it was to the situation in Britain where resale of leased lines was banned. Partly for bureaucratic reasons, the MPT had avoided the problem of segmenting the market into 'basic' and 'enhanced' services. Had it done so, MITI would have claimed 'enhanced' services as its territory. VANs therefore had to be regulated by size of company involved. This method of segmenting the market allowed data networks to develop while protecting the voice monopoly of NTT. This pattern of development was aided by the horizontal integration of the domestic manufacturers across telecommunications and data processing technology. But by excluding large companies from operating their own VAN, the policy built up a domestic constituency of large, powerful opponents to NTT's monopoly who were aided in their pressure by Japan's vulnerability in trade with the United States, by MITI's interests and by the interests of American data processing companies in entering the NTT nationwide VAN market.

Nevertheless to a large extent liberalisation in Japan had been done without additional cost to local subscribers and local callers who were protected from increased charges by legislation. Under this form of liberalisation the main losers were trunk and international telephone users and those large companies in insurance, finance and information services who wanted to create their own national communications networks. Just as in the United States these user companies proved the match for AT&T, so in Japan the stage was set for their success.

Notes and references

1. Ezra Vogel, *Japan as Number One*, New York, Harper Row, 1979; G. L. Curtis, 'Big Business and Political Influence', in Ezra Vogel (ed.), *Japanese Organisation and Decision-making*, Berkeley, University of California Press, 1975; T. J. Pempel (ed.), *Policymaking in Contemporary Japan*, Ithaca and London, Cornell University Press, 1977. For a review of this

literature see: Jill Hills, 'Government Relations with Industry: Japan & Britain.' Review of Two Political Arguments', *Polity*, **XIV**, 2, Winter 1981, pp. 222–48.

2. Jill Hills, 'Industrial Policy of Japan', *Journal of Public Policy*, 3, 1983, pp. 63–80.

3. Keiji Tachikawa, 'Information Network System: New telecommunications converged with computers', *Studies of Broadcasting*, **19**, 1983, pp. 49–69.

4. Akira Hosoda, 'Telecommunications Administration in Japan' in H. Inose (ed.), *Telecommunications Technologies; Japan Annual Review in Electronics, Computers and Telecommunications* , **14**, 1984, pp. 305–21.

5. M. T. Hills, 'A Comparison of Switching System Development in Japan and the UK', *Telecommunications Group Report*, no. 116, Essex University, 1977, (mimeo).

6. Interviews, August 1984.

7. Yasusada Kitahara, *INS: Telecommunications in the 21st Century*. London, Heinemann Educational Books, 1983, p. 16.

8. Legislation quoted in Yasusada Kitahara, op. cit., fn. p. 15.

9. Yasusada Kitahara, 'INS (Information Network System)—Telecommunications for the Advanced Information Society', in H. Inose (ed.), *Telecommunication Technologies*, Tokyo, OHMSHA, 1984, p. 10.

10. *NTT Annual Report 1970–71*, pp. 2–3.

11. Carter Report, *Report of the Post Office Review Committee*, Cmnd. 6850, London, HMSO, 1977, p. 18.

12. Figures from; *NTT Annual Report 1984–5* ; *BT Annual Report 1985*.

13. Keiji Tachikawa, op. cit., pp. 52–3.

14. O. P. Sellars, J. J. E. Swaffield, J. F. L. Stubbs and S. Lunt, 'A Yen for Success', *British Telecom Journal*, Summer 1980, pp. 20–2.

15. Interviews, August 1984.

16. *NTT Annual Report 1978–9*, pp. 12–14.

17. Tetsuro Tomita, 'Japan's Policy on Monopoly and Competition in Telecommunications', *Telecommunications Policy*, March 1984, pp. 44–50.

18. The following account is based on M. T. Hills, op. cit.

19. Interviews, August 1984.

20. Arthur D. Little Inc., *The Japanese Non-Tariff Trade Barrier Issue. American Views and the Implications for Japan–US Trade Relations*, Tokyo, National Institute for Research Advancement, 1979, p. IV–19; *Industrial Review of Japan*, Tokyo, Nihon Keizai Shimbun, 1977, p. 86;

21. Ira S. Magaziner and Thomas M. Hout, *Japanese Industrial Policy*, London, PSI, 1980, pp. 82–8; Eugene Kaplan, *Japan: The Government–Business Relationship*, Washington D. C., US. Dept. of Commerce, 1972 .

22. *NTT Annual Report 1967–8*, p. 3.

23. Keiji Tachikawa, op. cit., pp. 51–2.

24. *Computer White Papers*, Tokyo, JIPDEC, 1982, p. 57.

25. *Report on Present State of Communications in Japan*, Tokyo, MPT and Japan Times, 1982, p. 11.

26. *NTT Annual Report 1983–4*, p. 24.

27. Yasusada Kitahara, op. cit., 1983, p. 30; R. Barrett, 'Development and Use of Facsimile Systems in Japan', *Electronics and Power*, 12 December 1984, pp. 1118–1121.

28. *NTT Annual Report 1983-4*, p. 25.
29. Keiji Tachikawa, op. cit., p. 49.
30. *International Herald Tribune*, 26 October 1983.
31. Yasasuda Kitahara, previous vice-president, NTT, quoted in *Look Japan*, 10 February 1979, p. 11.
32. Arthur D. Little, op. cit., p. V-18.
33. Ibid., pp. IV-16 & 17.
34. Kunji Maeda, 'Privatization of Japanese Telecommunications', *Telecommunications Policy*, June 1985, pp. 93-4; Peter E. Fuchs, 'Regulatory Reform and Japan's Telecommunications Revolution', *US-Japan Relations: New Attitudes for a New Era*, Program on US-Japan Relations, Boston, Mass., Harvard University, 1984, pp. 123-142.
35. Kunji Maeda, op. cit., p. 93; Interviews, August 1984.
36. Figures provided by CIAJ, 1984.
37. United States International Trade Commission, *Changes in the US Telecommunications Industry and the Impact on US Telecommunications Trade*, Washington D. C., USITC, 1984, p. 30.
38. Communications Industry Association of Japan, *Outline of Communications Industry*, Tokyo, CIAJ, 1984, p. 2.
39. *Washington Post*, 26 May 1985.
40. NTT, *NTT Telecommunications Bulletin*, no. 8, August 1984; *Japan Times*, 11 July 1985; *NTT Procurement Update*, Tokyo, NTT, 1984.
41. *KDD Annual Report 1984*, p. 25; *NTT Annual Report 1983-4*, p. 34.

5 Privatisation: Britain and Japan— a contrast of styles

Introduction

The term 'privatisation' can mean different things in different countries and contexts. In Britain the privatisation of BT has meant the sale of 51 per cent of the shares, without a transfer of managerial control; the creation of a private, rather than public monopoly and the creation of a quasi-governmental regulatory agency. In Japan, the privatisation of NTT has transferred it from the status of a public corporation to that of a special government-controlled company with shares still owned by the government. Whereas Chapter Three indicated that liberalisation increased the power of the British state bureaucracy, privatisation weakened it once more. In contrast NTT's privatisation extended control by the Ministry of Posts and Telecommunications, not simply over NTT, but also over all telecommunications companies. The use of the same term to describe processes and outcomes which differ in the two countries has led to considerable confusion and disappointed expectations on the part of British and American industrial analysts surveying the Japanese scene.

The purpose of this chapter is to compare the process of privatisation of the public telecommunications monopoly in Britain and Japan. The previous chapters outlined the background to telecommunications in the two countries. Since privatisation in each country began from different points and one would therefore not expect the prices to be the same. Also all mechanisms of intervention are influenced by the historical tradition of relations between state and industry, by the ideology attached to that intervention, by differences in political institutions and by differences in domestic and international markets. Both external and internal pressures influence policy, as may the very style of political life.

Despite the social democratic consensus of the post-war years, today's style of politics in Britain is confrontational. Whereas the Japanese Liberal Democratic party had the power to force through legislation but did not, the British government did. It overrode opposition to privatisation, making only those concessions into which it was forced. Despite the fact that the British telecommunications equipment manufacturing industry is much weaker than that in Japan, its concerns were more or less ignored.

In Britain privatisation came out of a long-standing ideological debate on the virtues of 'competition' against those of 'public control' and nationalisation. But the major impetus to privatisation came from the ideological framework of the Thatcher government, from a belief in monetarist policy which demanded a decreasing share of public expenditure within GDP. The proceeds of the sale of BT were to be used to offset actual unscheduled increases in the PSBR brought on by increased expenditure on defence, law enforcement and unemployment payments, coupled with a decreased tax-take. Capital was to be used as revenue. A desire to make a 'successful' sale, both to maximise the benefit to the Treasury and because the previous sale of oil had been undersubscribed, resulted in the overriding of other interests and conflicted with other ideological goals, such as the increase of competition within the telecommunications market.

In contrast, this chapter suggests that the privatisation of NTT resulted from competition between elements of Japanese industry allied to the competing interests of Japanese bureaucrats, within an international trade system where Japan is dependent on the United States. It suggests that it has been competition between Keidanren, representing the old established companies, and newer large non-establishment companies such as Kyocera and Sony, coupled with competition between the Ministry of Trade and Industry (MITI) and the Ministry of Posts and Telecommunications (MPT) which has brought about the privatisation of NTT. Nevertheless impetus was given to the movement towards privatisation from the 'small government is best' ideology of the Nakasone government and from American pressure. That pressure has had a crucial influence on certain aspects of the outcome and has reduced the power of the MPT. Despite these conflicts and despite competition between these various protagonists, the actual process of privatisation allowed the accommodation of many of these interests. Japanese style, this chapter illustrates that politics is not necessarily a zero-sum game.

In both countries trade unions were excluded from the central debate, except through their links with opposition parties, yet in both it was the trade unions which managed to raise the debate to consider some of the long-term effects of privatisation. Both used American experience within their campaign. In Britain the unions took on a gladiatorial role opposing both liberalisation and privatisation by industrial action. In Japan, with strategy limited by the seeming impossibility that a socialist government might ever be elected, after first presenting outright opposition to NTT's privatisation the union accommodated itself to the legislation.

But perhaps the most interesting aspect of the privatisation process in both countries has been that the beneficiaries of the new system are not those domestic interests which expected to do well. Instead in both countries the winners have been American and global companies and the privatised entity itself. In both countries the losers have been domestic manufacturers and in Britain the residential telephone customer.

Britain—from liberalisation to privatisation.

The Post Office and British Telecom were split in October 1981 and, officially, some liberalisation of equipment began at that moment.

Even before the split between BT and the Post Office had taken place, BT's chairman was arguing that he should be allowed to raise money outside the Public Sector Borrowing Requirement. He put forward three suggestions. BT could issue subscriber bonds, on the lines of NTT in Japan. These might be either voluntary or compulsory. Secondly BT might issue bonds to the fixed interest market. Or thirdly BT might issue bonds more akin to equity with yields related to BT's performance and turnover. Of the three the Department of Trade and Industry (DTI) originally favoured the third option in return for stricter monitoring of BT but the Treasury was against the concept in principle. Whether in retaliation against BT's persistence in pushing for bonds, or from the perspective of savings to the PSBR, in the summer of 1981 the Chancellor of the Exchequer began publicly to float the idea of the privatisation of BT.

The problem with the phone bond was the interest return which investors would require. It seemed that the City institutions would want 3 per cent or 4 per cent more interest than was available on government stock and were worried that the government would restrict BT's profits. For the Treasury the question at issue was whether it made sense for BT to borrow at a higher rate of interest than it could borrow from the Treasury and whether this borrowing should count within the PSBR. A further problem was posed by the lack of incentive for efficiency if BT were released from control of its tariffs. The Treasury won the argument that the borrowing should be within the PSBR, which immediately took away the point of the bond. If it was to count within

BT's allowed external financing then all that was needed was for the government to raise BT's external financing limit and it could then borrow from the Treasury without issuing the bond.

The fighting between the Treasury and the DTI went on for a whole year, with the announcement of the bond postponed several times. There was some suggestion, officially denied, that further capital borrowing by BT was being postponed because of BT's dilatory behaviour following liberalisation; that its desire for capital was being used to pressure it to behave less monopolistically. Efforts were also made to attract employees into investment in the bond.[1]

The bond eventually received government approval in principle in March 1982, but by then BT's financial circumstances had considerably improved from that of the previous year. Instead of overshooting its £380 million limit for the financial year it was expected to undershoot by £130 million, a reversal brought about, so BT argued, by lower than expected inflation, delays in delivery of equipment and an increase in the use of the network. It reported more than doubled profits of £450 million in the year to 1982.

Its radically altered financial forecasts were reflected in reductions of 35 per cent in trunk charges and a 33 per cent cut in international tariffs in the early months of 1982. These cuts, said to be in line with reductions in costs, also coincided with the business areas in which BT would face competition with Mercury. At the same time BT upgraded its business services, so that in July in describing the beneficiaries of liberalisation, the Minister was able to state:

... perhaps most important of all ... the prospect of competition and the advent of new technology are stimulating BT to respond to market opportunities. BT is providing a new array of services, especially the City Overlay in the City of London, using microwave radio and other techniques'.[2]

The very threat of competition had galvanised BT into providing new services to meet the unmet demand which had been the justification for Mercury's inauguration.

By March 1982 the new Minister of Industry had revived discussion of the privatisation of BT as a possible alternative to the bond. One major problem was the need to gain the co-operation of the trade unions, particularly the POEU, but it was thought that by extending BT's presence in new areas they could be won over. The union's policy was that BT should stay within the public sector but that it should be able to enter new services—hence BT's arguments that it should be allowed to lay the cable for cable TV companies was supported by the unions. The prospect of numbers of cable TV companies wanting to lay cables also made urgent the revision of the Telegraph Act, which gave only BT the right to way-leaves for cable-laying.[3]

The 'busby bond' never saw the light of day. Instead the announcement of BT's sale came in July 1982. BT reacted with surprise. It had not been consulted nor informed of the decision prior to the public announcement—an indication of strained relations between BT and ministers. Its view was that it had quite enough to do coping with liberalisation without privatisation as well. But the prospect of being free of government control was clearly appealing and BT gave the statement a guarded welcome.[4]

The original statement by the industry minister justified the privatisation measure in terms of the government's ideology, in terms of increased competition which would ensue and in terms of BT's need for capital. The Government aimed, he said:

> to promote consumer choice ... we believe that consumer choice and the disciplines of the market lead to more stable prices, improved efficiency and a higher quality of service. . . . In the past monopoly power has allowed BT to raise prices to finance investment without doing all that could be done to increase efficiency. Around 90% of BT's investment programme has been self-financed ... I mean of course 'customer-financed'; BT's charges to customers not only cover current running costs, but are also paying 90% of new investment. As a result charges have risen steeply but investment is not enough'.

The implication was that BT's self-financing ratio was both BT's own decision and an inherent feature of public ownership, rather than something imposed upon it by government policy. He stated that the new legislation would free BT from government control. In other words, when privately owned, BT would be able to borrow from the money market without affecting the sacred PSBR.

However, contradicting himself on BT's new freedom, he added that because BT would continue to dominate the British market for some years yet: 'there will be a need for regulatory arrangements for the industry to balance the interests of those supplying telecommunications services, their customers, their competitors, their employees, their investors and their suppliers'. BT's role in licensing its competitors would be ended. Instead a new Office of Telecommunications would be established, modelled on the Office of Fair Trading, under a government-appointed Director General. He would have powers similar to the Director General of Fair Trading, and would operate with the same independence from government. It would be his job to ensure 'fair competition and fair prices'.[5]

The telecommunications unions began a massive public campaign against the bill even before it was published, arguing that further jobs would be lost, that pension arrangements would be at risk and that rural areas and other disadvantaged customers would suffer further deprivation if cost-based services were allowed. A study of the break-up of AT&T was used to demonstrate that residential charges would be increased as a result of privatisation. But at its annual conference in the summer of 1983 a substantial minority (48,000) of members refused to take national industrial action, preferring to wait and see what the government actually proposed. Instead the union took selective action, ensuring that BT managers had to carry out the interconnection of Mercury, and taking action against the business community, particularly in London's international telephone exchanges. Mercury's court action against the union was eventually successful on appeal.[6]

The union's narrow strategy was to put such pressure onto the business community that it in turn would bring pressure to bear to stop privatisation. But it was also at the forefront of a wider parliamentary and publicity campaign against the measure. Opposition was fanned by uncertainty. During the year in which the bill was debated various estimates of job losses came from Ministry sources ranging from 15,000 to more than 45,000.[7]

At this stage it was estimated that BT would be capitalised at about £7–8 billion, making the sale of 51 per cent the largest share sale in history. The initial reaction of the City institutions was luke warm. BT was regarded as a 'utility' with a low return on capital. After liberalisation the Treasury had set it a target of 5 per cent return on capital per annum but BT's prices were not allowed to rise by the rate of inflation. It was therefore forced to reduce unit costs by 5 per cent each year. BT was not a particularly attractive buy and the City was unsure that it could actually finance such a huge issue. Soundings in Japan and the United States produced equally tepid responses.

For the government the response was worrying. It had already failed to place all the shares in the British National Oil Corporation issue and could not afford another embarrassing failure. It considered the possibility of selling BT in pieces, but BT effectively argued against such a break-up.

The government was in a difficult situation. On the one hand it was ideologically in favour of increased competition and a more efficient telecommunications entity. On the other it was both reliant on BT for information and on its co-operation in the privatisation process and also needed a successful sale. To make sure that the sale succeeded, regulation of privatised BT would have to be as light as possible. To gain the co-operation of the trade unions demanded that privatised BT should be allowed to expand into new areas, such as manufacturing. Limitation of competition was necessary to protect BT and its monopoly over the existing residential market and to protect the consortium Mercury's investment. Given the timetable, it seems that the government's ideological position in favour of increased competition took second place to its desire for a successful sale. Concern for the existing British equipment manufacturing industry also came second to placating the trade unions.

National chauvinism entered the scene—nationalism being one of the easy ways of stilling opposition. The privatised BT was to be a company which could compete with IBM and AT&T on the world market. The model held up was that of GTE, which both manufactured equipment and acted as a transmission carrier, but later it was suggested by a minister that BT would become another AT&T.[8]

The bill was not published until mid November 1982 and was presented to Parliament only twelve days later, leaving politicians little time to consult interested parties. The government's intention was that it should be on the statute book as quickly as possible in order to allow Mrs Thatcher manoeuvrability in setting the date for a general election in 1983. Anticipating criticism that it had not mentioned privatisation of BT in its 1979 manifesto and had received no mandate for it, the government announced that the actual sale of shares in BT would not take place until after the next general election.

The government's various conflicting priorities led to a bill in which some of the glaring anomalies of the liberalisation bill were altered, but where rather little was done to weaken BT's existing dominant position. BT's power to licence its VAN competitors was removed, but this power had *de facto* been removed by the DTI in April 1982. BT still retained the right of installation of the first phone and the right to manufacture equipment. Its previous obligation as a nationalised industry to provide service throughout the country was weakened by a provision that these services, such as public call box services, emergency services and services in rural areas should provide a reasonable return on investment. And although the Office of Telecommunications, modelled on the Office of Fair Trading, was established by the bill it was not to be on the lines of the Federal Communications Commission with autonomous power. The Minister reassured Parliament that: 'We intend BT to have the maximum commercial freedom to operate in the market. We intend that the licensing and regulatory system shall, as it were, constitute a light rein and that there should be the minimum of interference with legitimate commercial decisions.'[9] Such reassurance was, of course, aimed at the City rather than Parliament.

The bill was fought by a variety of interests. A coalition of the National Farmers' Union, the Scottish local authorities and Welsh consumers opposed the weak phrasing on services to rural areas in fear that uneconomic services would be axed. The bill was also criticised by the consumer body, the Post Office Users Council (POUNC), whose functions were to be taken over by OFTEL. It argued that the director could not both be responsible for consumer interests and for ensuring an adequate rate of return for BT. The provisions of the bill were subsequently strengthened to take into account the pressure of Conservative politicians on these issues.[10]

The bill was also opposed by the telecommunications equipment manufacturers who saw it as the means by which BT could squeeze them out of much of the domestic market, and who alleged that they had already begun to suffer from BT's predatory behaviour. They wanted BT restricted to operating the network and providing telecommunications services. They argued that BT currently had about 95 per cent of the telephone apparatus market, that it had consistently lost money on the supply of apparatus and that it would be able to cross-subsidise sales from network revenue. They wanted BT's market share of apparatus restricted to 25 per cent, and restrictions on both BT's right to manufacture and on its right to maintain equipment attached to the network. Many of these proposals conflicted with the interests of the trade unions and were rejected by the government, but the bill was subsequently altered to allow subscribers to provide their own first telephone.

In the middle of the debate on the bill the government received a report which it had commissioned from Professor Stephen Littlechild, another academic economist, who had been asked to examine the problems of regulating a privately owned BT. He argued that behavioural regulation was inherently unsatisfactory and that only competition would control BT's behaviour. His proposals included competitive access to international switched circuits, the resale of private circuits and an 'open skies' satellite policy allowing private companies to provide transmission capacity. He also recommended inter-modal competition between cellular mobile radio and BT, cable TV and BT and private satellite communications and BT. As an interim measure he recommended that of the various behavioural regulatory schemes put to him, that of restricting price rises on monopoly services by less than the resale price index measure of inflation was the best, and that this restriction should last for five years.[11]

The government accepted the principles of the report and the Minister promptly stated that restrictions on Mercury would be eased, that BT's monopoly of maintenance over all new equipment would be ended and that resale of capacity would be allowed after discussions with BT. Also it was agreed that competing networks would have the right to interconnect to the public network but that Mercury and the two existing cellular radio services would have to pay access fees to BT.[12] These access fees would cover the cost of emergency calls and losses on call boxes and rural services. The only provision of the report with which the government disagreed was the recommendation that cable TV companies should be allowed to compete with BT and Mercury.[13]

The trade unions reacted bitterly to the report and the government's acceptance of it, stating that they had been called in to the Minister's office without having seen a copy, or even having knowledge that it was being prepared. The POEU stated that 'The report has been produced in secret and the Government has accepted most of its recommendations without any discussion in Parliament or with users.'[14]

Protracted negotiations with BT followed the Littlechild recommendations. The major questions surrounded the RPI—X formula. The greater the value of 'X' the more BT would have to reduce costs. BT pressed for 2 per cent, the government for 3 per cent. Eventually a compromise allowed BT to raise prices by RPI—3 per cent overall. There remained the question of what services this overall limitation would be applied to, and whether there should be restrictions on BT's ability to rebalance its charges to cost-priced charges for individual services. In other words, how far should BT be allowed to rebalance costs onto the residential consumer and local call charges? The final agreement was that the basket of services would include residential and business rentals and all direct-dialled inland calls. International calls, private lines, public call box calls were not included. BT also agreed to a voluntary undertaking that it would not raise the cost of customer rentals by more than the level of inflation plus 2 per cent, and would continue to operate a low user rebate scheme. But this agreement took one year to complete.

Held up in Committee, the bill fell with the general election of June 1983 only to be reintroduced following the Conservative victory. That election brought into parliament many politicians on the right of the

Conservative party and attitudes hardened. It also brought the appointment of yet another new Minister for Trade and Industry, Cecil Parkinson. He stated that he intended to sell BT as one whole because it would take too long and would be too complex and costly to break it up. The objections of the equipment manufacturers were brushed aside. He also rejected the idea that BT should be forbidden to sell apparatus and specialist services. But, implicitly accepting that there was a danger of cross-subsidisation, he agreed to explore whether the apparatus supply and services provided by BT Enterprises (one of the four profit-centres within BT) should take place in a separate company.[15] This option was later rejected. The government also rejected the provision that BT and Mercury licences should be subject to the approval of Parliament, although the government gave in on the latter under pressure from the House of Lords.

Pushed through the House of Commons by virtue of the guillotine 300 amendments to the bill were introduced in the House of Lords. One of the most vociferous opponents of the bill was Lord Weinstock, the Chairman of GEC. He argued that the government was not considering telecommunications as a whole, that it was handing out numbers of monopoly licences embracing cable TV, cellular radio and satellite transmission, yet had no coherent policy. Lord Weinstock complained that the government had licenced a duopoly of companies for cellular mobile radio, one of which was backed by BT, and was in the process of licensing other small geographical monopolies for cable communications, in which BT was present. BT was being allowed to extend its monopoly into competing technologies.[16]

He also pressed the manufacturers' case—that if BT chose to manufacture equipment it would have an unfair advantage and leave too small a share of the market for independent suppliers. GEC would have preferred BT to have been split on the lines of AT&T with separate arms for manufacturing, equipment and local network. In fact, GEC had been interested in buying a piece of BT had the government split it for sale, but instead, giving in to BT pressure, the government had limited any one holding to 15 per cent preventing any one company influencing BT.

Reading the reports of the debates of both Houses the overwhelming impression is that the government was thinking on its feet and really had little knowledge about what it was doing, the problem being that each amendment which strengthened regulation, or which increased competition, was antipathetic to the prospective sale of BT. The result was that even amendments to which the government could have been expected to agree in the interests of competition had to be defeated in the interests of keeping the City happy.[17]

To a large degree the sale itself diverted attention from many of the issues of regulation. Its promotion as a measure to democratise share ownership was a public relations coup brought about by such measures as a special train taking the chosen merchant bankers around the country promising 2 per cent commission to solicitors who advised clients on the BT sale. Special rebate vouchers were designed to attract telephone customers. Employees became eligible to buy shares (145,000 did so) and large blocs of shares were sold in America and Japan—the latter seemingly on the basis that British investors would then be able to invest in NTT's privatisation. By 1985 however the number of BT shareholders had decreased from the original 2.3 million to 1.7 million suggesting that many small shareholders had taken a quick capital gain.

The share sale was oversubscribed many times over, with shares changing hands within a day at almost 100 per cent profit. In total the sale cost £323 million, which went predominantly to City institutions. It also provided a capital gain for shareholders of 1.3 billion.[18]

OFTEL had been established as soon as the bill had completed its passage through Parliament. The government chose as director general an accountant, Professor Bryan Carlsberg. The agency was not only tiny compared to the American FCC, but also took on a variety of competing objectives. Together with the Minister it was made primarily responsible for ensuring 'such telecommunications services as satisfy all reasonable demands for them', except insofar as such provision was 'impracticable or not reasonable practicable.' Subject to that main duty, which also included emergency services, public call boxes, directory information services, maritime services and services to rural areas, it was also responsible for promoting the interests of consumers, purchasers and other users, and for promoting the interests of manufacturers. It was not only responsible for promoting effective competition in telecommunications services in Britain, and for their 'efficiency and economy', and for promotion of their R & D, but it was also responsible for attracting multinational investment into Britain, for 'the provision of international transit services' and for promoting exports of telecommunications services from Britain. Many of its responsibilities conflicted with each other.

Most of its powers were indirect—the provision of advice to the Ministry. Its direct powers were limited to revision of the licences of BT and its competitor, Mercury, in order to promote more effective competition, subject to the agreement of the Monopolies Commission. Even its power over tariffs was limited by the decision of the government to accept the Littlechild recommendation and to control BT's price rises to the overall level of the RPI minus 3 per cent.[19]

Despite these handicaps, the agency has nevertheless made a reputation for itself as being pro-competitive and tough with BT. To some extent by regulatory decisions it has been able to inject a competitive element lacking in the privatisation legislation. Its first action was to ask individuals and companies to report complaints of anti-competitive behaviour by BT. In the first year it received almost 3,000 complaints, many of them relating to individual telephone bills. But other major causes for concern were BT's discriminatory pricing for connection and wiring, depending on whether the apparatus to be connected was from BT or not, BT's accounting practices which did not differentiate between services and its code of practice intended to prevent the passing of customer information from one section to another.

The agency's first major action was to intervene to advise the Minister against allowing the proposed VAN network between IBM and BT on the grounds that it would prevent competition. The proposed Jove network had been opposed by both the major British computer manufacturer, ICL, and the Micro-computer Manufacturers Association, on the grounds that it would use IBM's System Network Architecture (SNA) standards which would preclude the attachment of other manufacturers' equipment to the network. Following this decision the Minister subsequently announced that all VANs must make provision for Open System Interconnection (OSI) standards, allowing interconnection to all makes of equipment.

This advice by OFTEL to the Ministry was followed by its recommendation that BT should be excluded from the mobile radio communications services, which the government was about to licence to use the old 425 television spectrum space. Again the government took OFTEL's advice.[20]

But the limitations on OFTEL's powers and its competing responsibilities were made evident in its intervention in the dispute concerning BT's decision to second source its exchange equipment from overseas. The whole matter of BT's behaviour in the apparatus market was fraught with allegation and counter allegation. Even during the sale process, the effects of the liberalisation legislation had not worked through. The government acknowledged that even after privatisation BT would still be responsible for testing its competitors' products for approval. Nor, despite the fact that in April of 1984 the Ministry had agreed that the current standards were too strict, had the relevant technical standards been rewritten in order to shorten the approval process.

The various delays had acted to the advantage of BT. In 1985 a market survey showed that during the period since liberalisation BT had not only begun to manufacture its own telephones and micro-computers but had gained such market dominance in equipment sales that it was likely to crowd out competition for several years. Seventy per cent of the small PABX had been replaced since 1981 and, of that proportion, BT had replaced 90 per cent. It also still held 82 per cent of the market in telephones.[21]

In the large exchange market BT had begun to squeeze its British suppliers of System X, complaining of delays in delivery. In 1982 STC had dropped out of manufacture of System X. Plessey had become the prime contractor, although it and GEC competed for the manu-facturing contracts, but software problems delayed the introduction of the System X local exchange. From 1982 onwards BT threatened to go abroad for 20 per cent of its requirements in large exchanges and made good the threat in 1985 with an agreement with Thorn-Ericsson for System Y.

Asked by an all-party parliamentary committee to investigate the matter, OFTEL agreed with BT that the second sourcing might benefit the consumer in the long term. But with its responsibility to the British manufacturers in mind, it suggested that BT should keep the propor-tion of its ordering from Ericsson to 20 per cent for the next three years. Lacking any form of legal power to back up the recommendation, OFTEL was quickly told by BT to mind its own business.[22]

In 1985 BT announced that it was taking over Mitel, its ailing Canadian supplier of PABX. Although ownership of Mitel presented the opportunity of entry into the North American market, the prospect of a vertically integrated entity within the home market placed British telecommunications suppliers under even greater threat of being excluded from the domestic market. OFTEL, once more in the position of representing conflicting interests, advised that the merger be referred to the Monopoly Commission with the recommendation that it should be approved with certain safeguards. These safeguards included the separation of manufacturing from network management.[23] The Monopoly Commission recommended against the merger, but the Minister, Leon Brittan, overruled it, just before his resignation in January 1986. BT's future 'flag-ship' position was clearly of primary political importance.

Particularly on the question of BT's competitor, Mercury, OFTEL has proved itself to be in favour of competition, even if the instigation of that competition would mean a reduction in BT's profits. Mercury asked OFTEL to intervene in its negotiations with BT on interconnection. These negotiations had not been completed before privatisation.

Mercury began service internationally in the summer of 1984, linking London to New York. Its original plan was a figure of eight interconnection of major cities using optic fibre cable, but by the spring of 1984 only 150km of the 1,100km planned had been laid. In order to start some form of service, it began by providing business links between London, Birmingham and Manchester via microwave.

Although Mercury had originally received a licence under the liberalisation legislation, in which it was guaranteed for five years its position as BT's only transmission competitor, the privatisation legislation meant another licence was required. This draft licence had been published in July 1984 following lengthy negotiations with the Ministry in which the company had engaged an American consultant to advise them. Mercury had resisted pressure from the Ministry to extend its network to the whole of the UK and to give priority to poorer areas, such as the north-east and Scotland. Mercury had argued that it wanted to concentrate initially on large business in London, Birmingham and Manchester and to expand in line with demand. It was unwilling to provide unprofitable services unless it received a subsidy.

By the time of the issue of the draft licence, British Petroleum had withdrawn from the Mercury consortium to be followed shortly after by Barclays Bank. Neither C&W nor Barclays were willing to commit more than the £125 million already committed, without some prospect of a commercial return. The £1 billion or more required to lay a national network was out of the question.[23]

The draft licence had reflected Mercury's priorities, requiring only that it should provide services to fifteen key cities within two years and should extend its activities as far as commercially practical. But after its publication the government had come under pressure from Scottish and Welsh business wanting access to the alternative network. The final licence therefore required it to extend its services to four major cities in Scotland and Wales. It was also required to publish tariffs and to prevent cross-subsidisation between arms of its business.

Because Mercury would have to rely on BT's local network, full interconnection was obviously of paramount importance. OFTEL's involvement arose because, under pressure to allow BT its licence prior to privatisation, Mercury had entered into an interim agreement on interconnection with BT in the summer of 1985. BT argued that the interim heads of agreement, which were in BT's favour, were binding on Mercury. Mercury asked OFTEL to adjudicate but BT argued that the matter was outside OFTEL's jurisdiction. Eventually the two sides went to court and the judgement in Mercury's favour opened negotiations again. OFTEL stepped in when the two sides failed to reach a commercial decision.

The decision announced by OFTEL in October 1985 was highly beneficial to Mercury. The two principles which OFTEL adopted were first that any person should be able to dial any person and that a customer should be able to choose which network would carry the call. For access to the network Mercury was to pay the equivalent of a bulk discount on BT calls, based on BT's costs rather than its tariffs, meaning that Mercury would make a profit on the BT part of the call—an incentive for BT to make these entry calls toll free. The decision also stated where and when physical interconnection between the networks should take place—they had to be linked at thirty-six trunk exchanges by March 1986—and Mercury had to pay only 50 per cent of the capital and labour costs for increased capacity. The ironic situation is therefore that OFTEL actually intervened to force BT to provide at cost what in any normal competitive environment would be provided at some profit. The manipulation is actually a cross-subsidy from BT subscribers, in favour of subscribers to Mercury.[24]

BT's reaction to the ruling was that residential and small business customers would end up paying more to offset the benefits of Mercury's interconnection to large business customers but for the moment there was 'no immediate reason to review' either its voluntary undertaking that it would not increase telephone rentals by more than two percentage points above inflation or to review its low-users rebate. The ruling had followed increased charges from BT in which residential rentals rose by 8.6 per cent, business rentals by 9.4 per cent, connection charges increased by 7.5 per cent and the unit charge increased from 4.7 pence to 5 pence. At the same time BT had lowered charges on some trunk calls and some international calls (the major ones). The average increase at 3.7 per cent was less than the 4 per cent allowed (RPI measured inflation at 7 per cent), but under the terms of its licence BT could compensate by increasing prices more in the following year. OFTEL's reaction to BT's public statement was a sharp warning that it would not hesitate to use all its powers if BT broke its commitment.[25]

The real problem with BT's regulation is that the formula of RPI minus 3 per cent is no more than rate-of-return regulation which hardly prevents BT piling charges onto its monopoly services and cross-subsidising its competitive services. OFTEL has itself demanded that BT provide better accounting for its current costs and has initiated both an international comparison of tariffs and a study to determine the extent by which rentals should be cross-subsidised by call revenues to encourage access to the network. For the first time the advantages to be gained by national, rather than semi-national, coverage of the telephone network are being debated. But OFTEL cannot take action on charges outside the basket of services which BT fixed prior to privatisation, or on what constitutes BT's assets. For instance although OFTEL could investigate charges for access lines (external extensions) which BT had increased, it could not immediately alter the whole area of charging on leased lines. BT and Mercury are also in conflict on the question of numbering. BT regards telephone numbers as its own asset; OFTEL and Mercury regard them as a national asset. OFTEL is unable to rule on telephone numbers until after 1989, when the current interim period of regulation is reviewed.

While OFTEL's responsibilities have concerned the regulation of BT and Mercury, the Ministry, responsible for issuing licences, has been caught in a considerable muddle over its VAN policy and the question of resale of leased lines. Between 1981 and 1985 it licensed about 600 VAN on the basis originally set out during the liberalisation debate, that the services must add something to the basic conveyance service. A problem arose when the IBM–BT VAN was proposed. The system would have connected together the computers of banks, insurance companies and manufacturing industry into a large integrated network.

A question arose as to whether it was a VAN as previously defined by the government or part of a basic conveyance service. The government ducked the question by vetoing it on the grounds of competition. But there then arose a problem of distinguishing between types of systems called Managed Data Networks and other VANs. The Department had actually been unable to come up with a suitable blanket definition for VAN beyond that which it had already applied—where 'each message is subjected to some significant action additional to that associated with basic conveyancing'.[26] Under this definition MDN could not be VAN. The Ministry then overcame this difficulty by stating that it would issue a special licence for MDN on the grounds that MDNs were part of the basic conveyance system. Under the terms of BT and Mercury's licence no other competition in basic conveyancing could be allowed until

1989. The problem then arose that if MDNs counted as basic conveyance BT could provide and cross-subsidise them from other network services.

MDNs are appropriately dominated by the computer companies entering into transmission—IBM, ICL—and by communications subsidiaries of large companies such as Electronic Data Systems, a subsidiary of General Motors. IBM was therefore furious at the prospect that its MDN for insurance companies might be subject to subsidised competition from BT. The ruling was bound to upset everyone bar BT because it subjected MDN to an individual decision by the Department rather than being part of a general licence requiring registration. Further, if MDNs were basic services then they were transferred from being optional for BT and Mercury to being compulsory services for nation-wide development. Mercury also argued that the decision effectively contradicted the 1989 'duopoly' agreement, under which the government would licence no other competitors for five years from privatisation.

Faced with this barrage of criticism, at the end of 1985 the Ministry issued another consultative document in which it proposed to open all data communications and value added services to competition, even including those which would include some voice communication as part of a 'deeper' service, such as videoconferencing. OSI standards were to be used wherever possible. Changes in the licences of BT and Mercury would be negotiated with OFTEL with the only exclusive services left to BT and Mercury being ordinary phone conversation and telex. There would also continue to be a ban on simple resale of leased lines. VANs had gone and Value Added and Data Services (VADS) had replaced them. The decision reflects the advice given by Professor Beesley in 1982 that no technical distinction could be made between VANs and basic service.[27] The effect is a duopoly in voice and telex transmission and open competition amongst licensed carriers for other services, but under conditions of fair trading which prevent abuses by large service providers. Service providers should not be able to lock customers into their own equipment. The Ministry also ducked defining those of the newly defined VADS which would be allowed internationally under CCITT rules, arguing that it was up to the provider to negotiate with partners in other countries and that the CCITT regulations were capable of differing interpretations. The effect, by default, was to open basic data transmission as well as 'enhanced' services to international transmission by private companies, without publicly breaking CCITT regulations.

There is little doubt that while BT was regulated by the Ministry there was little public pressure or spokesperson to represent the interests of competitors to BT or to represent the interests of residential consumers. The government was in fact perfectly prepared to accept that increased residential charges would decrease the number of residential connections.[28]

But perhaps the major problem is that lack of access and reduction in the network have been presented politically as simply a problem of the disadvantaged, rather than a cost imposed on each telephone user. The goal of a universal telephone is contained in BT's licence, but the inauguration of OFTEL has removed telecommunications policy from the parliamentary arena. In 1981, 5 million households were without a telephone, predominantly outside the south-east and in poorer economic groups, although one estimate puts the proportion of Londoners without a telephone at 13 per cent.[29] In 1985 because of an increase in the number of households the number without a telephone was approximately the same, and with connection charges equivalent to 25 per cent of an average monthly wage penetration seems set to fall. Liberalisation and privatisation have not benefited the average telephone user.[30]

Nor have BT's trade unions fared particularly well under privatisation. BT's internal organisation has been changed from a three-tier hierarchical system to one based on divisional profit centres reporting to the board. The domestic network is now split between local customer services and national networks, and one layer of the hierarchy in LCS has vanished. New technology threatens to deskill on the one hand and demand additional training in software on the other, while the unions anticipate increased managerial control will go hand-in-hand with the computerisation of customer services. From paternalistic management BT is seen as moving to 'macho', autocratic management, responding to its changing, uncertain, competitive environment with increased authoritarianism towards a more segmented workforce. The takeover of Mitel by BT also introduces a non-unionised company into a fully unionised enterprise, further weakening trade union power.

The change was only to be expected since part of the original reason for the privatisation of BT was to attack trade union power. Between 1982 and 1985 almost 17,000 jobs disappeared, surpassing the target set by BT management in 1982. With this size of job loss BT can rely on the trade unions to back its initiatives to expand into new fields.[31]

The major beneficiaries from privatisation in Britain have been large domestic and international companies, benefiting from lower priced trunk and international calls. Domestic and foreign computer service and equipment companies have benefited by entry into VANs, and overseas equipment suppliers have benefited from increased penetration of the British market. The City benefited directly from BT's sale. But the major gains so far have been made by the shareholders of BT and Mercury, the former by their capital gains and the latter by the subsidy given their company by BT's customers. Direct losers are residential consumers and domestic manufacturers.

Japan—from liberalisation to privatisation

Because of the conflict between MITI and the MPT over data processing in the 1970s and early 1980s, and because of American pressure for the liberalisation of telecommunications imports, NTT's monopoly of telecommunications transmission was not something which went undiscussed in the ten years prior to privatisation. In particular, NTT's vision of INS, with its concept of a single network providing data, voice and video transmission was unappealing to elements both within American and Japanese industry, specifically those concerned with computer and information services, those affected by the prospect of charges by 'bit' of information, and those with an existing investment in private data networks, which would be made redundant. Private VANs were estimated in 1983 to provide a market worth $700 million rising to $4 billion in 1990.[32] INS would also increase the power of MPT against MITI because it would once and for all take away MITI's influence in data processing and information services. From the equipment manufacturers' point of view, although domestic telecommunications growth had slowed computer growth had not and value added networks promised to be the growth market of the future. The manufacturers were no longer so dependent individually on NTT.[33] It was possible that they could do better by selling to the private VAN market and to the first telephone market both of which were being held back by NTT. NTT still held the monopoly of the first telephone and from 1983 began to sell rather than rent these telephones, primarily so that it could market more up to date telephones. In so doing it raised the question of whether its marketing operation was as good as the manufacturers' own sales organisations. In addition to the large user companies wanting to provide their own private VAN, the railways and power companies who operated their own telecommunications systems wanted to sell spare capacity. Also

NTT's computer services division competed with private companies without any safeguards on cross subsidy.

There was therefore a constituency of large, powerful companies in favour of a full liberalisation of the telecommunications market. With net earnings of $1,544 million in 1983, and with data communications and leased circuit revenue showing annual growth of 14 per cent, it was hardly surprising that some large companies cast envious eyes at NTT's profits and wanted to get into this growth market.[34] Taiyu Kobayashi, chairman of Fujitsu, also chairman of Keidanren's Committee on Data Processing and a prime proponent of NTT's privatisation stated:

The development of sophisticated communication means such as data and video communications is expected to contribute importantly to economic activity and social evolution. Therefore it is urgently necessary to make an overall review of the existing legal basis for the telephone network and develop a new system suited to the age of advanced communications[35]

Large business not only complained about its inability to set up nation-wide VAN or VAN between companies, but also about the high trunk call charges, about NTT's monopoly of the first telephone and about lack of customised billing.[36] There was also a feeling that NTT was a large bureaucracy and as such unresponsive to industry's needs—it was too powerful and not sufficiently demand-orientated.[37] In other words, 'something had to be done about NTT'.

Although these feelings surfaced during the wrangle between MPT and MITI over the further liberalisation of data communications in 1982, the issue of NTT's privatisation was first raised formally by the Second Ad Hoc Commission on Administrative reform, headed by the octogenarian Mr Toshio Doko, a previous head of Keidanren. The Commission was originally appointed by Prime Minister Zenko Suzuki in 1981 for a two year term with a remit to review the civil service and government deficits and to recommend a form of administration suitable for the twenty-first century. It was basically a cost-cutting exercise in line with the Thatcher government's reduction of civil service numbers in Britain and the Reagan administration's original intention to reduce the size of the American federal bureaucracy. Some opinion in the industry suggested that the Commission turned its attention to NTT because its profits were too great a temptation to large-scale business, who wanted a slice of the action. MITI's competition with the MPT may also have had an impact at this juncture—MITI certainly later championed the committee's proposals—and MITI had just been beaten by the MPT in its attempts to bring software under patent rather than copyright law.[38]

The Commission presented its basic report to the government in July 1982, which contained its proposals for NTT, although its final report was not submitted until March 1983. It recommended that NTT should be split up on the lines of AT&T before its deregulation. NTT would be split into regional operating companies servicing local exchanges and subscribers, while the main body of NTT would remain responsible for research and long-distance calls.[39] The dispersal of NTT would not in fact have mirrored that of AT&T before divestiture because NTT was not an international carrier, nor had it a manufacturing arm. It is not at all obvious why this organisational framework should have been suggested for NTT, except perhaps that it would have made cross-subsidy of those services most likely to be subject to competition more difficult for NTT, and that in the crudest sense it mimicked American experience.

While NTT was to be broken up in this way, it was also to be privatised. The commission considered that the private sector was most responsive to industrial innovation. The argument went like this: the Americans had deregulated AT&T and were in the process of breaking it up; even the possibility of break-up had stimulated a whole plethora of activity in the telecommunications market in the United States; this new activity was necessary both because of the convergence of tele-communications and data processing and because the telecommunica-tions market had reached maturity in existing services; NTT should be privatised and decentralised, giving industry the opportunity to enter into competition with it.

The original proposal suggested that the reorganisation should take place over five years and that in the meantime NTT's status should be shifted to that of a special corporation whose stock would be held by the government. NTT was to be divided into a long-lines company and local companies, but with the intention of following the pattern of AT&T's divestiture over a period of time. The central company was to be responsible for the construction, maintenance and operation of the basic trunk lines, to own and run the telecommunications laboratories and to provide local companies with technical advice. In addition data facilities and some maintenance should be split off from the new company. Competition would be gradually introduced into the basic trunk area with the licensing of competitors. The government should hold the stock in the company for the time being but should sell it off over five years. The central long-lines company should also sell stock in the local companies until they became independent. In addition NTT should carry out various rationalisation plans reducing the number of its personnel, and should immediately improve certain of its services, such as maintenance and repair work.[40]

Both Keidanren and the Communications Industry Association of Japan (CIAJ), the equipment manufacturers association, presented their views to the committee. Keidanren represents the interests of over 800 companies, the most powerful being Toyota, the motor manufacturer and the heavy industries, Nippon Steel and Tokyo Electric. It has about ten foreign companies within its membership, including NCR, Olivetti, IBM and Philips. NTT and KDD are also members, but were precluded from the decisionmaking on telecommunications. IBM was a member of Keidanren's Telecommunications Policy Committee. Keidanren presented testimony to the Ad Hoc Commission in favour of NTT's privatisation.[41]

In contrast to the predominance of large companies represented by Keidanren, the CIAJ represents 178 companies manufacturing telecommunications equipment, the largest group of them (44 per cent) having a turnover of less than ¥100 million ($500,000). Only thirty-three of its companies have a turnover of more than ¥5 billion ($2, 500 million) Although it seems that most of the CIAJ members would in fact have preferred to keep the status quo, in Japanese fashion, bowing to the prevailing wind, the CIAJ also presented a short statement to the Ad Hoc Commission in favour of the innovatory force of private industry and the privatisation of NTT.[42] The major concern to the manufacturers was the question of R & D, which was divided up between NTT, doing the more basic research, and manufacturers doing the development work. NTT family manufacturers did not have to pay NTT a commercial fee for rights to use patents whereas a privatised NTT would sell them for profit. There was also concern that NTT would turn to more short-term research if privatised. There was some hope too that, once privatised, NTT would revert back to its old equipment family of suppliers and would not have to open its equipment purchases to the Americans.[43]

The Ad Hoc Commission's report was made public in July 1982 and accepted as a basis for action by the government. It was then referred to the Telecommunications Policy Committee within the LDP. Keidanren presented its detailed views in October of that year, formulated by a sub-committee on which IBM was represented. It wanted complete liberalisation of line usage for voice and data, the liberalisation of hardware (the first telephone), the easing of regulation of NTT at the same time as its conversion into a stock company, the divestment of NTT's related business of computer services and its limitation to the supply of communications circuits.[44] Although Keidanren's draft position paper was in favour of the break-up of NTT, that stance was dropped following opposition within the organisation and it asked only for a review of NTT's position after five years.[45]

It seems that the first reactions of MPT to the proposals were hostile, but within a few months the top personnel had changed, bringing in bureaucrats more sympathetic to the privatisation and more receptive to international trends towards privatisation. For MPT the reorganisation of NTT provided an opportunity to re-establish its authority against MITI, which had always been the lead Ministry. Some form of regulation would also allow MPT to re-establish its authority over NTT. In similar fashion to the British DTI's relations with BT, the Japanese bureaucracy seems to have had problems in controlling a very large technological public corporation. If some form of 'regulatory control' of NTT were to be established by legislation, then MPT would gain considerable power.

In the battle over territory MITI stood to gain from complete privatisation and the break-up of NTT, which would take it outside MPT direct control into the private market where it would come under the direct influence of MITI. This inter-ministry competition and conflict has also to be interpreted in the light of MITI's own failing influence, brought about by the liberalisation of the monetary system and by the increasing internationalisation of companies. In addition MITI is now the focus of American pressure. From being a ministry involved mainly in the protection of growth industries within Japan, in order to buy off the possibility of protection abroad, it has become the ministry most likely to push for liberalisation of domestic markets.

Publicly the privatisation and liberalisation were presented as a matter of increasing efficiency within NTT, although ministry officials were unable to elucidate on exactly how 'efficient' was defined.[46] It most certainly did not mean 'efficient' in the sense of the British euphemism for labour force reduction. Although NTT was thought to have too many employees, and was proposing to lay off 90,000 workers from its 320,000 workforce over fifteen years, the proposal was seen as a means by which personnel could be re-employed in new services, rather than laid off.[47] Ministry officials argued that it was impossible to tell how efficient NTT was because there was no similar company for comparison. However NTT's rising personnel costs, its employees' short working week (thirty-seven hours ten minutes) compared to manufacturing industry and its 90 per cent dependence on revenues from the mature telephone market were causes for concern.[48]

Perhaps what is most interesting to an outside observer is the lack of attention paid to the considerable achievements of NTT or to its technological plans for the future. The arguments presented by proponents of privatisation were that NTT had done its job well; there were now no waiting lists for telephones, the network was laid and it was time to hand over to the private sector.[49]

Personnel within NTT seem to have been divided over the proposed changes. At the top President Hisashi Shinto, with strong links to Keidanren, and other top management were very much in favour. The privatisation proposal would allow more managerial autonomy and would solve the problem of NTT's yearly budget. They saw it as a means of moving away from the maturing telephone market to the more profitable related markets of information services.[50] Others, particularly those working on INS planning, were not so happy, mainly because the privatisation meant that INS would no longer be developed nation-wide, as a public service.

Once the Ad Hoc Commission's recommendations had been made public a round of consultations started. The political wind was in favour of privatisation of some kind. At this stage NTT and its trade union, Zendentsu, held talks to decide what kind of bill they would want. NTT seems to have left much of the later politicking to the trade union.

In fact, as employees, NTT personnel were likely to gain personally from privatisation and were therefore likely to feel ambivalent towards the proposals. The gains were likely to come from the fact that they would no longer be civil servants under a privatised NTT and therefore not constrained legally by a no-strike clause. Also, as private employees, their pay would no longer be constrained by equity with other loss-making public corporations such as Japan National Railways. In 1983, as if to rub the point home, as an austerity measure the government froze their pay award.

Together with NTT management Zendentsu was united in being totally opposed to the possible break-up into local and long-line companies. It argued that in order to safeguard the provision of INS, NTT must have a firm financial base and that such a base could not be had purely from long-lines business which would be subject to competition. In other words NTT had already seen and rejected the possible scenario of an AT&T-operating company split as too financially risky.

Zendentsu's demands were all based on its position that telecommunications should remain a publicly controlled service, but were nevertheless designed to improve the position of a privatised NTT and its employees. Zendentsu was aiming for a new type of company with some form of co-operative ownership. Opposed to privatisation or to NTT's division along either geographical or functional lines and to the unconditional entry of new competitors, it nevertheless wanted NTT's obligation to provide universal service continued. But, perhaps most saliently, it wanted the right to strike presently denied to it—the rights of public sector workers to be equal to those in the private sector.[51]

In effect, once the political decision had been made to privatise NTT, both NTT's interests and those of Zendentsu were in making a privatised NTT as free from ministry control as possible. Zendentsu argued that it was reasonable for the ministry to control the basic telephone tariff, but that all other tariffs should be subject to NTT's commercial decision-making. Both wanted NTT to be able to expand its business into new areas without having to ask for ministry approval.

As a 'company' union Zendentsu's strength within the trade union movement itself would be affected by any diminution in numbers. That in turn would be likely to affect the alignment within the trade union movement between those unions aligned with the Social Democratic party (the right) and those such as Zendentsu aligned with the Japan Socialist party. If NTT were given the right to enter new services, then there remained the possibility that new employees might be taken on, as well as existing employees redeployed.[52]

Gaining from the experience accrued by BT's unions in their fight against liberalisation and drawing on American evidence, Zendentsu emphasised the impact that splitting NTT might have on rural telephone bills. Rural members of the LDP, of whom there are many, became convinced that such regionalisation would adversely affect their areas. This possibility, together with the fear of the unknown implications of a radical restructuring of NTT, was enough to swing opinion away from LDP approval of the break-up of NTT, and to a commitment to keep local tariffs steady. Three bills were presented in April 1984 to the Diet.[53]

The NTT bill allowed for the privatisation of NTT. It did not authorise its regionalisation or its split into functional divisions, but a 'sunset' clause after five years meant automatic review and a possible break-up. The bill contained a clause limiting strikes to fifteen days but also failed to forbid NTT to manufacture equipment—a possible sop to Zendentsu. The bill placed NTT's entry into new services under the control of the ministry, which also had control of tariffs. Whereas the Ad Hoc Commission had recommended competition only on long-lines the Telecommunications Business bill allowed competition in the local network as well. But both competitors and NTT were to be subject to regulation by the MPT.

What seems to have happened is that MPT's interests in extending its regulatory control over NTT and telecommunications coincided with a compromise position on the issue of privatisation itself. The concept of regulatory control by MPT was a half-way house between the full break-up of NTT wanted by MITI, some member companies in Keidanren and the Ad Hoc Commission and its continuation as a public corporation. In addition Zendentsu, NTT and MPT all had something to gain from privatisation, although this did not override Zendentsu's original position that telephone and telegraphy should remain a monopoly of NTT in order to ensure INS as a public service.

Within the Diet, Zendentsu aligned itself with the opposition parties—the Japan Socialist party and the Japan Communist party—in opposing the privatisation of NTT. Debate produced some concessions. The MPT's control over new services was eased. And although there remained a 'no strike' provision during a period of forced arbitration the bill was amended to include a clause giving a review in three years' time.

By this time however, the telecommunications manufacturers had become seriously concerned about the NTT bill. As it stood NTT was to be allowed to manufacture equipment in direct competition with the manufacturers. They presented a petition to the Diet, provoking an undertaking from NTT that it would not undertake manufacture for the 'time being'. Various interpretations were put on this phrase, but the manufacturers seemed reasonably certain in 1984 that NTT would not be undertaking manufacture for a long time. They anticipated that NTT would have considerable difficulty adjusting to its newly privatised situation and in gearing up for competition.[54]

Throughout the summer of 1984 the opposition parties aligned with Zendentsu opposed the bill. Then, just when it seemed that the bill would not be passed before the parliamentary year finished, Zendentsu switched strategy. In early September it publicly came out in favour of the NTT bill being passed as quickly as possible. By this time all the possible compromises had already been reached. Future credibility and possible repeal of the 'no strike' clause depended on the public attitude to Zendentsu and whether it was seen as a 'responsible' trade union, rather than a wrecker.

By then the bill was primarily held up by inter-factional fighting within the LDP. That fighting seemed to be aimed at the imminent re-election of Prime Minister Nakasone to the leadership of the party. A failure to pass the bill, which had his personal backing, could be seen as a reflection on his status and it seems to have become a pawn in the leadership stakes. It was not until after the leadership election at the end of December that the bill was finally passed.

Throughout the passage of the bill the two ministries, MPT and MITI, were engaged in competition and conflict revolving around MPT's victory in gaining increased powers over the whole telecommunications industry, including data networks. MITI was even accused by the MPT of being a spokesperson for American interests. It seems more likely that MITI's interests happened to coincide with those of America which wanted to see a fully liberalised market with ease of access for American firms.

Major clashes came over the terms of entry of foreign enterprises into competition with NTT and the form of control which MPT should have over VANs. The Americans had argued during the spring and summer of 1984 that foreigners should be allowed to buy the shares of a privatised NTT which the bill expressly forbade. Unsuccessful in this, the Americans continued to pressure for easier access for American firms into the new competitive market.

As the telecommunications bill stood originally there were to be two types of carriers. Type 1 carriers were to be licensed by MPT to carry basic voice services. Type II carriers were to be VAN suppliers, leasing circuits from the Type I companies but they also were split into Special and General Types. In fact what the ministry was trying to overcome once more was the problem of distinguishing between 'basic' and 'enhanced' services, so that it did not play into MITI's hands, while at the same time giving itself the power if necessary to stop the domestic and international market from being swamped by nation-wide value added networks provided by overseas companies. 'Special' Type II services were those which were to be provided on a wide scale serving many companies or unspecified individuals or the international market. Both Type I and Special Type II carriers were to be licensed by MPT, whereas General Type II services—those for instance providing intra-company VANs—had only to notify MPT. Foreign enterprises were denied the right to enter into the Type 1 carrier business.

One difference between MITI and MPT revolved around the definition of what constituted a 'foreign' enterprise. The original MPT definition was that 50 per cent Japanese ownership was required to qualify as 'domestic'. The Americans wanted this definition scrapped, arguing that their companies should have absolute right of entry.

A second point of contention was the question of what form of control MPT should have over VANs, whether it should be able to refuse entry to companies, or whether it should purely hold a register of VANs. MPT wanted the larger power. MITI's interests and those of the Americans were in favour of no control. The conflict between the two ministries became so severe that the impasse was eventually solved only by the intervention of the LDP's specialist parliamentary committee on telecommunications. The eventual compromise allowed companies with 30 per cent Japanese capital to enter the Type 1 market and reduced MPT licensing of Special Type II VANs. However, because the telecommunications business bill has a three year review period, the question of a completely open market and MPT's powers will reoccur. The bills were finally passed in the closing days of December 1984 and the provisions came into force in April 1985.

The compromises that went into the passage of the bills resulted in an NTT bill with conflicting goals. On the one hand NTT had imposed upon it certain public service obligations. It had to provide appropriate and stable telephone services throughout Japan (a reference to the rural areas dispute) and it had to promote research for practical use and also basic research on telecommunications technology. The legislation actually has written in that ¥10 should remain the unit for pricing. The implication is that NTT may possibly alter the time and distance allowed for the unit price, but that no large increases can be made in local telephone call tariffs. The further implication is that decreases will have to be made in NTT's costs and it will need growth in usage if it is to continue to make a profit as inflation erodes its revenue. Unlike BT, NTT will not be able to protect its revenue by increasing costs of local calls in a significant manner. Coupled with the possibility of a full break-up in five years' time, control of NTT is therefore much stricter than that of BT.

On the other hand the bill allowed NTT to operate domestic tele-communications and business incidental to this. By omission it neither precluded NTT from manufacturing nor precluded it from entry into the international market. The assumption at the time was that the major competition to NTT would come through Type I carriers, whilst the major competition to KDD would come through Special Type II carriers.

But the real worries of KDD were three fold. First it feared that NTT would enter the international market. Second it feared that KDD would have to agree to lease international lines to any Special Type II carrier which wanted them, thereby affecting the numbers it had for its own business and leading to decline. Third it worried that because the legislation omitted to mention the question of the resale of international circuits, resale was allowed by omission. Early on in the bill's discussions KDD had determined that the only answer to its worries about NTT and its own decline was to enter the VAN business itself, giving it something to sell to the end user. On the question of resale of international circuits and the possible contravention of CCITT Regulations D1 and D6, the MPT position was that nothing in the legislation actually contravened the regulation. If there were any conflict then Japan would campaign to alter the regulation, rather than break it.[55]

While the bills were still going through the Diet, other organisations were also considering the possibility of entry into NTT's market. Within Keidanren the president of Fujitsu had actively campaigned on the possibility of using satellites of an SBS variety to provide an alternative to NTT's network. At this time Japan had two communications satellites and one partially crippled DBS satellite in use. The communications satellite was used predominantly as a back-up in time of earthquake and for transmission to the outlying islands. Despite American pressure the policy of the MPT had been that the further use of communications satellites had to wait until the launch of a Japanese satellite in 1990. Using the Ka band the satellite being developed would provide tens of thousands of telephone circuits. In contrast, Keidanren was in favour of buying Ku band satellites from America and in deference to Mr Kobayashi of Fujitsu, during 1984 Keidanren staff worked on a feasibility study on the use of satellites for long-distance transmission. The argument over satellites was to surface once the bills had been passed.

Once again MITI and MPT were in conflict over the proposal. Satellites represented one area in which the United States held an advantage in telecommunications and it therefore continued to press the Japanese to reduce the balance of payments deficit between the two countries by buying satellites. MITI took the American position while MPT was concerned with the development of domestic communications satellite manufacturing capacity. The issue remained unresolved when the bill was passed, but shortly after, with protectionist pressures within the American Congress increasing, and a deadline of 1 April 1985 for resolution of the Japanese-American trade talks, the Japanese government altered its position. Although NTT would not buy American satellites, its private competitors were to be allowed to do so. On 9 April Prime Minister Nakasone confirmed the promise and the Export-Import Bank of Japan was authorised to finance their purchase.[56]

In April, MPT licensed five competitors, one of which, Dai Ni Den Den, was originally seen by MPT as probably capable of providing a future national competitive voice communications network. Dai Ni Den Den, using microwave circuits, a company formed by the Japan National Railways and a third formed by the construction ministry, both using optic fibres laid along their existing rights of way, will provide telephone and leased circuits on Japan's most used route—between Tokyo and Osaka. Two further competitors will provide leased lines nation-wide via satellite transmission, and, inevitably these will concentrate on the long-distance market. One consortium, consisting of C. Itoh and Mitsui, two large trading houses, formed a joint venture with Hughes Communications of the United States (Hughes taking one third) to buy two communications satellites from Hughes. These are scheduled for launch at the beginning of 1988. Mitsubishi, another trading house, and Mitsubishi Electric Corp. have signed up with Ford, while a third company backed by Sony and Marubeni, a further trading house, is collaborating with RCA. However, by the end of 1985 the MPT had not yet decided whether to license this third venture, on the grounds that there might not be enough business for all three.[57] In addition in January 1986 it was reported that a cable TV company had launched an application as a Type I carrier, competing with NTT in the local market.[58]

Originally the major Type I competitor to NTT, Dai Ni Den Den, a company headed by the 'new' Japanese capital of Kyocera (a ceramics company specialising in microchip wafers) and Sony had anticipated using satellite transmission. The problem with satellite use in Japan is one of economics: the distances are not large enough for them to compete on cost with terrestrial transmission via optic fibres. The situation in Japan, where NTT has modernised its network and where demand for telephone communications is already being met, is somewhat different from that in the United States where AT&T had been slow to introduce new technology. To use satellite transmission in Japan is to compete against an NTT whose marginal costs are likely to be lower than those of satellite users. Since MPT controls tariffs, the result would likely be that NTT's charges would be kept artificially high in order to allow the competition to make a return on its capital investment. And from the experience of SBS in the United States it seems highly unlikely that a satellite system could pay for itself in a competitive market situation by data and voice transmission alone. In fact, Keidanren in conjunction with the MPT proposed that the three competitors should be unified into one satellite competitor, but were opposed by the Fair

Trade Commission. Keidanren's action suggests however that the services as they stand will not be competitive with NTT, and that unless traffic grows by something in the region of 30 per cent on the Tokyo–Osaka route all are likely to lose money.

In the international market, 25 per cent of which is made up of calls to the United States, of which 75 per cent are data communications, the major problem in the use of private satellites is that the obvious regional market for satellite transmission with neighbouring countries is small. The major route between Tokyo and the United States is a monopoly of Intelsat using which, in 1986, KDD announced a new fast data transmission service between Japan, Britain and the United States. An optic fibre link of which KDD is an owner, being constructed between Japan and the United States, will also be a major competitor with satellite communication. Unless the Intelsat monopoly is broken, or unless Japan is going to buy satellites as a form of development investment for the smaller south-east Asian countries to use, although DBS and cable TV present possible markets, there is rather little room for their use within Japan in the telecommunications market. Japan is not unlike Britain in this respect.

Within the United States cable TV provided the alternative usage for the transmission capacity of satellites. It is noticeable that in agreeing its contract with Mitsui and C. Itoh, Hughes was said to envisage: 'an enormous pent-up demand for communications satellites in Japan.' In particular it was expecting a large growth in cable TV programming in Japan, more efficient distribution of broadcast TV via satellite as well as telephone traffic and computer data transmission.[59] It seems therefore that although entry of satellites into Japan has been gained from pressure on telecommunications it is in fact the market for broadcasting which is the primary target for some satellite operators. Just as in the United States, cable TV will in fact provide the alternative use for sunk investment in satellites, although this targeted usage may have implications for the current broadcasting entities in terms of advertising revenue. It seems likely that once satellites are in service, pressure will mount for usage with existing cable TV (which is expanding), to be followed by American pressure on programming. Japan currently has one of the lowest proportions of American programmes on television in the world—it is one of the few countries where 'Dynasty' has flopped.

The second kind of competition to NTT is in the provision of Special VAN services using leased circuits. They must be registered with the MPT—meaning that they have to satisfy the MPT on standards. A further row between MITI, the Americans and the MPT blew up over what standards would be set and who would judge the equipment. Prior to its privatisation, NTT was responsible for setting and adjudicating on standards. After privatisation the MPT proposed that a board should be set up consisting of representatives from the manufacturers. The American companies immediately protested that the system contained inbuilt bias against foreign manufacturers. After much argument, the Americans prevailed. An independent board was established and standard specifications were reduced to make it easier for foreign companies.[60]

By the end of 1985 the MPT had registered eight companies providing Special Type II services, and 172 General Type II companies had notified the MPT of their existence. In all ten, American companies have announced VAN services in conjunction with Japanese partners. These include AT&T, GTE, Tymnet, General Electric and Uninet. European firms, such as Cable and Wireless have reported difficulty in entering the Type 1 market, but Philips and Kyocera have two Type II joint agreements to market home information systems and telecommunications control systems. NTT is a partner in several VAN services, and is looking to compete with KDD for its South Korean business, which provided KDD with more than 13 per cent of its telephone and 7 per cent of its telex traffic in 1983. Although KDD is said to have liberalised the leasing of private international circuits in line with CCITT regulations, these regulations are themselves subject to wide interpretation and in 1985 KDD still precluded the entry of competitive international VANs by only renting international private circuits for direct company-to-company use.[61]

NTT has also set up a consulting/construction company jointly with a number of trading houses with the main purpose of doing business with China, but the equipment manufacturers have been excluded from the venture. In 1985 it signed an agreement with AT&T to exchange product development, marketing and management know-how.[62] The intention was to develop a new generation of digital switching and a standardized computer protocol for linking incompatible computers. Nothing however has caused such a furore as NTT's agreement to enter the VAN market with IBM using NTT's data network and IBM's computers. The link-up between the two was opposed vociferously by the CIAJ and the two largest equipment manufacturers, Fujitsu and Hitachi. From 1979 Fujitsu had been taking a larger computer market share in Japan than IBM, which dropped to third place behind NEC in 1984. The proposed VAN enables IBM to use NTT's local offices to sell its hardware. The intention of the alliance is to produce a mini-computer designed to interconnect IBM's SNA standards to the DCNA (Data Communications Network Architecture) standards of NTT, to provide telecommunications services including the design and installation of VAN and to sell IBM compatible software, and mini-IBM machines. It also intends to provide interconnections for the international networks of multinational corporations. DCNA had been developed by NTT in conjunction with all the major Japanese computer manufacturers, and with 70 per cent of on-line users using non-IBM machines, there is a suspicion that NTT intends to manufacture a special computer for use with its telecommunications services.[63]

The link-up between the two took place despite the public hostility of all the major manufacturers. They argued that such a tie-up would not be allowed under anti-trust legislation in the United States, and had been forbidden in Britain. Nevertheless, the MPT did not oppose the proposal. With a huge trade surplus with the United States and anti-Japanese feeling running high in Congress, the ministry stated: 'We did not oppose the idea at all. If we did, you know, the United States will make it an issue.'[64]

The result of NTT's ambition—President Shinto argues that 'what we are doing now is only on a small scale'—has been not only a cooling of relations with AT&T but also non-co-operation from the Japanese manufacturers. They can afford to distance themselves from NTT because, unlike the British manufacturers, they are not reliant upon it.

To conclude, in the political process which went with the passage of the NTT bill and the telecommunications bill it seemed that Japanese-style politics is one of numerous trade-offs. Trade unions, manufacturers, NTT itself, the Americans, MITI and MPT all lost on some issues and gained on others. Even KDD, the international carrier, which had its monopoly broken and seemed most vulnerable to competition gained the power to enter the domestic market for the first time. All interests seemed to end up with some accommodation, and the contrast with Britain could not be more obvious.

Yet despite this difference in process, the privatisation of NTT has benefited similar interests to those in Britain. It has predominantly benefited the large trading houses and multinationals, who have entered the computer services and transmission field, and NTT itself. Once privatised, NTT, like BT, took on a set of different interests geared to profitability and expansion. It has also benefited MPT, which, according to one person close to the scene, 'gained such wind-fall power over telecommunications as it never dreamed of two years ago'. Yet the MPT's problems are not over. With the illness of former Prime

Minister Kakuei Tanaka, it lost a most powerful patron. And although it seems to have gained the role of policing telecommunications, in practice it has been unable to hold much ground under concerted American pressure.

Conflicts over interconnection and tariffs are yet to come, but the assumption must be that NTT's long-distance tariffs will be kept up by the MPT, so that its competitors may make a profit. A further assumption must be that overcapacity will provide the incentive for attempts to expand cable broadcasting massively.

With threats of reciprocal trade legislation by Congress never far away, the only ground which will not give is that already settled by legislation. NTT will not buy a satellite because in the words of American officials: 'A decision by NTT to buy an American satellite system would effectively spell the end to Japan's program to develop its own space communication capability.'[65] Japan's space industry will continue to develop because it is specified in legislation.

Overall the major winner from NTT's privatisation has been IBM. Because IBM's installed base in Japan is much smaller than its 70 per cent base in Europe, there was much less reason for NTT's interests to coincide with those of IBM than for BT's to do so. But just as there is talk in Britain that BT may manufacture an IBM compatible computer, so in Japan domestic manufacturers are threatened by a similar prospect. In the privatisation stakes, Japan's domestic manufacturers, like those in Britain, have been major losers.

Notes and references

1. *Financial Times* 30 June 1981; 15 October 1981; 30 November 1982
2. *The Future of Telecommunications in Britain*, Cmnd. 8610, London, HMSO, 1982, p. 4.
3. On cable TV in Britain see: Cabinet Office, *Cable Systems*, London, HMSO, 1982; *Cable TV Expansion*, Cmnd. 2866, London, HMSO, 1983.
4. Guy de Jonquieres, 'A Direct Line To the Market', *Financial Times*, 24 July 1982; *Cable and Broadcasting Act 1984.*
5. Department of Industry, *The Future of Telecommunications in Britain*, London, HMSO, 1984, pp. 1–2.
6. See: David Thomas, 'The Union Response to Denationalization' in David Steel and David Heald, (eds.), *Privatizing Public Enterprises*, London, RIPA, 1984, pp. 59–75.
7. David Goodhart, 'On the edge of a "black hole"', *Financial Times*, 12 October 1983.
8. Guy de Jonquieres and David Freud, 'BT: the 51% Solution' *Financial Times*, 27 September 1983; *Guardian*, 8 December 1983.

9. *Hansard*, 29 November 1982, col. 138.
10. *Financial Times* 14 December 1982; 3 February 1983.
11. Stephen Littlechild, *Regulation of British Telecommunications Profitability*, London, Department of Industry, 1983; *Guardian*, 8 February 1983; *Financial Times*, 17 January 1983.
12. *Financial Times*, 8 February 1983.
13. The Cable and Broadcasting Act 1984 set up the framework for expansion of cable TV. The government decided cable TV should be privately funded but then took away the necessary capital allowances. Limited local franchises are regulated partly by a new Cable Authority and partly by OFTEL. BT has been allowed to invest in half the original eleven cable TV systems and the cable companies are not allowed to act as common carriers except in conjunction with either BT or Mercury.
14. *Guardian*, 8 February 1983.
15. Cecil Parkinson, *Hansard*, 18 July 1983, Vol. 46, 1983–4, col. 26–38.
16. Lord Weinstock, *House of Lords Debates*, 16 January 1984, cols. 860–63. Also interview in *Financial Times*, 28 March 1984.
17. See for instance Second Reading Debate, *Hansard*, 29 November 1982, Vol. **33**, 1982–3, col. 31–110.
18. Michael Smith, 'How Maggie sold us £2bn short', *Guardian*, 4 December 1984.
19. *Telecommunications Act, 1984*, Part I, 3 (1) and (2).
20. See: Bryan Carsberg, 'Oftel–the Challenge of the Next Five Years', *Information Technology and Public Policy*, Vol. **4**, No. 1, September 1985, pp. 1–11; OFTEL, *First Report 5 August–31 December 1984*, London, HMSO, 1985.
21. MZA Report quoted in *Financial Times*, 17 May 1985.
22. *Financial Times, 24 July 1985.*
23. *Financial Times*, 26 June 1985.
24. *Financial Times*, 16 October 1985; OFTEL, *Determination of Terms and Conditions for the Purposes of an Agreement on the Interconnection of the BT System and the Mercury Communications Ltd System Under Condition 13 of the Licence Granted to 241 BT under Section 7 of the Telecommunications Act 1984, London, OFTEL, 1985.*
25. Department of Trade and Industry, *Future Licensing of Value Added and Data Services: Revised Proposals*, 30 December 1985, Mimeo.
26. Memorandum accompanying a statement by Sir Keith Joseph, 21 July 1980.
27. Guy de Jonquieres, 'The muddle that is slowing VANs', *Financial Times*, 10 September 1985; Michael Beesley, *Liberalisation of the use of the British Telecommunications Network*, London, HMSO, 1981, pp. 3–5.
28. See for instance: *Hansard*, 29 November 1982, Vol. **33**, 1982–3, col. 94.
29. Gareth Locksley, 'London Calling: A Policy for Telecommunications after Privatisation', *Telecommunications Policy*, September 1984, pp. 178–80.
30. Extrapolation from 1981 figures gives approximately 20.5 million households in 1985, of which about 15.5 million had telephones.
31. Post Office Engineering Union (now the Union of Communication Workers) *Making the Future Work: The Broad Strategy*, Approved by Special Conference, November 1984. On the interests represented in the

privatisation debate see: John Kay, 'The privatization of British Telecoms', in David Steel and David Heald, (eds.), op. cit., pp. 77–86.

32. *Asahi News Service*, 7 October 1985.
33. Peter E. Fuchs, 'Regulatory Reform and Japan's Telecommunications Revolution' in *US–Japan Relations: New Attitudes for a New Era*, Annual Review 1983–4, Boston, Mass., Center for International Affairs, Harvard University, 1984, p. 131 quotes NTT's share of sales for Oki Electric at 14 per cent, NEC 9 per cent, Fujitsu 8 per cent, and Hitachi 1. 5 per cent in 1983.
34. *NTT Annual Report 1982–3*, p. 36.
35. Taiyu Kobayashi, 'Hopes for an Open Policy in Telecommunications', *Keidanren Review*, no. 85 February 1984, pp. 5–9.
36. Yasusada Kitahara, 'INS–Telecommunications for the Advanced Information Society', in H. Inose (ed.), *Telecommunications Technologies*, Tokyo, OHMSHA and North-Holland Publishing Co., pp. 9–10.
37. Interview, August 1984.
38. Edwin T. Whaley, 'Legal Protection of Software', in *US–Japan Relations: New Attitudes for a New Era*, op. cit., pp. 143–60.
39. *Report on Present State of Communications in Japan 1982*, Tokyo, MPT and Japan Times, 1982, p. 11.
40. Ikuo Ohashi, 'The Effects of Telecommunications Deregulation', in *US–Japan Relations: Towards a New Equilibrium*, Annual Review 1982–3, Boston, Mass., Centre for International Affairs, Harvard University, 1983, pp. 85–97.
41. Interview, August 1984.
42. Interview, August 1984; CIAJ statement, 13 March 1984.
43. Interview, August 1984; CIAJ, *Outline of Communications Industry*, Japan '84, Tokyo, CIAJ, 1984.
44. Taiyu Kobayashi, op. cit., pp. 7–8.
45. Interview, August 1984.
46. Interview, August 1984.
47. See Hisashi Shinto in NTT Advertisement, *Financial Times*, 24 May 1985.
48. See Akira Nishii, NTT Senior Managing Director, *International Herald Tribune*, 26 October 1983.
49. See Moriya Koyama, 'The New Communications Age in Japan', *Telecommunications Policy*, September 1985, pp. 182–84.
50. Hisashi Shinto, 'Reform of the Telecommunications System in Japan', *Japan Quarterly*, 31, 1984, pp. 380–83.
51. Postal, Telegraph and Telephone International, *Privatisation and Liberalisation of Telecommunications Services in the PTTI Asian Region*, September 1984, Section 4. 1–4. 20.
52. Interview, August 1984.
53. *Nippon Telegraph and Telephone Company Bill, 1984.* .
54. Interview, August 1984.
55. Interview, August 1984.
56. *Washington Post*, 12 January 1984; 10April 1985; 26 May 1985; 26 September 1985; *Japan Times*, 18 July 1985.
57. *Financial Times*, 29 March 1985.
58. *New Era of Telecommunications in Japan*, no. 9, 1 February 1986, p. 5.

59. *Washington Post*, 26 May 1985.
60. *Japan Times* , 19 July 1985.
61. *Asahi News Service*, 1 August 1985—In 1985 KDD allowed exclusive lines only to link companies in Japan with foreign offices or subsidiaries.
62. *Asahi New Service*, 27 September 1985.
63. *Asahi News Service*, 26 September 1985; 7 October 1985; *Washington Post*, 26 September 1985.
64. *Asahi News Service*, 7 October 1985.
65. *Washington Post*, 26 May 1985.

6 Deregulation of international communications: the United States versus Intelsat

Introduction

This chapter is about the export of American-style deregulation into the area of international telecommunications. Specifically it is about American attempts to break into the market of Intelsat, the international consortium for international satellite transmission. The Reagan administration, in 1985, decided that private American satellites could be placed over the Atlantic, thereby ending twenty years of international consensus that this market in satellite transmission should be open only to Intelsat.

The decision follows many years of attempts by the FCC to export its deregulatory concepts into international telecommunications—attempts which to a large extent have been thwarted by the European PTTs. The argument in this chapter is that not only will deregulation of Intelsat's market benefit the American space industry by increasing demand for domestic satellites, but will also place greater pressure on European PTTs to liberalise their telecommunications markets, thereby aiding American business. The problem for the American administration has been how to justify to international opinion this about-turn in its policy.

Just as American domestic telecommunications were split until the 1980s into telephone, telex and data services, so international transmission was similarly divided, with the additional complication that it was split, not only by service offered, but also between cable and satellite technology. Hence international transmission was divided between AT&T carrying telephone; several international record carriers, such as Western Union International and RCA, which were responsible for international telex and data transmission; and Comsat, responsible for access to international satellite communications. Gradually the FCC has erased distinctions between telephone and telegraph, between domestic carriage and international and between satellite and terrestrial transmission. Over a period of years the FCC, courts and Congress allowed new companies such as AT&T's primary competitors, GTE and MCI, into the international market as carriers.

By 1984 all the original international carriers could provide all services, while others, such as Satellite Business Systems could provide enhanced services.[1] The intended impact was increased competition over a range of services.

Despite this integration of services, and the integration of technologies within the domestic market, in the international market the technologies remained separate. Comsat remained the carrier's carrier providing the domestic linkage to international satellite transmission. With the deregulation of Comsat's ownership of earth stations in 1985, the FCC completed the process of service and technological unification at the American end of the international transmission market. It has opened access to international satellite communications to AT&T and others. The earth station connection, rather than the international satellite link, represents 90 per cent or more of the cost of an international call. The ensuing price differentiation between American carriers puts pressure on PTTs in Europe to match those lower prices and increases the economic possibilities of private satellites. AT&T has bought several Comsat earth stations and is providing a new business service in conjunction with BT using Intelsat for its international link. It could equally well use a private satellite.[2]

During this introduction of competition the PTTs complained vociferously that the FCC increased their costs of interconnection each time it approved another carrier and that it was throwing the international market into confusion. Although BT agreed in 1982 on a data communications service interconnecting with SBS via Intelsat, and interconnected with GTE and MCI in 1984, the reluctance of PTTs to connect with additional carriers limited the effectiveness of the original policy. Nevertheless, in 1984, the regulations on Mercury's international interconnection were considerably eased by the British government and it was allowed to make its own arrangements with foreign carriers. And, in Japan, the American idea of numbers of competitors in the international market has been repeated. NTT is looking to provide international communications to South Korea.

It has been in this deregulatory atmosphere in the United States, mirrored in Britain and Japan, that the 1983 application made by Orion Satellite Corporation to the FCC to place a private satellite over the Atlantic has been discussed. Intelsat was a 'monopoly' which had to be deregulated. The policy is not only commensurate with deregulation in the domestic telecommunications market, but also fits with other policies on the liberalisation of service industries being pursued through GATT.

The efforts of successive American administrations to achieve that liberalisation through GATT have met with little success. Renewed emphasis reflects the increased importance within the American domestic economy of service industries compared to manufacturing as well as failing American competitiveness in manufacture. The developing countries have not been anxious for any such liberalisation, fearing that their cultural autonomy as well as their sovereignty might be overwhelmed. Some of these fears concerning broadcasting have been expressed through UNESCO, from which the United States withdrew in 1985 followed by Britain. Within GATT the developing nations have at last found a bargaining counter against the industrialised West which has systematically precluded exports from the developing world in order to protect its own industries. They have demanded that the industrialised countries show some evidence that they will abide by the GATT article agreed in 1975, that they would positively help the developing countries' industries to export. The 1985 GATT meeting therefore followed the pattern of others in reaching no agreement on the liberalisation of trade in services.[3]

Just as the American withdrawal from UNESCO coincided with a failure of its influence within that organisation, it so happens that the desire to breach Intelsat's monopoly coincides with a loss of American influence within Intelsat, a diminution of its share of that organisation's capital, and a decrease in the benefit of Intelsat to the American space industry. Although the American satellite industry has benefited to the tune of $3.4 billion from Intelsat contracts over the past twenty years, the current programme will provide more than enough capacity for many years to come. To underline the point that industry had little to lose, in 1985 the FCC calculated that whereas the American satellite industry would have sales in that year of $6 billion the amount it would gain from Intelsat contracts would be $100 million.[4]

Intelsat came into being in the 1960s with eleven member nations to provide a global system of satellite communications. By 1985 it had 109 members, twenty-five countries used its services for domestic communications and non-members used it for international communications. From its original capacity of 460 telephone circuits over the Atlantic it had expanded to provide 1700 pathways globally, and took all international TV transmission and two-thirds of international telecommunications traffic. It was to combat this global monopoly that in 1983 an American company, Orion Corporation, launched an application to the FCC for a private trans-Atlantic satellite.

Intelsat was intended primarily to serve the interests of the developed countries and only in recent years has begun to consider carefully the needs of the underdeveloped. Even now it is not completely clear how far the demand for international facilities for the underdeveloped have in fact been demands from American or other global corporations based in those countries. Until the initiation of its Vista service for the underdeveloped in 1983 Intelsat's technology was based on the C band demanding heavy up-front investment in ground stations on the part of the receiving country, rather than the Ku band which would have allowed more primitive receivers. Concentrating as it did on low-cost satellites with high capacity, the technology was designed to benefit the industrialised countries with their demand for high-volume capacity, while Intelsat's financial structure benefited the PTTs of those same countries and Comsat in the United States.

It seems that various American entrepreneurs perceiving Intelsat to be locked into the older technology saw the possibility of providing specialised services to international business more cheaply by Ku band satellites. The original application was said to have been boosted by American banks and broadcasting organisations, who expected to depend even more heavily on international communications 'to tie together new generations of computers and to transport programs for new television services'. More recently it has been said that one or two of the applicants are expecting to sell out their 'space slot' to larger businesses, rather than launch satellites themselves.[5]

From 1983 there has been an ongoing debate on the *de facto* deregulation of Intelsat's monopoly by the private entry of American satellites on the trans-Atlantic route, a debate in which the problems of regulation, cross-subsidies and cost-based pricing have all been raised within an international context. The timing of this challenge to Intelsat is important insofar as the technology of optic fibres threatens the viability of satellites. Both trans-Atlantic and trans-Pacific optic fibre cables are due to start operation in 1988.

At the same time the expansion of cable TV and SAMTV in Europe and the deregulation of financial and telecommunications markets in Britain have provided a market incentive for Ku band private satellite provision. If American operators do not break into that market now, the chance may be missed. Both France and West Germany have advanced plans for DBS broadcasting, with a satellite launch expected in 1986.[6] Debates in the American House of Representatives have made clear that the new entrants are expected to facilitate the export of American programming, while Mark Fowler, the chairman of the FCC, has argued that the new entrants will open up to American business the ability to use new communications links to Europe and will be important in changing the trade imbalance of the United States.[7] In addition, one of the applicants Finansat, wanting both Pacific and Atlantic slots, is aiming specifically for financial customers.

The domestic American policy-making process has been influenced by a complicated mixture of private companies, international carriers, the FCC, the State Department, the Department of Commerce and congressional interests. Although since 1977 the FCC has had informal sessions of consultations with foreign PTTs. the lack of any one agency to co-ordinate American international telecommunications policy has been a cause for considerable concern to international business, the FCC and Congress.[8] The American policy debate has demonstrated this fragmentation and also American isolationism.

To the European observer one of the strange facets of the American domestic debate on Intelsat has been the implicit assumption that Intelsat should serve American interests; that it is American. For some time after 1983 the question of private satellites over the Atlantic was treated as a domestic issue and Intelsat's opinion or that of its members was ignored. When eventually Intelsat began a public fight-back it was accused not only of being anti-American, but of being pro-Soviet.[9]

The legal background

The prospect of American-style deregulation in the international market in telecommunications transmission illustrates the differences between domestic and international law. Domestic law can be characterised as a system of rules of conduct which are legislated by Parliament, Diet or Congress, administered by the executive and backed up by legal sanctions and force if necessary. On the other hand international law is created to a large extent by the participants themselves. Sovereign states need not accept a new rule unless they agree with it. They do not need to appear before an international tribunal unless they agree to do so and there is no centralised executive over and above the states themselves which can enforce the law. On the other hand most states want to obey the rules, partly because international law is made up of rules which states have made themselves and partly because states are interdependent.[10] In no field are they more interdependent than in that of telecommunications, which is why it now seems unlikely that the private satellite operators will have their services ready before over-capacity hits the trans-Atlantic market.

Within international law the two most important sources of law are treaties, which establish the rules recognised by two or more states which enter the treaty, and international custom (i.e. the actual behaviour and practice of states). In deciding whether a state has contravened a treaty to which it is a signatory, both the intentions and discussion at the time of signature will be analysed to see whether the current action fits the original intention of the state. Its actual behaviour since that signing will also be looked at to see whether it fitted the original intentions of the treaty or not.[11]

The difficulty for the American administration has been that it wishes to extend domestic law into international law and to extend deregulation of the domestic telecommunications market into the international market. This desire is not something new. In previous attempts the FCC has come up each time against the fact that the international market is governed by certain rules which can be used by PTTs to defend their positions.

One primary rule is that established by regulation D1 of the International Telecommunications Union. This rule prohibits the resale of leased lines in the international market. Although the ITU has representatives of industry at its meetings, it is primarily the province of the PTTs and the rule represents their interests in preventing 'cream-skimming' competitors. The rule is in fact a compromise, allowing international business to lease private lines from the PTTs. These leases allow them to transmit data at low prices. They pay for the line, not the amount of information which passes along the line, thereby avoiding the charges which they would pay if the transmissions went through the public networks. But, on the same basis as within domestic VAN debates, many of these businesses have excess capacity and could resell that capacity thereby reducing costs. International business gains by the D1 rule, but not as much as it might from resale.

The international banking network, Swift, was the first world-wide private data network, allowed mainly because it took PTTs by surprise, but later encompassed by regulation D6 which allows private group communications under certain circumstances.[12] Since its inception other private networks have been allowed, provided that the capacity was not sold to a third party and the private operators did not thereby become carriers. The desire of businesses and government agencies for secure communications over which they have control has led to increased demand for leased lines. PTTs in Europe, despite opposing this development have allowed the calls to be routed outside their public networks. They have argued that they have lost revenue by the development but have accepted the compromise involved in the D1 regulation.

Ignoring this international protocol in 1980 the FCC held that international business users could resell their leased lines. The intention was to lower business costs and to export to the international market the equivalent deregulation of the internal American market. The fear on the part of business that the European PTTs would retaliate by switching their private circuits through the public network and would charge by volume of data prevented companies from availing themselves of the ruling. The ability of PTTs to frustrate American information service companies had already become apparent with the refusal by Japanese NTT to allow Tymshare, CDC and other American vendors of on-line bureaux services to lease private lines. There were also petitions against the ruling by the established carriers and an angry letter from the Chairman of the CCITT Committee to the State Department. Although the provision has not been acted on and there has been no final ruling by the FCC, the idea was exported.[13]

One year later the point was taken up in Britain. The 1981 Beesley Report in Britain argued for resale of domestic leased lines on the basis that it would encourage resale in the international market. Beesley's view was that Britain would benefit by the increasing location of multinationals in Britain, which domestic and international resale would encourage.[14] And when BT was privatised in 1984 one of the specific goals of OFTEL, the regulatory body, written into the legislation, was set as the encouragement of the entry of multinational users of telecommunications into Britain.[15] The 1986 decision not to prevent the newly defined VADS from entering the international market is a further mechanism designed to loosen CCITT bonds and attract multinational trans-Atlantic traffic.

In Japan also the telecommunications business law, setting the framework for competition to NTT and KDD, does not specifically preclude resale of leased lines in the international market. The ministerial view was that nothing in the legislation was antithetical to CCITT regulations.[16] Nevertheless the omission suggests that Japan also is biding its time for the D1 and D6 regulations to be renegotiated, despite KDD opposition.

Quite obviously the signing of an international treaty is done for what is perceived as the best interest of the nation at the time. But interests alter as do leaders' perceptions of those interests. Behind the alteration in America's attitude to Intelsat, and to international telecommunications in general, lies a shift in the perception of American economic interest. In contrast to the 61 per cent equity it held in Intelsat at its inception, by 1985 with 23 per cent and with 108 other members America's stake in the organisation had been reduced. Also, in 1982 the United States lost the argument when it opposed the formation of Eutelsat, the European regional satellite, which provided the European space industry with a market outlet. Hence the United States's economic interests had altered since its original signing of the Intelsat treaty. Not only was Intelsat no longer the beneficiary of the space industry that it once had been, but Europe was fast gaining ground on the American industry through its regional satellite system. The original defence of private satellites over the Atlantic had a flavour of 'If Europe can do it, so can we'.[17]

Being a signatory to a treaty and not wishing to be seen as a country which breaks its contracts, the task for the Reagan administration has been to show that what it proposes to do does not contravene the treaty. To do this it has attempted to define the term 'public' within the treaty as it has been defined within the regulation of the domestic telecommunications market. Here 'public' refers to non-private. Leased lines are private in that they are used by one private business communicating with another. Within American domestic telecommunications although the distinction between the two kinds of services is recognised by the FCC as being political, not technical, the most important traditional distinction was between 'basic' telephone service and 'enhanced' services—'enhanced' being data management and value added services. Even prior to the break-up of AT&T the FCC worked on the basis that private and enhanced services should not be regulated. These distinctions made within the United States between public (open to anyone) and non-public and between basic telephone service and enhanced services are central to the arguments over deregulation of international satellite transmission services. Also because the intentions of the signatories have a direct bearing on Intelsat's current arguments, it is necessary to understand some of the background of Intelsat and the politics of its beginning.

The background to Intelsat

Intelsat was not formally established until 1971, but international co-operation began in the 1960s. In 1961 J. F. Kennedy called for the United States to develop satellites 'for global benefit'. The intention was ambivalent—that the satellite system should be run by private enterprise, but in such a way that it should benefit the parts of the world which would otherwise be excluded from the satellite revolution. In Brenda Maddox's words, the system was to be both American and international: both commercial and altruistic. She contends that there remained an unbridgeable gap between those who argued that international satellites should become part of the private telecommunications network and those who felt that, because satellite development had been financed by the public through NASA, satellite transmission should be a public service. She argues that this tension, evident from the 1960s, was inherent in the arrangements made at the conception of Comsat.

Comsat was initiated as a private company in 1961 to develop American international satellite communications. International telephone traffic was still very much in its infancy, the first cable for telephone conversations having been opened in 1956. According to Maddox, AT&T wanted private ownership of Comsat restricted to the existing international carriers. The FCC concurred with AT&T. However the Kennedy vision of a part private, part public service precluded this arrangement and the final structure of the company allowed the carriers to own half, with the other half sold to the public.[18]

Kurt Borschadt argues that the sole purpose of Comsat was in fact to act as a buffer between AT&T and the aerospace manufacturers. 'The establishment of Comsat was designed to preclude on the one hand government operations of satellites and on the other AT&T's activities on an exclusive basis into satellite communications. [It] was also designed to achieve the further antitrust objective of assuring access by nonintegrated hardware manufacturers, (primarily aerospace manufacturers). . . .'[19] Comsat could not provide services directly itself, it could provide services only to the carriers. It was also the authorised representative of American interests in international satellite negotiations. Comsat negotiated with PTTs and then with governments for international agreements on satellites. West Europe negotiated as a group and a five year interim agreement was signed in 1964. The amount of investment in the international service was determined by Comsat on the basis of the amount of international traffic the country was expected to have in 1968. The United States took the controlling share of 61 per cent and the interim agreement made Comsat the manager of the satellite system and responsible for contract decisions.

The arrangements of the interim agreement ran into considerable trouble however because of Comsat's position as an American carrier, making it subject to FCC regulation. After several political storms over the concept of an international body being subject to American control, when 1969 came and with it the opportunity for renegotiation, Intelsat was formally established as a body separate from Comsat. Comsat remained as the interface between American domestic carriers and Intelsat. It acted as the recipient of revenues from the American share of Intelsat, but without a real role.[20]

Although Intelsat is currently referred to as a 'monopoly' the term is inaccurate. It was founded by treaty under international law and claims to be a co-operative, non-profit making body which provides satellite transmission facilities for member and non-member countries. Members contribute to and get back revenue from the co-operative and through a governing council they determine its research and development and investment programme. The reason for the pejorative use of the term 'monopoly' against it now comes from the fact that within Intelsat there has been cross-subsidisation from the revenues of the busiest routes (thick routes) to those of less-developed countries (thin routes). Under the terms of its charter Intelsat must charge the same price to each participant and this unitary pricing has had the effect of the traffic between the developed world subsidising the traffic from and between the underdeveloped.

Of the 1600 routes Intelsat now operates 50 per cent of its income comes from 10 per cent of its routes and 10 per cent of its income comes from another 50 per cent of its routes.[21] The effect is therefore similar to unitary pricing under government regulation of a natural monopoly, with the difference that the pricing policy of the organisation is determined not by an external regulatory authority but by the recipients of its services who are also predominantly its owners. Richard Colino has pointed out:

Since the system owners are also in most cases, the system users, they have every incentive to lower rates whenever possible. This also means they are typically 'paying themselves' in terms of compensation for use of capital . . . But, not all users are also owners. For this reason the utilisation charges include a 14 per cent compensation for capital fee that is similar in every respect to an interest payment. It is, very simply, the cost of using capital.'[22]

Intelsat argues that it has reduced the costs of its circuits seventy-five times since its inception, the last time being in 1980, and that it is not a 'monopoly' in the normal sense.

It is also possible that in other circumstances monopoly theorists might well admit Intelsat's arguments that because it faces competition with sub-marine cables, its prices could not be monopoly prices. One of the effects stemming from the method of control devised for Comsat and the denial of control of satellite communications to AT&T was that its investment in submarine cable became commensurately more attractive. This investment counted towards its rate base, which in turn affected the profits it could make under regulation. It provided PTTs in Europe, anxious also for control of international transmission and for fixed capital investment, with an American partner for the provision of trans-Atlantic submarine cable. However, the economics of satellite transmission made it 40 per cent cheaper than coaxial cable and by 1984 satellites carried 60 per cent of trans-Atlantic traffic.[23] Despite the seeming cost advantage, because AT&T might otherwise have favoured its own facilities, until 1982 it operated under an FCC regulation by which it had to send traffic through both satellite and cable. Since facility planning on the most important trans-Atlantic route was designed at that time to minimise over-capacity, it could not be said that there was true competition between the two technologies. However by 1988, with the introduction of optic fibre cable that competition will be severe.[24]

There is a further slight flaw in Intelsat's argument that it is not a 'monopoly'. Its users and investors are not one and the same. Increases in tariffs can be passed on by PTTs to their consumers, while PTTs themselves benefit from the average 15 per cent return on capital made by Intelsat investment. There has been little incentive for PTTs to reduce the price of international telephone services. Some critics have argued that the European PTTs have kept charges artificially high, not simply to cross-subsidise their residential market, but also as a form of non-tariff barrier to make American companies locate in Europe.[25] Traditionally the European PTTs have milked the international trans-Atlantic market by keeping tariffs for their terrestial part of the link high. One feature of Mercury's entry into the British market has been BT's reduction in international tariffs. The proposal is therefore likely to lose the European PTTs money both directly, by taking traffic, and indirectly by producing alternative cut-price services. The proposal also makes possible the beaming of American cable TV into Europe and raises the question of how far European governments want their cable service dominated by American programming. With SAMTV already legalised in Britain the pressure will be on other European governments to act similarly, and it is argued that as happened in the United States and Canada telecommunications liberalisation will follow from broadcasting deregulation.[26]

Intelsat's revenue has gone to financing R & D, carried out by Comsat and to financing new generations of satellites each carrying more telephone conversations than the last. As larger numbers of lesser developed countries joined the system so a conflict of interest arose between them and the developed. The developed, in particular France and Britain, wanted a share of Intelsat's satellite contracts. In contrast developing countries wanted cheap communications and were unwilling to pay for the learning curve of European industry. As a result, although some European companies shared in contracts for the III series in the late 1960s and there was some small foreign participation in the IV series, begun in 1969, following developing country objections, the second series of the IV contracts saw almost no non-American participation. The advantage of Intelsat to the European countries thereafter was primarily in terms of the revenues they gained, rather than in contracts and technological experience for their aircraft industries.

This situation had two effects. First the Europeans resisted attempts to lower the cost of satellite circuits for the benefit of developing countries. Second, from 1975, the Europeans began to develop their own space industry through the European Space Agency in competition with the United States. During the negotiations on the original treaty, France, anxious to develop its own space industry, argued for a system of regional satellites. America, which then had the lead in the technology, wanted no systems other than Intelsat. The resulting treaty was a compromise between the two positions, leaving room for the development of a European space industry.[27]

The exclusion from Intelsat contracts made it almost inevitable that the Europeans would wish to see the European market developed for European industry. Where developed and developing countries joined forces was in opposition to Intelsat's R & D programme. From Europe it looked like a subsidy to American manufacturers. From the perspective of the developing countries, many of whom could hardly afford the investment necessary for ground-stations, the prospect of upgrading of technology which might make their investment redundant was singularly unappealing. Developing countries made clear that they were uninterested in further R & D for technical development of the system. The prospects of inter-satellite links or on-board processing or new systems held out little attraction to those who had just invested resources in ground stations which would become out of date with new technology. Intelsat's future market looked as if it would be primarily a replacement market and therefore of less benefit to the American satellite industry whose technological development it had subsidised.[28]

In general the treaty provisions of Intelsat have enabled wealthy countries to develop their own domestic satellite systems. Canada was the first to provide itself with a domestic system in the early 1970s. In the United States Comsat filed with the FCC for a broadcasting satellite in 1966, followed by Western Union. Europe followed in 1977 with Interim Eutelsat, set up as a private company to make a profit for European PTTs and following the same pattern as Intelsat. The operating agreements were signed in 1982 making the ESA responsible for building, launching and operating Eutelsat's satellites. Arabsat, a regional company for the middle East financed by OPEC revenues was agreed in 1982, (but not established until 1985) and domestic systems have been established in Australia, Indonesia, India, Brazil and Mexico. An Africasat regional satellite system is being discussed.

Although it is obvious that Intelsat must lose some revenue because of their total capacity, each of these systems has been able to argue individually that it has done no significant harm to Intelsat. While Intelsat continued to have a virtual monopoly over the India and Pacific oceans and while voice traffic over the Atlantic continued to grow, this loss of capacity seems to have caused little concern. In all, Intelsat agreed to twenty nine applications for co-ordination and turned none down. Intelsat argues however that none sought to duplicate existing Intelsat services.

By 1980 Intelsat had 109 members and nineteen non-members used its capacity. Its annual charge of $60,000 per circuit in 1965 had dropped to $10,000. Its charges could have decreased further had the developed countries been willing to allow differentials in circuit costs to the less developed, but under its charter Intelsat charges the same on all routes and to all, both members and non-members. Even so, to some extent its policy has developed to take into account the needs of its less wealthy members. Countries unable to afford their own domestic satellite system have been able to lease capacity from Intelsat. These leases were originally based on Intelsat's spare satellite capacity (needed for possible breakdowns). They worked on the basis that if a breakdown occurred then the international market took precedence. The availability of these leases delayed the development of domestic satellite systems, the costs of which include not only the satellites themselves, but launch costs, insurance costs, the costs of a control system and those of earth-stations. Using leased capacity developing countries needed only to provide the earth stations and internal microwave or terrestial distribution. But the very number of lessees—seventeen in 1981—created problems. Intelsat was running out of spare capacity by the early 1980s and was also concerned at the effect of a withdrawal of service in the event of breakdown. So it began to construct satellite capacity for leasing for domestic systems.

In the 1980s both technical and economic factors coalesced to make buying domestic satellites a more attractive proposition. With the advent of the American shuttle and the French Ariane launches became easier to find and cheaper. And for a time, until the failure of both launchers in 1984 insurance rates seemed set to come down. The cost of satellites has also been decreasing. For the developing countries India—pursuing its own space programme with a broadcasting, tele-communications and weather satellite—acts as an example of the advantages of satellite transmission in a far-flung, multi-lingual country. Among the Third World countries Indonesia, Mexico and Brazil have their own domestic satellite systems. This potential market for both domestic satellite systems is held in check by Intelsat and is out of the economic reach of many.

Intelsat has expanded its capacity both to cater for domestic systems and to meet the demands of business. But because of the down-turn in the world economy the result has been overcapacity. The greater its capacity, the lower its prices, the more advantage there is in leasing rather than buying and the less possibility there is of entry into the domestic satellite market .

Catering to what seemed an ever-increasing volume of traffic, in the early 1980s Intelsat launched the first of its V series, designed to give 12,500 two way circuits and two TV channels. It also planned the VI series providing 30,000 voice circuits and three TV channels, scheduled for launch in 1986. But then the market began to be saturated as the world recession continued. Intelsat's profits sank and in 1983 its revenue shortfall was $30 million. As recession has continued Intelsat has diver-sified its services. Domestic leases now make up 9 per cent of its revenue, full-time TV leasing 3 per cent, occasional TV leasing 6 per cent, and business services 2 per cent.These services are faster growing than its public switched services.

Besides the advent of Eutelsat, the slowing of R & D benefits and diversification of Intelsat, a further factor may have influenced the private satellite proposal. Despite French and West German protest, in 1982 BT initiated its Satstream data service for Europe with SBS-type direct satellite links, thus evading the continental public networks of the PTTs. Although the service has been too expensive to attract much custom it is a first breach of the PTT monopolies. Also BT announced in 1982 that it had reached agreement with SBS to provide a satellite gateway to Europe. Although the service in fact uses Intelsat for the international part of the transmission, it seemed at first that BT might be preparing to break the Intelsat agreement. To some extent therefore not only has the international system already been privatised in the interests of big business, but the initial signals on the possibility of a European partner to any American move to break PTT monopolies may well have been given by BT, an impression perhaps compounded by the inclusion of a business communications service in the original plans in 1982 for a British DBS satellite.

From March 1983 when Orion Satellite Corporation first applied to the FCC for permission to launch two satellites pressure in the United States built up. Intelsat's original response was to send a letter of protest to the State Department but without any request for action. The deregulators made all the running on Capitol Hill. By November 1984 a further five companies had filed applications. In total there were four applications for the trans-Atlantic route and two for the north-south America route. A further application in 1985 for slots to cover both the Pacific and Atlantic oceans for an interconnected service was made in 1985. RCA American Communications Inc. was the only applicant wishing to extend the coverage of an existing domestic satellite to the Atlantic. The others intended to construct new satellites.

The legal arguments

When the original treaty was signed the United States was in the lead technologically in satellite production and launching, and in the negotiations which took place it argued that no other satellite systems should be possible other than Intelsat—which of course it dominated. On the other hand the French were in favour of a federation of regional systems allowing the possibility of the development of non-American satellite manufacture. The resulting treaty was a compromise between these two conflicting interests. Article XIV (d) states that if any party to the treaty:

> intends individually or jointly to establish, acquire or utilise space segment facilities separate from the Intelsat space segment facilities to meet its public telecommunications services requirements, such Party ... prior to the establishment, acquisition or utilization of such facilities shall consult with the Assembly of Parties through the Board of Governors to ensure technical compatibility of such facilities and to avoid significant economic harm to the global system of Intelsat...'

In fact Intelsat never defined what constituted 'significant economic harm' partly, it argued, because it had never had to. It considered that the second part of the same clause, under which, once notified, the Assembly of Parties shall express its recommendations: 'regarding the assurance that the provision or utilisation of such facilities shall not prejudice the establishment of direct telecommunications links through the Intelsat space segment among all participants. . . .' meant that new provisions should not prejudice Intelsat's ability to continue to provide global interconnections at a reasonable rate. In other words it argued that the second part of the clause itself defines what is 'significant economic harm'.

Under the Intelsat treaty telecommunications services fall into two categories—either 'public' or 'specialised' services. Specialised services have to be co-ordinated technically with Intelsat, but do not have to pass the 'significant economic harm' test. Intelsat argues that it was clear when the treaty was signed that the distinction between the two was made on the basis that 'specialised' services, were those to ships or aircraft and government services and that all other services were 'public'. It contends that it has consistently defined public to mean any service which may by its nature be made available for use by the public. The only exception is DBS which is specifically mentioned as a specialised service under Article I(l). Included within the definition of 'public' services in Article I(k) are fixed or mobile telecommunication services including telephony, telegraphy, telex, facsimile, data transmission, transmission of radio and television programmes and 'leased circuits for any of these purposes'.

In addition to the 'specialised' services set out in the original treaty, each of the three regional systems—Palapa, serving Polynesia, Arabsat and Eutelsat—has been able to justify itself as not significantly affecting Intelsat's income. In the case of Palapa serving a predominantly rural area the system hardly affects overall income. In the other two cases it was possible to argue that signals would have otherwise been terrestially transmitted. Intelsat had also agreed to domestic systems expanding to contiguous countries and thereby becoming international. In each of these systems Intelsat had looked at the possible economic harm to itself on a case-by-case basis.[29]

But as an Office of Telecommunications Policy report pointed out the regional systems had more serious economic and political effects. The cumulative effect of all the systems might entail a drop of over 50 per cent in Intelsat's envisaged income. In addition:

. . . Intelsat's business decisions are made by its Board of Governors and . . . these same individuals also represent their own regional and national satellite systems interests. In a competitive environment it is clear that in the long run the national interests of each Governor and Signatory will have priority over the interests of the Intelsat system.

The report concluded that if regional systems were allowed to proliferate then Intelsat would eventually 'be managed by its competitors' and would become uncompetitive. The report alerted Intelsat to the dangers inherent in regional systems.[30]

At first Orion contended that the satellites should not be classified as providing 'public' (i.e. open to the public) services but 'specialised' and therefore only needing technical co-ordination with Intelsat. The question revolved around what were 'public' services. The United States wanted to define the term to mean common carrier services, i.e. those with general public access as used in American domestic policy. Intelsat responded that the United States could not suddenly transfer this term into the international arena, thereby avoiding its duties under the treaty. Orion countered by saying that the term 'public telecommunications' was already in use in domestic American telecommunications when the Intelsat agreement was signed and was familiar to the participants in that agreement as meaning 'availability to the public at large and not just selected customers, a key element of common carriage'. Intelsat replied by pointing to the previous practice of the FCC. The FCC had not equated the terms 'common carrier' in the domestic market and 'public' in the international market. When the domestic 'open skies' policy was announced during the 1970s, those American companies which purchased transponders, although not designated 'common carrier' by the FCC, still co-ordinated their services with Intelsat under the provision for 'domestic public telecommunications services' and not as 'specialised' services. Intelsat also argued that its own leased circuits to private companies have been 'public telecommunications services'. It further held that the services could not be denoted 'regional' systems in the same way as Eutelsat because Intelsat already provided services in the areas proposed for coverage. It therefore believed the proposals would contravene Article XIV of the treaty.[31]

As the legal argument has progressed so the American administration seems to have shifted its position, away from arguing that the services are 'specialised' towards arguing that they need not do Intelsat serious economic harm. It contends that the services will only take 2 per cent or 3 per cent of Intelsat's income and that Intelsat can minimise the damage by lowering its prices on the Atlantic route to compete with the newcomers. They argue that under its present charter Intelsat may charge marginal cost prices for different services. Intelsat responds that under its Charter it is bound to provide non-discriminatory tariffs. The organisation is in a no-win situation. If it does not lower prices on its thick routes its position is likely to be comparable to that of AT&T after divestiture—regulated by an external entity (in this case its Charter) unable to vary prices and therefore losing market share. On the other hand, should it vary prices on its busiest routes the revenue gained and the cross-subsidy possible for its thin routes will be less, thereby raising prices for the developing countries to an extent which they could not always afford. Access would be reduced and Intelsat would become a shrinking organisation.

Intelsat critics argue that its problems are to a large extent its own making in that it has over-expanded capacity and spent large sums on R & D, capital investment which it will no longer have the revenues to pay off, particularly since growth is now 10 per cent per annum rather than the envisaged 20 per cent. The criticisms are based on the assumption that Intelsat is a monopoly seeking to extend its rate base, rather than an organisation subject to facility planning by the FCC and foreign PTTs.[32]

President Reagan's decision, delayed in announcement for some time because of competition for the lead in international communications between the Departments of Commerce and State, came in November 1984. It allowed competition to Intelsat in intra-company communications. The private satellites would not be allowed to carry communications between companies or telephone calls between individuals, hence it was argued that 85 per cent of Intelsat's revenue would be protected. Operators would be allowed to lease long-term or sell capacity on their satellites to individual business users for data transmission, video conferencing and the distribution of programmes for cable networks. Orion Corporation had already announced that it intended to sell all its transponders to private companies,—TV networks, multinationals, governments and banks being its target market. The proposals closely parallel the beginnings of deregulation in the American market in the 1970s where 'private' services in both terrestial and space communications were allowed and where these carriers were not designated 'common carriers' under the 1934 Act because they did not provide a 'public' (open for access to the general public) or 'basic' telecommunications service.[33]

The presidential decision taken in the 'national interest' required that the satellite companies have partners in another country before launching the service. International reaction was hostile. As *Le Monde* put it, the question became who would provide the bridgehead in Europe? It singled out Mercury as the most likely candidate. It also pointed out that because the PTT would have to respond to the cuts in international telecommunications charges which would result, the pressure for liberalisation in France was thereby increased.[34]

The Reagan decision was taken over Intelsat's protests that it had not been fully consulted and despite protests from developing and developed countries in 1983 and 1984 (including Britain). The FCC followed in July 1985 with a decision on the private satellites broadly in line with the Presidential decision, but with two commissioners abstaining. Intelsat fought back within the American domestic policy process. Congressional 'education' by Intelsat resulted in action in 1985 bringing some further clarification of policy. Under the terms of the State Department Authorisation bill (H.R. 2068) and the 1985 Supplemental Appropriations legislation (H.R. 2577) in August of 1985 the Presidential condition that the new private satellites should not be interconnected with the public switched network was reiterated. In addition the legislation stated that the United States' government should support an amendment to Intelsat's articles which would allow it to establish rates for individual traffic routes. The FCC was not to award construction permits without adopting appropriate measures to enforce the Presidential determination. While America was to adopt procedures to co-ordinate with Intelsat, if the Intelsat Assembly were to reach negative conclusions the President must then determine once again that it was in the American interest to establish the separate systems. If he did so, then a report would go to Congress where unless action was taken within sixty days the United States would be deemed to have met its obligations under the Intelsat Treaty. According to this legislation co-ordination with Intelsat was voluntary not a binding condition of the treaty.[35]

The month following this legislation the FCC issued its final written decision on five of the applications. Its report concluded that separate satellite systems would be beneficial to international communications users by meeting specialised service needs, stimulating new services and technologies and reducing user costs through improved efficiency. Under the decision a final operating licence would not be issued unless 'one or more' foreign authorities also authorised use of the new systems and also agreed to enforce the 'no-interconnect' restriction. As the FCC admitted there existed no practical means for it to discover individual violations since company PBX can normally route calls to either the public or private network. The FCC agreed with critics that only if widespread violations occurred would it become aware through statistical evidence of a drop in public switched traffic, but argued that only if there were widespread violations would Intelsat be affected.

The FCC also weakened the Presidential directive's commitment to customised service by allowing resale and shared use of leases and by requiring only a one-year lease period, rather than the 'long-term leases' previously specified. And finally, despite the Congressional legislation, the FCC broke with previous practice to allow the applicants to begin construction of their space segment at their own risk. Previous practice had held that construction prior to full authorisation might influence a decision. Four of the applicants were allowed to proceed with construction, while the fifth had to provide further financial details.

The FCC made no decision on how many systems in total it would allow, or their cumulative effect on Intelsat. It argued only that 2 per cent of Intelsat's revenue would be diverted from existing customised services and that growth would provide additional compensatory revenue. The arguments were very similar to those used in domestic telecommunications decisions. The decision left little doubt that the FCC intended to see private satellites in place as soon as possible.[36]

In response to the privatisation proposal and its existing over-capacity, in addition to the new business services which were already planned for introduction in 1985, Intelsat took several countervailing measures. At its November meeting it agreed to sell spare capacity for use within domestic systems, and reduced charges for leased capacity, undercutting the opposition. Its critics argue that it is guilty of predatory pricing. They believe that by over-expanding capacity and leasing circuits cheaply Intelsat is actually behaving in a monopoly fashion. Its supporters might argue that having failed to win the legal argument Intelsat is setting out to win the economic and by grabbing market share which might otherwise go to the possible satellite competitors or might be routed via submarine optic fibres when they come on-stream. In particular the sale of transponders preempts market share for many years to come.

Intelsat has also taken steps to define more rigorously what constitutes 'significant economic harm' by writing in to the treaty a condition that the cumulative impact on Intelsat must be taken into consideration. Critics argue that the step has been taken purely to prejudge the issue on the proposed American satellites. Also in a further defensive mechanism, Intelsat has raised the possibility of going elsewhere than America for its replacement satellites.[37]

The threat which private satellites in the Ku band present to PTT monopolies may be keeping the French and West German governments behind Intelsat for the moment, but British and Japanese backing seems more ambivalent. Following from a meeting of Intelsat signatories in 1985, no immediate action was planned to alter the pricing mechanisms adopted by Intelsat to that of cost-based pricing. Despite the Congressional legislation, the State Department was said to be unwilling to act as the initiator of a motion to alter the treaty, officially for fear of the foreign policy repercussions, unofficially for fear that Intelsat might start predatory pricing on its customised services. Although two Third World countries put forward an amendment to Article V in favour of such flexibility at the October 1985 meeting of the Intelsat Assembly, it was left on the table on the grounds that no representative present admitted to holding talks with the private satellite bidders, therefore there was no immediate hurry to alter the treaty.

Meanwhile being both the American representative on Intelsat and severely affected by the proposed changes Comsat has been making itself domestically unpopular by opposing the private satellites' entry. Predominantly concerned with its failing DBS project Comsat had been rather slow off the mark to understand the implications of the breaching of Intelsat's monopoly. But, in an exchange of letters in 1984 the Executive made it clear that it wished to see Comsat's monopoly over access to Intelsat replaced by open entry to Intelsat facilities. Debate continues, threatening Comsat's major source of revenue. Intelsat on the other hand wants to see Comsat free of regulation so that it also may compete on price.[38]

If and when the private satellite entrepreneurs put their proposals to Intelsat, it seems almost certain that they will be turned down for their 'significant economic harm' to the global system. The entrepreneurs still need partners elsewhere and one would expect Britain to be the most likely candidate, but the economic and political arguments are finely balanced. The break-up of Intelsat might produce domestic satellite orders for the British aerospace industry in the long-term, while private satellites together with a link to either or both BT and Mercury might lower costs of international business and attract it to Britain. On the other hand, the prospect of all-American cable programming might finally stop any possible British DBS project. The British government previously rejected the possibility of using an American satellite for that purpose.[39] And the prospects of competitive pricing against their proposed submarine cables from Intelsat, and the prospects of trans-Atlantic overcapacity might not suit the two carriers.

The chances are however, that the European space industry and multinational business within Britain are lobbying for the demise of Intelsat. In Japan the arguments may be less finely weighted. NTT has already made it evident that it wishes to challenge KDD's dominance of international transmission. To open access to Japan for private satellite operators would be a relatively simple process, particularly if a service could be in place before the satellite competitors of NTT get off the ground. On the other hand KDD's investment in an optic fibre link with the United States to come on-stream in 1988 will make it a formidable competitor on that route, and it might make more economic sense to concentrate on intra-regional traffic, building on existing links with South Korea and the Philippines. In either case the Japanese satellite industry is unlikely to benefit in the short term, while the earth-station industry would benefit to a greater extent from the second option. Nevertheless American pressure is likely to be exerted on Japan, particularly as one existing proposal concerns the placement of a private satellite over the Pacific.

It is likely that whatever the outcome of this latest American attempt to impose its domestic policy on the rest of the world, the days of Intelsat as it presently exists are numbered. The American challenge comes just before the TAT 8 optic fibre (owned by AT&T, BT and the French PTT) and the Cable and Wireless/Tel-Optic fibre over the Atlantic and that linking the United States and Japan come into being in 1988. The logic of the FCC's decision-making during 1985 is difficult to understand. A report in August 1985 showed that if all the private satellites were built for an estimated demand for voice-equivalent circuits of 82,000 on the trans-Atlantic route by 1995, the actual supply would be about 650,000. Most of this capacity—390,000— would be provided by the two undersea cables whose construction the FCC had authorised in 1985. Tel-Optic and Cable and Wireless's optic fibre cable, constructed for private leasing would provide 80,000, Submarine Lightwave Cable would provide 230,000 and the TAT-8 and TAT-9 cables owned by European and American carriers would provide a further 80,000. The six satellite systems would provide 120,000 and the Intelsat system more than 100,000, while existing cables provided 10,000. The report concluded that even if all the venture capitalists pulled out, leaving RCA's satellite, and the cable consortia, the number of circuits would still be more than 300,000. It pointed out that the large shift to cables 'would make it more likely that Intelsat would become seriously unprofitable' and suggested that the FCC approval of 330,000 voice-equivalent circuits, 'without much attention to its [Intelsat's] planning process, indicate that the commission is acting without much regard for this link'.[40]

Perhaps the FCC is expecting over-capacity to produce demands for increased regulation of the international market, thereby subjecting Intelsat to itself. Perhaps it is hostile to Intelsat for defending itself. More likely is the expectation that overcapacity will provoke demands for resale and the breaching of CCITT regulations. Whatever the reason the FCC's action betrays a greater concern for American interests than international co-operation. The cables have a higher proportion of American ownership than does Intelsat—for instance, AT&T will own 35 per cent of the Atlantic and 56 per cent of the Pacific cable.

By creating these optic-fibre links the industrialised countries have reduced the influence of the developing countries over their international communications. Both the new optic fibre cables and the proposal for private satellites are a reassertion of the interests of the industrialised, and particularly the American against the developing world. Deregulation of PTT monopolies in Europe, deregulation of Intelsat's monopoly, increased broad-band cheap transmission all increase the global penetration of American industry and services.[41] Unlike the domestic scenarios in America, Britain and Japan there is no Congress, OFTEL or MPT to re-regulate the international market or to see that in the stampede for profit the interests of the poorest are in any way represented.

Notes and references

1. On ITU regulations and FCC decisions see: Anthony M. Rutkowski, 'History of ITU and Current Developments'in Jane H. Yurow (ed.) *Issues in International Telecommunications Policy: a Sourcebook*, Washington D.C., George Washington University, 1983, pp. 51–84.
2. Lee McKnight, 'Implications of Deregulating Satellite Communications', *Telecommunications Policy*, December 1985, pp. 276–81.
3. On GATT see: *Financial Times*, 2, 12, 18, 24 July 1985; 1, 9, 14, 25 August 1985; 3, 12 September 1985.
4. *Telecommunications Report*, **51**, 30, 29 July 1985, p. 38.
5. *New York Times*, 5 October 1985;*International Herald Tribune*, 26 October 1983; *Communications Daily*, 8 October 1985; Tom Kerner, 'North Atlantic Fury', *Satellite Communications*, August 1985, p. 23.
6. On existing American competition for European cable markets see: 'Europe Braces for Free-Market TV' *Fortune*, 20 February 1984, pp. 50–54; on satellites in Europe see: David Gregory, 'Future directions in space communications' *Information Technology and Public Policy*, **4**, 1, September 1985, pp. 12–16.

7. Rep. Timothy Wirth, *Congressional Record* H. 3058, 9 May 1985; Mark Fowler, quoted in: *Broadcasting*, 29 July 1985, p. 29.
8. See Joel S. Winnick, FCC, 'Political, Institutional, Economic Constraints in International Telecommunications', pp. 206–8 and Norman C. Lener, 'Legislative and Regulatory Changes in US International Telecommunications; an evaluation of US and foreign impact,' pp. 228–34 in *Proceedings of 1st International Telecommunications Exposition*, Vol. 3, *Telecommunications and Economic Development*, 1978, Dedham Ma., Horizon House International. Also: Report by the US General Accounting Office, *The Federal Communications Commission's International Telecommunications Activities*, Report to the Chairman, Subcommittee on Government Information and Individual Rights, House Committee on Government Operations, CED-82-77, Gaithersburg M.D., USGAO, 1982; Congressional Research Service, *International Telecommunications and Information Policy: Selected Issues for the 1980's*, Report prepared for the Committee on Foreign Relations, US Senate, Washington D.C., US Government Printing Office, 1983.
9. Richard Colino, 'Intelsat: Myths and Realities', speech to Satellite Summit 84, 26 April 1984.
10. Michael Akehurst, *A Modern Introduction to International Law*, London, George Allen & Unwin, 4th edition, 1982, pp. 23–8.
11. Ibid., pp. 28–42.
12. 'S. W. I. F. T: A fast method to facilitate international financial transactions', *Journal of World Trade Law*, 1983, Vol. **17**, Sept/Oct., pp. 458–65; *Financial Times*, 10 September 1985. The Society for Worldwide Interbank Financial Communications was established in 1973 as a non-profit, bank-owned co-operative organisation and began operations in 1978. In 1985 it handled an estimated 650,000 messages per day.
13. *Business Week*, no. 2647, 28 July 1980, pp. 66–8. On the application of Computer II to international telecommunications see: Leslie A. Taylor, 'Current Trends in Regulation', in Jane H. Yurow (ed.), op. cit., pp. 95–6.
14. Michael E. Beesley, *Liberalisation of the use of British Telecommunications Network*, 1981, HMSO, London, pp. 27–8.
15. *Telecommunications Act 1984* Part I, Section 3, (2) (e): 'to encourage major users of telecommunications services whose places of business are outside the United Kingdom to establish places of business in the United Kingdom.'
16. Interview with MPT personnel, August 1984.
17. See William Schneider Jr., Under Secretary for Security Assistance, Science and Technology: 'In our deliberations of proposals for non-Intelsat international communication satellite systems, we should be aware that a number of regional non-Intelsat satellite systems are being implemented by Intelsat members. The policy question we face is not whether regional systems are incompatible with Intelsat obligations but whether US participation in such systems, particularly across the North Atlantic, would undermine the viability of the global system.' Statement before the Subcommittee of Telecommunications, Consumer Protection and Finance of the House Energy and Commerce Committee, 25 July 1984, reproduced in: *Department of State Bulletin* October 1984, pp. 45–6.

18. Brenda Maddox, *Beyond Babel*, Indianapolis, Howard B. Sams, 1972, p. 85.
19. Kurt Borschadt, *Structure and Performance of the US Communications Industry. Government Regulation and Company Planning*, Boston, Harvard University, 1970, p. 102.
20. Brenda Maddox, op. cit., pp. 87–114.
21. Richard R. Colino, 'Global satellite communications: winners and losers', speech to the Parliamentary and Scientific Committee of the House of Commons, 22 January 1985.
22. Richard R. Colino, 'Questions and Answers', Testimony to the Subcommittee on Arms Control, Oceans, International Operations and Environment, Senate Foreign Relations Committee, 19 October 1983, p. 11.
23. OECD, *Telecommunications. Pressures and Policies for Change*, Paris, OECD, 1983, pp. 58–68.
24. On facilities planning in the North Atlantic see: Leslie A. Taylor, op. cit., pp. 114–5; Richard R. Colino, 'Questions and Answers', op. cit. pp. 6–8; William Schneider Jr., op. cit., pp. 43–6.
25. For an early version of this argument see: Brenda Maddox, op. cit., p. 76.
26. Lee McKnight, op. cit., p. 279.
27. *The Economist*, **281**, 21 November 1981, pp. 39.
28. In 1985 the Office of Technology Assessment concluded that from a market standpoint the Ka band satellites might not be needed either to avoid significant overcrowding in the geostationary orbit or to meet currently foreseeable demand. *Telecommunications Report*, **51**, 30, 29 July 1985, p. 39.
29. Richard R. Colino, 'Questions and Answers', op. cit., pp. 11–19, 37–47.
30. Future Systems Inc., *The Impact of Future National and Regional Communications Satellite Systems on Intelsat*, prepared for the Office of Telecommunications Policy, Gaithersburg, Md, Future Systems Inc., February 1978, p. 4.
31. Davis R. Robinson, 'Memorandum of Law', 21 November 1983; 'Summary of Certain Legal Inhibitions of Intelsat: Comparison with Certain proposed International Systems', (Supplied by Intelsat).
32. See Richard R. Colino, 'Questions and Answers', op. cit., pp. 6–7
33. Letter to Mark Fowler, chairman of FCC, from George Schultz, Secretary of State and Malcolm Baldridge, Secretary of Commerce, 28 November 1984.
34. *Le Monde*, 1 December 1984.
35. H. R. 2068, 21–22, signed into law 16 August 1985.
36. *Broadcasting*, 29 July 1985, pp. 29–30; Intelsat, 'Analysis of FCC decisions on separate systems', attachment no. 2 to AP-10-39 E W/10/85. (Supplied by Intelsat.)
37. Richard Corrigan, 'Intelsat Balking at Opening the Skies to International Satellite Competitors', *National Journal*, 11 May 1985, pp. 1019–23; *Broadcasting*, 21 October 1085, pp. 62–4.
38. *National Journal*, 11 May 1985, p. 1022.
39. On DBS see: Albert D. Wheeler, 'The future of Communications Satellites', *Intermedia*, **12**, 2, March 1984, pp. 40–9.

40. On overcapacity see: report of Office of Technology Assessment, *International Co-operation and Competition in Civilian Space Activities*, quoted in *Broadcasting*, 5 August 1985, pp. 44-5.
41. On American actions to increase the liberalisation of trade in telecommunications services through the OECD and GATT see: *International Telecommunications and Information Policy*, hearings before a Subcommittee of the House Committee on Government Operations, 97th Congress, 1st and 2nd Sessions, 2 December 1981 and 29 April 1982, Washington D.C., US Government Printing Office.

7 The impact of liberalisation and privatisation

The argument of this book has been that regulation, liberalisation and privatisation represent the interests of different sections of the domestic and world community. Deregulation and privatisation of telecommunications transmission involve a redistribution of resources away from the least advantaged towards the most advantaged. Two trends are increasingly visible in the telecommunications market—increased integration of networks and the privatisation of information.

Impact on Europe

The seminal work on the telecommunications market in the United States prior to AT&T's divestiture produced a map of a segmented structure.[1] It suggested that it was conceptually and technically possible to distinguish between equipment, long-lines and local network markets. Whereas the equipment and long-lines markets were suitable for and experiencing some competition, the local network was still a 'natural monopoly'. With its loss of 'natural monopoly' services, the divestiture of AT&T took place upon the basis of that segmentation. But technology had moved ahead of regulators, and the pressure exerted by both IBM and AT&T to deregulate the division of their equipment and transmission companies bears witness to the reintegration of the two brought about by the digitalisation of transmission. Technically, once the network can take over parts of the function of the customer premises' equipment, it is necessary to have control of both. Companies and particularly American companies recognised this fact before either American or European administrations.

Using analogue transmission the impact in the United States of the deregulation of equipment was to increase pressure for deregulation of transmission. Using digital transmission pressure to liberalise transmission following any liberalisation of equipment has become inevitable, particularly if much of the installed capacity comes from one dominant supplier. While West European governments consider the possibility of opening just the equipment market to liberalisation, they work within a marketing framework which is no longer valid.

The impact of technological convergence coupled with deregulation has been physical convergence between companies from different markets into that of telecommunications. The communications market now consists of those transmitting information, those manufacturing equipment for the transmittal of that information and those providing the information itself. Gradually the largest companies are integrating horizontally into all three. For this reason IBM has diversified into transmission and information provision while AT&T has diversified into data processing. It is also the reason for pressure from the publishing industry to prevent AT&T's entry into electronic publishing under the 1981 consent decree. Other information providers such as Reuters, various airlines and the banking industry have moved into transmission through 'enhanced' services. And other large users of communications services such as General Motors have taken over companies in the information technology sector. End to end transmission of information in the global market has become the aim, and comparative advantage goes to the integrated company.

While digitalisation coupled with deregulation has meant that companies in one or other of the traditional computing or telecommunications industries have needed expertise and often manufacturing capability in the alternative, the integration of transmission and equipment has increased vertical concentration once more. The result is both horizontal and vertical integration. The divestiture of AT&T in which it retained Bell Labs and Western Electric was intended to give it the incentive to exercise its technological leadership in world markets.[2] In Britain, BT is attempting to diversify from transmission into equipment manufacture and into alternative transmission modes. BT, with its virtual monopoly of telecommunications transmission has taken interests in cable TV systems, was part of the abortive consortium with British Aerospace (Unisat) to build a British DBS satellite, has taken over Mitel, a Canadian manufacturer of telecommunications equipment and is now moving into the area of information provision.

Where European companies have not had the wherewithal to take-over other companies, the result has been a plethora of technological and marketing agreements, often cross national with a strong American or Japanese component. In 1983 of the 200 agreements made by European companies, 50 per cent were made with American companies, 30 per cent with Japanese and only 18 per cent with European.[3] Deregulation of the American market has both opened opportunities to export to the United States and brought increased competition from IBM and AT&T. Companies have felt that they must join forces to reach a global market and the partners they have chosen for their attempts have tended to be the strongest, and therefore American or Japanese.

Although the effect on industry structure seems to have been one of capital concentration, companies have been brought into the telecommunications market from what had been traditionally separate industries. Hence satellite manufacturers come predominantly from the defence market, and cable TV operators from the world of the media. Within the America domestic market, traditional telecommunications markets such as PABX have been entered by a variety of firms.[4] In Britain, companies such as Racal from defence electronics have entered the cellular radio market, while Cable and Wireless, previously operative predominantly in Hong Kong, has financed Mercury, the opposition to BT. In Japan, Kyocera and more than ten other companies have formed Dai Ni Den Den, and Mitsui and other trading houses are now involved in setting up telecommunications transmission competition to NTT. Because many of the technologies are fungible, the effect is that governments, by choosing a particular technology or product standard, favour one particular company or industry at the expense of another. For Europe the problem is that each government has chosen different standards and still backs its national champion in any one technology—from satellites to cellular radio. Fragmentation of European industry is pitted against the horizontal and vertical integration of the two major companies with their huge home base in the American market.

Traditionally, one of the major problems for the European sector has been the dominance of American companies in data processing. IBM alone has 70 per cent of the installed capacity in Europe. The impact of IBM on Europe has been accentuated since 1981 by that company's diversification into smaller computers, by its increased aggressiveness in both the European and Japanese markets following the dropping of the Justice Department anti-trust case against it, its settlement of the European Community's anti-trust case and by its entry into transmission facilities using its own standard System Network Architecture. Whereas previously companies which did not wish to meet IBM head-on could diversify into mini or micro computers or industrial process control this option has been foreclosed by IBM's own diversification and could be further foreclosed if IBM were to be allowed to dominate privatised transmission systems.

The liberalisation of the American market has allowed AT&T to compete on the world market for the first time since it sold its international interests to ITT in 1925. Divested of its local operating companies AT&T has responded to its newfound freedom by buying into the European market. First it entered a joint venture with Philips of The Netherlands to market its digital public telephone exchange. Then it bought a 25 per cent stake in Olivetti, the Italian office equipment manufacturer, and concluded an agreement under which Olivetti will market its exchanges in Europe—an agreement which seems to have been especially favourable to AT&T. Then it made a bid for the Anglo-American microchip company, Inmos, making it clear in the process that it simply wanted a base in Europe for its microchip business. Then it concluded an agreement with Spanish manufacturers.

In view of IBM's dominance of the data processing market in the United States, AT&T needs the European market if it is to break into the equipment market. Similarly, in view of AT&T's dominance in transmission in the America and the relative failure of SBS, IBM needs foreign markets if it is to provide end-to-end transmission of information. Hence much of the competition between IBM and AT&T has been transferred to Europe and Japan where both companies are involved in the introduction of Value Added Networks for data transmission.

Where liberalisation of the telecommunications transmission market has taken place impetus has been given to the entry of the two dominant American companies. Much policy in Europe can be seen as moving between an attempt to prevent further domination by IBM in particular, and a desire not to offend a company which provides considerable employment and claims to transfer technology to its host countries. France has undertaken farreaching rationalisation of its electronics sector in order to create companies of a size which can compete with American companies. There is now only one French telecommunications equipment manufacturing company. And in Britain one of the original intentions of the government in privatising BT—to create a company capable of competing against the American giants—has been followed by government instigation of a merger between the two manufacturers, GEC and Plessey.

Fuelled by increased aggressiveness on the part of American companies and by the difficulties created by the American Export Administration Act, which European companies and governments see as a protectionist mechanism to limit European exports of high-technology equipment, a new movement has arisen within Europe. Much of the impetus has come from private companies themselves. Companies have joined together in cross-national R & D inside EEC-inspired projects, such as Esprit for computing equipment. They have taken private joint initiatives such as that between ICL, Siemens and Philips and initiated rationalisation of production such as that between British Channel 4 TV and its French and German counterparts. And they have begun to create European companies such as that for microchip production being set up by the previous managing director of ICL. European companies, rather than governments, are acknowledging that they can only compete on the world market from the base of a unified European market.

Growing direct American political pressure on the French and West Germans to liberalise their telecommunications markets is reinforced by pressure from multinationals established within Europe and the possibility of their relocation in Britain, where trans-Atlantic call rates are the lowest in Western Europe. The West German decision made in 1984 that it would in future charge by the volume of messages transmitted via leased data processing lines, rather than a flat rate as previously, which threatened American defence establishments and multinationals, brought forth immediate trade pressure from the American administration. The Americans threatened protectionism against West Germany if telecommunications trade was not increased. The Dutch have recently decided that their telecommunications equipment market, dominated by Siemens and Philips should be liberalised.[5] And in West Germany a state commission considering the possibility of telecommunications liberalisation will report in 1987.[6] The effect of Britain's liberalisation and privatisation of its telecommunications markets has been to open the door to multinationals to play off one country against another and increase pressure for liberalisation.

Inevitably the major beneficiaries of any liberalisation within Europe will be the dominant American companies, which under EEC law must be treated equally with domestic European companies. Second only to the Americans are the Japanese, who until the mid 1980s concentrated on exports to the American market. In 1985 NEC announced that it would establish manufacture in Britain. Other Japanese companies such as Matsushita are already present in the British market with sales of facsimile machines to BT. Liberalisation in British banking has already produced the result that one quarter of all British banking assets are held by the Japanese and liberalisation of telecommunications for the first time in 1982 produced a trade deficit in the sector.[7]

But just as the provisions of GATT in the post-war world, which liberalised trade in manufactured goods (excluding telecommunications) were tempered by the ability of governments to erect non-tariff barriers, so the liberalisation of telecommunications markets has been tempered by similar actions. Only governments under extreme pressure can allow their domestic manufacturers to be completely crowded out of the domestic market, especially in high technology industries. Hence having liberalised the data transmission and 'enhanced service' market in Britain, the British government is attempting to claw back some of the control of its economy lost thereby.

The British government and others within the EEC have begun to emphasise the importance of manufacturers' standardisation of equipment. A battle of standards is taking place, between Open Systems Interconnection on the one hand—the international standard accepted by AT&T, all the Japanese computer manufacturers and European manufacturers—and Systems Network Architecture (SNA), IBM's standard. Standards have become politicised. Part of the *raison d'être* for the EEC-backed Esprit programme was to spawn European standards for equipment, to challenge the SNA standard of IBM. There was considerable concern therefore when IBM was allowed into the project, even though it was given only some minor funding on the grounds that it was a European-based manufacturer and could not be excluded.[8]

The strategy adopted has been to demand that equipment used in the public network in Britain and in the EEC data network should conform to the OSI standards developed by the International Standards Organisation. The decision in 1984 by the British government to refuse permission for BT and IBM to develop a VAN which would have used SNA standards was taken on the grounds that it would have excluded all British manufacturers from the supply of equipment to customers. This decision was followed by another that all VAN should adopt OSI rather than SNA standards. Despite this decision the development of EFTPOS, the point of sale method of deducting money from bank accounts is going ahead between BT, IBM, retailers and the banks based on IBM equipment. In its fair trading licences the government has set out the proviso that OSI standards must be adopted as and when they become available—the problem being that they are not complete. The monitoring of IBM's technical practices has been handed to OFTEL—for the first time IBM's European business practices will be subject to regulation by a public agency.

Since IBM has always dominated the data processing market and imposed its standards *de facto* on the rest of the world, the concerted move of European countries towards OSI has apparently given it pause for thought. But the Europeans have never seriously contemplated creating their own standards which would be incompatible with American—the ISO is in fact dominated by American interests. It seems that fearing IBM more than AT&T their interests and those of AT&T coincided. The strategy of adhering to standards compatible with AT&T but not with IBM depended crucially on the cohesion of the major manufacturing countries. That cohesion has now been broken by Japan's NTT with its decision to enter into a VAN with IBM. Although NTT has argued that the equipment used will have to conform to its own standards there seems little doubt that unless Japanese manufacturers produce IBM compatible equipment they will be excluded from that major market. And if IBM and the Japanese manufacturers together adopt the same standards for VAN equipment then Europe will be left clinging to AT&T's coat-tails. The hope for Europe must be that the Japanese manufacturers may succeed in their rear-guard action of non-co-operation with NTT.

To the outsider the planned destruction of the domestic base of the Japanese telecommunications manufacturing industry is as incredible as the confusion evident in Europe is to the Japanese. The French in particular have been emphasising co-operation. In 1984 the French PTT approached BT with a proposal that since there was only one French telecommunications manufacturer (the Mitterand government had amalgamated the two existing manufacturers against PTT advice) and it wished to second source its equipment, it would buy System X from Plessey and GEC if BT would buy the French made Emily public exchange. BT turned the offer down amid much French bitterness, deciding instead to second source from Ericsson of Sweden (a non-EEC company) and cutting back on its orders of System X, thereby ensuring that both Plessey's and GEC's shares decreased in value. BT itself claims to be uninterested in Europe and is primarily concerned with the North American market.

While the EEC is torn by the need to reassess the Community Agricultural Policy and with the entry of Spain and Portugal faces the difficulties of an increased number of poorer members, EEC projects such as RACE, designed to help telecommunications manufacturers develop standardised equipment in preparation for the advent of European wide ISDN, have been delayed by the wider conflict over the budget. RACE's projected funding has been reduced. The Eureka project, proposed by France to bring together West European defence-related R & D is similarly seen by Britain as a mechanism of co-ordination, rather than one which will need funding. Other co-operative ventures, such as the decision that France and West Germany would open 10 per cent of their telecommunications market to each other, and that they would jointly develop a radio-phone have fallen by the wayside. Cellular radio standards in France, West Germany and Britain are incompatible. The British government chose an American standard, leading to immediately increased imports and very few British jobs.[9]

In all, for Europe, the deregulation of the American market and the break-up of AT&T coupled with the liberalisation of the British market and the privatisation of BT has produced considerable problems compounded by events in Japan. The two British carriers, BT and Cable and Wirelesss look towards the lucrative market on the other side of the Atlantic and the international market connecting the two. The British government dithers unable to decide whether Britain's best interests lie with the EEC or with the United States, paying lip service to the one, but deliberately increasing imports of companies, equipment and technology from the other. As Janet Morgan, a member of the Central Policy Review Staff of the Thatcher Government implied in testimony to an American Congressional Committee—the British government had delayed responding to the EEC's proposals on RACE because it was unsure that its interests lay with Europe.[10]

The lesson within Europe is that what has happened nationally within the American domestic market—that transmission carriers' interests in a competitive environment become identified with the largest user companies—is replicated on an international level. The largest user companies of international communications, which prior to BT's liberalisation was its fastest growing market, happen at present to be American. With the liberalisation of financial markets and the increased penetration of Japanese manufacturers, communications between Britain and Japan take on increased importance. Hence it is no surprise that BT announced in 1986 that a fast data link had been established between the United States, Britain and Japan, or that Japanese companies are planning to establish a telex link from London.

Impact on the deregulators

The impact of liberalisation of the American market took some time to work through, but a spectacle similar to the British government 's attempt to regain control over its domestic market has been evident in the United States. The Carter-phone decision of 1968, which allowed customers to attach certified equipment to the telecommunications network, coincided with an expansion in the Japanese market. Therefore it was only from 1980, when the Japanese market had reached saturation point, that Japanese companies began to export in any quantities to the United States. The break-up of AT&T and the parallel expansion of optic fibre cabling by its major competitors have given Japanese and newly industrialising manufacturers of telecommunications exchange equipment, of optic fibres and of customer premises equipment the opportunity to penetrate further into the American market.

In turn this penetration coupled with the high value of the dollar and the decline in competitiveness of American manufactured products has increased American pressure on Japan in particular to open its market to American companies. The traditional American answer in all trade areas is to press for deregulation and liberalisation where its industries are strongest, but to allow protectionism or to negotiate bi-lateral agreements where it has begun to suffer from technological lag. Problems of world over-supply in microchips and the recession in sales of computer equipment in 1985 have exacerbated these tendencies. The decline of the sector has led to increasing calls for protective legislation or bi-lateral agreements on microchips, the world market in 256K microchips being under Japanese domination. Decline has also led to software legislation to protect American microchip designs from copying by the Japanese and to increased pressure on the Japanese both to open their telecommunications market, and to allow increased technological transfer to American companies. In 1985 the Japanese responded by giving IBM access to the patent rights of the Japanese government in computer technology. The slump coupled with liberalisation has fuelled an anti-Japanese phobia with scare stories of American loss of technological leadership reminiscent of the late 1970s.[11]

Deregulation of the American telecommunications market is seen as having benefited foreign companies and American manufacturers have expected reciprocal benefits. The opening of the American telecommunications market has therefore also increased pressure on European countries to reciprocate. They, such as West Germany, argue however that if computers are taken together with telecommunications, then their trade balance is still very much in the United States's favour. In other areas which have traditionally been the province of American industry, such as satellites, the increased competitiveness of Europe has altered the trade picture. The deregulation of international telecommunications is no more than a traditional American response to such increased competition with the aim of taking on the European satellite industry before it can become further established.

The immediate effect of the liberalisation of AT&T's monopoly and its divestiture has been to increase the services available for business users and to reduce long-distance rates within the domestic market. Although AT&T took the view of a private entity faced with competition, that all the costs of the local network should be transferred to the local subscriber, a form of social regulation has papered over the logical effects of liberalisation. Residential charges have been held down by actions of Congress. The impact of liberalisation on ordinary consumers has therefore not yet been fully felt. AT&T's pressure for further deregulation and its bypass provision of alternative local networks via satellite is in effect a method of ridding itself of this social regulation, as well as a means of providing itself with a market for end-user equipment.

At first, unable to reduce long-distance rates until the end of 1984 because of FCC regulation, AT&T operated to $1 billion less profit than expected. It seemed that competition might establish itself within the long-lines market, but by the end of 1985 AT&T had re-established itself and still takes 80 per cent of the market. Meanwhile the seven regional operating companies' and the independents'profits increased through the time hallowed practice of increasing tariffs, while there were fears that some of those challenging AT&T's long-line business might go bankrupt because the competition on tariffs had grown so fierce. As the threat that large customers would bypass the local networks of the state operating companies grew, the local operating companies have entered into alliances to reduce their share of local network costs. But with the delimitation of the market of the previous Bell operating companies to local telephone service, the same questions of deregulation which were fought out at federal level have been transferred to the state level. Competitive local networks, access charges, interconnection—all the issues previously battled at federal level are now the subject of legal confrontation at state level. Whereas satellites produced the possibility of economic alternatives to AT&T's transmission of long-distance traffic, they now allow it to bypass the local networks. And optic fibre technology has produced the possibility of a further economic alternative to the operating companies local network via broad-band cable TV.

The question is: who is better off as a result of AT&T's break-up? The answer must be not the average consumer, now presented with a number of different companies to contact for a telephone and several bills. The break-up has not been popular among residential consumers. No firm evidence exists as to how many have been unable to pay increased telephone charges, but it was assumed that some consumers would drop out of the market.

What is evident is that a form of social regulation which attempts to offset the loading of costs onto the local caller, and which attempts to prevent the loss of universal service, cannot last in a fully competitive market. The interests of the dominant entity and of large users will be in trunk and international calls taking no share of the capital costs of a public local network which they do not use. As companies increasingly use private dedicated information networks for intra- or inter-company communication, both nationally and internationally, so the costs of access to the network for everyone else will rise. Hence the American picture is one of increased access costs for entry to the public network, and a trend towards privatised information services which exclude many of the population.

In each of the domestic markets the incompatibility between full private competition and universal access has been papered over by the re-regulation which has followed liberalisation, re-regulation which is an attempt to achieve a compromise between these two opposed aims. Each of the three governments has imposed social regulation on its dominant transmission carriers for domestic political reasons, thereby limiting the transfer of the full burden of the capital costs of local networks from being imposed on the individual local consumer. But just as AT&T has pressed for full deregulation of its services by the FCC so it can be expected that when they face truly competitive situations similar pressures will emanate from BT and NTT. They are likely to demand either to be released from their social obligations for uneconomic services, or to demand a subsidy to carry them out.

The post-privatisation scenario in Britain is hardly different from that in the United States. Whereas AT&T has re-established its dominance, BT's dominance has not yet been effectively challenged. Rather the goal of a successful sale of BT prevented the introduction of too much competition within the market, or too rigorous a method of regulation. BT has been enabled to act as AT&T did between the first and second world war, investing in competitive technologies, such as cable TV and DBS, and effectively securing its future against competition, while its major competitor has taken longer to get off the ground than anticipated. Redistribution of the costs of the local network has already begun, higher charges being borne by local calls and rentals and lower tariffs going to trunk and international calls.

In contrast, NTT's market was already further liberalised before privatisation than BT's and it will face a variety of competitors. In particular competition from VAN suppliers has already begun. In Japan the number of VANs has increased since privatisation allowing increased penetration of foreign, predominantly American companies. In Britain, the spread of VAN has been held up by the problems of a regulatory definition of data links between computers. In both countries it has been IBM which has been at the forefront of demands for a liberal regulatory policy and which will commensurately benefit.

Although the liberalisation of the equipment market increased the numbers of multinationals operating in the telecommunications market in Britain, privatisation has allied BT's interests with its largest users, particularly international companies, and has loosened its ties with domestic manufacturers. Similarly, in Japan, NTT's interests have shifted to alliances with IBM and AT&T and away from its traditional family of suppliers. And it is through NTT's transmission network that the American companies, particularly IBM, will secure the penetration of NTT's procurement and of the Japanese computer market which it had previously been unable to dominate.

In both Britain and Japan, the liberalisation and privatisation of the transmission network is a precursor of a privatised information society. In both countries the previously proposed public ISDN services have taken on the aspect of private VANs. Although the Japanese MPT has 'dreams' of the gradual integration of all private VANs into one national network, it has no power actually to integrate them. Both societies promise to see the development of a plethora of unco-ordinated private information systems unavailable to those without the money for access, and the development of increased numbers of private entertainment systems using American programming. In all three societies public access is being sacrificed to private gain.

The clash between public and private

It may seem that domestic liberalisation of telecommunications and international liberalisation can be seen as separate issues. But where integration of information, of transmission networks and of equipment gains comparative advantage, the international market becomes an extension of the domestic. In all three countries domestic liberalisation has met the interests of data processing equipment manufacturers and of service and information providers, allowing them access to the trans-mission market from which they were previously excluded and allowing them to use that liberalised transmission market to increase the penetration of their products. The privatisation of markets, the movement away from universal access towards specialised, differentiated markets under private control, is a necessary concomitant to this liberalisation. Whether in the domestic or international market, without privatisation much of the potential benefit of transmission capacity is lost to its provider. For the equipment manufacturer moving into transmission, private markets allow the imposition of standards amd lock customers in to proprietary transmission equipment. For the information provider privatised markets allow high access charges for admission coupled with low usage rates, making customer changes between service or information provider less likely. For government or international business private networks provide security of control over data flows and the evasion of regulation by sovereign governments. Hence the twin issues of liberalisation and privatisation bring together the interests of data equipment manufacturers, of software providers (both data bases and programming) and of large users, both domestic and international, governmental and non-governmental. Although the development of specialised, privatised services has been presented as the inevitable outcome of the technological convergence of data-processing, telecommunications and video reproduction, deregulation and liberalisation are the product of that convergence only inasmuch as it has altered the interests of powerful companies and governments.

Deregulated transmission has come to be seen as the means by which those countries falling behind in manufacture may benefit from their established position in service industries. Hence for the United States and Britain, both suffering from deficits in their trade in manufactured products, global penetration of their service industries may help to offset these imbalances. In the American case this global penetration can also be allied to its dominant position in the provision of programming and information sources, such as data bases, and to the dominant position in the world market of its data processing industry. The liberalisation of international transmission, with prospects of reduced tariffs, is also the means by which global companies may reduce their overhead costs, further contributing to their continued world domination of markets. As computers and telecommunications have converged, as global manufacture has increased in the continued search for comparative advantage by companies in the industrialised West, and as the American government has devoted increasing resources to its defence interests throughout the world, so cheap, fast, private communications have gained in importance. Technological convergence has produced a convergence of industrial, commercial, informational, defence and overtly political interests within the United States.

To take just one example, the decision to lay the trans-Pacific optic fibre in 1988, and the route which that fibre should take was influenced by the Pentagon's desire that Guam, with its central Pacific defense role, should be served by the fibre. The timing was influenced by the possibility of 50 per cent American participation in laying the initial cable—delay might allow other (Japanese and European) companies to take more of the contracts. And the need for optic fibre in the first place was influenced by the need for secure communications, under private control, compared to the comparative insecurity of satellite communications under Intelsat control.[12]

The transfer of international tranmission markets from public to private control is therefore in the political and economic interests of the United States. In the words of Timothy Wirth:

International telecommunications are of enormous importance to our economy. Those who manufacture the equipment that makes international telecommunications possible are on the cutting edge of high technology, developing satellites and fiber optics. And those who offer international telecommunications services make possible some of the few successes in our ability to compete internationally—in the high technology service sector ... While we may have a significant deficit in our balance of payments, we enjoy a strong surplus in our export of data processing services, financial services, legal services and so on ...'[13]

Together telecommunications and computing equipment are second only to agriculture in America's export league. The export of services and the export of computing and telecommunications equipment are equally important to the position of the United States in political terms. In the words of the former Deputy Assistant Secretary for Human Rights and Social Affairs:

Either we will design, produce, market and distribute the most advanced products and services spun off by the communications revolution—and in so doing, reinforce our economic, political, social and cultural advantage—or we will increasingly find ourselves in the position of consumer and debtor to those who do ...'[14]

As in other areas of trade the interest of the United States is in gaining free access to other countries' markets, free trade being that form of trade which benefits the strongest industry. Hence the regulation of domestic telecommunications markets is seen as a form of protectionism against the free flow of telecommunications services and product trade, as a mechanism of industrial policy by the governments of other industrialised nations. Public control of domestic markets is ranked with data protection codes enacted by industrialised and Third World countries as counter to American interests.

The issue of liberalisation and privatisation in communications is thereby presented as an issue of industrial political interest rather than as a basic conflict of philosophy—whether networks should be provided to gain comparative advantage for global private entities or whether they should be provided for universal benefit at reasonable cost to the individual user. Although it is acknowledged that systems of public regulation and the cross-subsidisation involved may represent the legitimate social goals of sovereign nations, the American administration's argument is that these goals are protectionist in intent, and that there is both a possibility of promoting fully competitive privatised systems and systems which achieve universal access at low cost. It is not acknowledged that by the redistribution of costs which take place under liberalisation and privatisation the two systems represent mutually incompatible interests.[15]

In the international market some countervailing political forces are still present to prevent the full redistribution of costs of Intelsat's thin routes onto those whom they serve. Neither the United States nor Britain wishes to acknowledge openly to the world that their intention is primarily to expoit the global market for their own economies and that their support of Intelsat is compromised. The attempt of both the American and British governments is therefore to accrue as much economic advantage as possible from the current regulatory situation without, if possible, raising the forces of opposition among European PTTs, while at the same time supporting the construction of new international facilities which may themselves provoke a complete overhaul of international regulation from 1989. Hence the Tele-Optik/Cable and Wireless private trans-Atlantic optic fibre leased line will enhance Britain's attractiveness as a location for American multinational enterprise within Europe, while at the same time, through increasing trans-Atlantic overcapacity, make Intelsat a less viable entity. Similarly the British decided that, although all those domestic services provided under its new definition of Value Added Data Services could not be internationalised under current CCITT regulations, it would nevertheless not attempt to define those that could be so provided. Instead the government would leave individual providers to find partners in other countries. The decision marries well with that of the FCC in the early 1980s (which has not yet been finalised) allowing 'enhanced' service to be provided internationally. The British decision opens the 'enhanced service' international market between Britain and the United States. British interests in the liberalisation and privatisation of the international transmission market have been perceived as almost identical to American.

The Americans are challenging the basis of Intelsat's global sharing of network costs directly by agreeing the construction of private trans-Atlantic satellites, the British are undermining it indirectly. Both are acting in favour of their own industries, the Americans in favour of their satellite makers, their programmers and information providers and American business in general, the British in favour of their aerospace industry together with financial and trans-national business markets.

To a large extent because of Intelsat's pivotal position, the conflict between public and private control within the international market has become a clash between the competitive technologies of optic fibres and satellites. European PTTs and AT&T have always preferred transmission via cable because of the private control which it gave them and optic fibres fulfill the same needs. In the past the technology of coaxial cable and the structure of regulation within the international market have prevented their exploitation of this cable provision. Coaxial cable has not been able to take the required capacity, Intelsat has produced a good return on investment for PTTs whose needs have been primary to its business and the FCC has required that the use of each transmission mode should be balanced in order to promote efficiency. These three features have each altered as optic fibres produce the capacity previously unavailable, as Intelsat pays greater attention to the needs of the Third World, as Europe has gained its own satellite system and as the FCC has reviewed its decisions on the balancing of international traffic between satellites and cable. The move to increase submarine optic fibre transmission is a move to keep trans-Atlantic and trans-Pacific enterprise under the control of PTTs and large multinational users. It precludes control by the other members of Intelsat whose interests run contrary to those of the leading industrialised countries.

But the additional provision of optic fibre has alternative implications. Trans-Atlantic and trans-Pacific optic fibre cables are both scheduled to go into operation in 1988, with AT&T owning 35 per cent of the Atlantic and 56 per cent of the Pacific cable. AT&T's preference for routing traffic through them will both threaten Intelsat and also provide even greater over capacity on the trans-Atlantic route which in turn is likely to increase pressure for the resale of leased international lines in an attempt to offset fixed costs—thereby further reducing the costs for international business. Yet satellites are useful for providing alternative access technology to local markets. And whereas internationally the existence of Intelsat has precluded the use of satellites under private control, in the American domestic market the development of satellites has gone hand in hand with the development of private ownership and deregulation. Sales of transponders and the incentives given by the American tax system to these sales by recognising transponders as private property for tax purposes, were essential to the development of satellites. It was this decision on the sale of domestic transponders which the FCC took as its precedent when it decided that Tel-Optik might provide a privately owned submarine trans-Atlantic optic fibre cable for private companies' use. With the saturation of the American domestic market in satellites it is hardly surprising that the answer sought has been in terms of private ownership of international satellite transponders, already a proven method for increasing growth.

Privately owned satellites on the trans-Atlantic route will   fulfill several functions. First they will accrue to American satellite makers and operators increased contracts and will increase markets for domestic satellites. Second they will cheapen communications for American multinationals and defence installations in Europe with their home base, thereby centralising control in the United States. Thirdly they will allow the penetration of American cable programme companies into the European market. Fourthly they will accrue to American companies the profits from the busiest communications route in the world, which at the present time are shared between the less industrialised countries.

And finally, the entry of private satellites will challenge the West European PTT monopolies. Whilst PTT monopolies remain, international business remains under some form of social control, and still must pay towards the costs of the local networks of the countries from which it operates. For years the FCC has attempted to deregulate the international market using cable facilities but has met limited success because of European PTT resistance and their control of cable landing points. But satellite broadcasting is less easy for PTT's to counter, especially since the principle of Ku band transmission between companies has already been accepted with BT's Sat-stream service. Private satellites give the prospect of achieving that which is in American business' best interest—liberalised, privatised telecommunications transmission systems throughout the industrialised world.

To American international business the possibility that PTTs might phase out the subsidy given to large users through the flat-rate tariff of private leased lines has been a cause of anxiety for several years. In 1983 the American Congress heard that the transfer of these flat-rates to a usage based rate would preclude the then current use of data communications. In the short-term it seems unlikely that leased lines will be phased out, for the simple reason that to do so would increase pressure on the existing networks which could not currently replicate the variety of specialised services demanded.[16]

But the concept of ISDN, which could make unneccessary the provision of those leased lines, and which would transfer tariff rates to measurement of amounts of information transmitted represents a long-term threat to American interests. The threat is both for those who have already invested heavily in their own communications networks and to equipment companies. The concept of ISDN, when put to PTTs by the Japanese, was welcomed, partly because it gave the prospect of increased investment for their bureaucracies, but it must be assumed because it also extends PTTs control to data processing equipment manufacturers. Depending on where it is decided to put the interface between network and consumer equipment, will determine whether equipment companies sell to a consumer market or to the PTT capital market. Already a split has occurred between the American view of where the interface should go—at a point which allows as much processing as possible within the consumer equipment and therefore allows the greatest diversity of equipment—and the CCITT view which would place the interface beyond the point of the processing currently done by customers' PABX.[17]

Equally there is a split between the PTT view that ISDN will provide a unified public service and the views of IBM which wants the retention of existing private networks and 'flexibility' in the concept of ISDN.

The liberalisation of current markets, the extension of numbers of private carriers and the integration of private transmission with equipment would make it considerably more difficult for European governments to introduce a full, public ISDN service. Short term American interests in penetrating these markets with information/transmission/equipment providers marry with longer-term objectives in relation to ISDN. It is hardly a coincidence that IBM has been at the forefront of the movement for deregulation of telecommunications throughout the world.

The international consortium arrangement which presaged the formal inauguration of Intelsat was a product of the 1960s and the Kennedy era of liberalism. It was in the interests of the United States while that country both dominated the organisation and received a subsidy in terms of contracts from it. Just as the organisation was a product of that time of hope and economic expansion, so the movement away from Intelsat is a product of the failing American economy and a movement towards the view that charity begins at home and should only go to those who 'deserve' it. The American efforts to release itself from the obligations of the Intelsat treaty are in tune with its reduction in aid to the poorest countries, its growing protectionism, its withdrawal from Unesco, its embargo of funding through the World Bank to those regimes it disagrees with, and its imposition of strict monetarist policies on Third World debtor countries through the IMF. It mirrors its failure to meet obligations under GATT to the Third World, and its opposition to Third World demands for planned use of the geosynchronous orbit at WARC 1985. The major difference between all these decisions and that concerning Intelsat is that the latter requires the United States to extricate itself from the burdens of an international treaty. Although there is no power which can stop America from withdrawing from that treaty, the force of international law is evident in the arguments which have been brought out by the United States to attempt to convince the rest of the world that its actions are commensurate with the treaty.

If there is any amusement to be had from its decision it is in the cries of 'foul' which have been aimed at Intelsat's retaliatory tactics and the allegations of 'monopoly' behaviour made against it. It so happens that the very contracts from which the American industry has benefited coupled with the world recession have helped to produce over-capacity in the international system, thereby allowing cheap leases of international satellite capacity from Intelsat. The charge levelled by Intelsat's opponents is that Intelsat, by lowering charges and by selling transponders, is undercutting the economic viability of private competitors and that this behaviour is evidence of Intelsat's misuse of its monopoly power. The fact that the United States, as part of the governing body of Intelsat was involved in the original decisions which increased its capacity and is therefore also responsible for bad forecasting tends to be forgotten. Also forgotten is the hidden subsidy paid to the American satellite industry and its R & D by poorer users of Intelsat over the years.

The fact is that two-thirds of the world's telephones are owned by the nine major industrial countries, with the other third distributed unevenly. Originally the interests of the industrialised and less industrialised seemed to coincide in the spread of telephone connections. It is particularly in the interests of the less industrialised faced with the problems of inaccessible regions, dispersed populations and low literacy to have access to cheap voice and image communications, cheap being in terms of low per capita income. Small, high powered satellites could provide the technology which requires only chicken wire as an aerial for TV reception and one-way conversations. But the interests of the industrialised countries and their concern with technological competition have been in providing either large, low-powered satellites, increasing the circuits each transponder can hold, or in providing high power satellites with digital Time Division Multiplexing (an expensive technology). In general present day satellites and digital technology with their heavy upfront costs are not suitable for the poorest countries' needs, although telecommunications is essential for their economic development.

It seems unlikely that if Intelsat as a result of private competition is forced to raise its prices and exclude the poorest countries from its market, that the result will be a flood of orders to American and European satellite industries. A basis of technological expertise is necessary before high-technology hardware can be of use in the developing world, and countries are becoming more aware through experience of the disadvantages of complex hardware. What may happen is that the global companies within these countries may increasingly provide their own private networks and that eventually a market may develop for cheap, intermediate technology satellites.[18] But given the current linkages of satellites to defence interests in Europe and to the SDI programme in the United States, it seems unlikely that the impetus for such development will come from the existing satellite industry. Perhaps India or Japan will begin to think in terms of such a market.

As the West develops and manufactures equipment predominantly for its vision of ISDN the effect is to exclude the less developed from telecommunications development. Equipment imported of a high technological level increases dependency on the exporting country for technical support, spares and maintenance training as well as being too expensive for other than piecemeal introduction within the lesser developed countries. The International Telecommunications Union in 1984 produced the Maitland report, acting in response to its increased membership from the lesser developed world.[19] The report called for a unified response to the problem of telecommunications development and some linkages with the World Bank to develop systems have been reported. But, although the lesser developed, by virtue of their superior numbers may influence the plenipotentiary meetings of the organisation, the detailed engineering decisions on standards now revolve centrally around data communications and ISDN on which the lesser developed are practically excluded. Technological emphasis on ISDN and deregulation with its emphasis on data rather than voice transmission are two mechanisms which in practice squeeze out the interests of two-thirds of the world community in favour of big business in the West.[20] Together the two represent a reassertion of control by the most wealthy. The domestic split between the haves with access to the new privatised information services and the have-nots is currently repeated at the international level of negotiation.[21]

While deregulation in the international market is a move by the rich against the poor, by emphasising data over voice communication, when data still represents only a small minority of all transmission, it favours major companies in the industrialised West. Deregulation shifts power away from sovereign governments to private capital in whatever market it takes place. But easy world-wide free flows of data make the global market a reality to the benefit of the strongest. Hence the freeing of exchange rates and financial markets, coupled with the development of private data networks, has made it easier for money and information to shift around the globe and more difficult for governments to control their economies.

Conclusion

This book began from a consideration of what the existing literature could teach us on the benefits of regulation, liberalisation and privatisation. Critics of regulation argued that it benefited the regulated industry and the regulatory bureaucracy but rarely the consumer. Implicity and explicitly deregulation and privatisation were held up as models for the benefit of that consumer. The problem with these analyses was however that they did not differentiate between different sets of consumers or explore the differences in interest between private dominant entities in a liberalised market structure and those of monopoly entities with public service orientations. They did not suggest that market strategy for privatised and liberalised carriers would be in catering for the needs of the largest business users and that their interests in data transmission would rapidly provoke their wooing of the manufacturers with the largest installed base of computers, or that the equipment market, the network market and the very provision of information would become unified. The analyses did not put forward the vision of either a domestic or world society where access to use of the telephone would increase in price to any remarkable extent, because the analyses did not foresee that carriers and large users interests would coalesce in evading the capital costs of the existing infrastructure.

Rather the majority of existing analyses emphasised the benefits of the new technology and the dead hand of bureaucracy upon innovation. Certainly in Britain and in Japan the years of control by the Post Office and the Ministry of Communication were not years of technical innovation in telecommunications, but these were also years when the network was starved of investment by governments. The expansion and technological upgrading of the Japanese network demonstrates that public control does not have to be antithetical to technological innovation.

The analyses of the proponents of deregulation and privatisation pointed to the weaknesses of regulation, to the difficulties in regulating large private companies and the failure of rate of return regulation or public ownership to control the costs of monopoly enterprises. But liberalisation and privatisation do not in themselves remove the need for effective mechanisms of monitoring and control. Rather the reverse—they demand better mechanisms to prevent predatory pricing and anti-competitive behaviour on the part of the dominant entity. And although privatisation has increased the power of the bureaucracy over the telecommunications industry in both Britain and Japan, the search continues for those effective mechanisms.

Nor did the proponents of deregulation and privatisation point to the benefits of the existing system for domestic manufacturers, and the difficulties caused by the liberalisation of small markets. Regulation suited the domestic manufacturers in particular. In Japan regulation gave them a large home market from which to export, and in Britain it enabled domestic procurement to support R & D and local manufacture, although this base was not converted into an export market. In both the United States and Britain it seems that the cost of this domestic support was passed on to the customer, but because it was accepted that the benefit of the local network (the most expensive part of the network) should be shared by all consumers, the result was a relatively low cost local service. In Japan, the stability of local call tariffs over twenty years and the rigidity of Japanese labour practices meant a greater degree of concern for manufacturing costs and productivity. But in all three systems local manufacturers benefited from regulation and in all three they have been major losers under liberalisation and privatisation.

Under the previous monopoly systems leased lines to large-scale business were subsidised, the major losers being those who used the trunk-line and international public switched service, where tariffs were higher than service costs would have led business to expect. The major problem with the behavioural regulation of AT&T, of the British Post Office and of KDD was the seeming inability, or lack of concern, of regulatory authorities to determine acceptable costs and efficient use of the network. In both Britain and the United States, the problem is now how to prevent the raising of costs of rentals and local calls, how to find a method of distributing the costs of the capital infrastructure of the local network which will prevent the diminution of the number of subscribers. Already in Britain there is customer resistance to the increased charges for local calls and the volume of traffic is decreasing. And in Japan, where the local call charge is set by legislation, the problem now is how to decrease the costs of trunk-calls when NTT's charges would in fact be lower than its competitors need for a return on capital.

In each of the three countries the pressure for liberalisation of the PTT monopoly came from large user companies in alliance with those equipment companies previously excluded from domestic PTT procurement. In America that pressure came first from oil companies and retailers and later from computer equipment and service companies as their products came to rely increasingly on communications capacities. A similar process is now manifesting itself in the international market with these integrated companies seeking to establish private global networks.

This book took as its starting point the concept of 'natural monopoly' and the regulation which went with it. Yet telecommunications in both the United States and Britain began in competitive market conditions with telephone transmission competing with and then replacing telegraph transmission. The way in which AT&T gained dominance of telephone transmission through control of interstate transmission is reminiscent today of the way in which American interests are seeking to privatise and gain control of international communications. Through that privatisation PTTs' control of their domestic networks can be isolated, in the same way as the independent telephone companies were isolated into their own geographical areas. Britain's overt intention through reductions in trans-Atlantic rates and the loosening of regulation of international value added data service traffic, to attract to BT the trans-Atlantic traffic of multinationals physically located in other Western European countries, impacts on those countries' ability to balance telephone tariffs and to provide cheap, universal access to the telephone. And by the intended funnelling of large-user communications from Europe to the United States it sets the scene for the electronic colonisation of Europe.[22] Hence the privatisation of international markets also concerns the distribution of world power—not only whether that power should rest with governments or with global private companies, but also how far power should be centered in the United States.

Gradually the rest of the world is being drawn into the competition emanating from the American domestic market, competition between satellites and optic fibres, competition between IBM and AT&T, competition between private companies and European PTTs, competition between the unbridled, capitalist free-market ideology of America and the desire of others to have a more socially equitable method of distributing the benefits of telecommunications. As access to both the basic technology of the telephone becomes restricted and information itself is dominated by privatised networks, public debate both domestic and international should centre on the issue of who *should* benefit from communication technologies and what mechanisms can increase the equality of their distribution.

Notes and references

1. *Telecommunications in Transition: The Status of Competition in the Telecommunications Industry*, Report of the Majority Staff of the Subcommittee on Telecommunications, Consumer Protection, and Finance of the Committee on Energy and Commerce, 97th Congress, 1st Session, HR 97-V, November 3rd 1981, Washington D.C., US Government Printing Off., 1981.
2. See for instance: Malcolm Baldrige, Testimony before the Subcommittee on Telecommunications, Consumer Protection and Finance of the Committee on Energy and Commerce, *International Trade Issues in Telecommunications and Related Industries*, 98th Congress, 1st Session, HR 98-36, 23 March 1983, Washington D.C., US Government Printing Off., p. 9.
3. *Financial Times*, 24 May 1984.
4. Manley Rutherford Irwin, *Telecommunications America. Markets Without Boundaries*, Westport, Conn., Quorum Books, 1984, pp. 45–58.
5. On the Dutch market see: Jens Arnbak, 'New Clothes for Old PTT Monopolies', *Intermedia*, **14**, 1, January 1986, pp. 22–7.
6. *Financial Times*, 6 January 1986
7. *The Guardian*, 6 March 1986.
8. On the European Information Technology Industry see: Maurice English, 'The European Information Technology Industry', in A. Jacquemin (ed.), *European Industry: Public Policy and Corporate Strategy*, Oxford, Clarendon Press, 1984, pp. 227–74.

9. Geoffrey Dang Nguyen, 'Telecommunications: a Challenge to the *Old Order*', in Margaret Sharp (ed.), *Europe and the New Technologies*, London, Frances Pinter, pp. 87–133.

10. Janet Morgan, statement to the Subcommittee of the Committee on Government Operations, *International Communications Reorganisation Act of 1981*, HR1957, 31 March 1981, Washington D. C., Government Printing Off., 1981, p. 40.

11. *Washington Post*, 22 September 1985; 8 October 1985.

12. Ronald Eward, *The Deregulation of International Telecommunications*, Dedham M. A., Artech House, 1985, pp. 292–99.

13. Timothy Wirth, Chairman, Subcommittee on Telecommunications, Consumer Protection and Finance, March 23rd 1983, op. cit., p. 1.

14. Quoted in Herbert I. Schiller, *Information and the Crisis Economy*, Norwood, N. J., Ablex, pp. 21–2.

15. Geza Feketekuty, Asst. US Trade Representative for Policy Development, statement to Subcommittee on Government Information and Individual Rights, 31 March 1983, op. cit., pp. 105–49.

16. Ibid. p. 120; see also Ronald Eward, op. cit., p. 343–6.

17. Ronald Eward, op. cit., pp. 186–7.

18. Hal Glazer, *Birds of Babel. Satellites for a Human World*, Indianapolis, Howard W. Sams, 1983.

19. ITU, *The Missing Link*, report of the Independent Commission for World-wide Telecommunications Development, Geneva, ITU, 1984.

20. Dan Schiller, 'The Emerging Global Grid—Planning for What?' *Media, Culture and Society*, 7 January 1985, pp. 105–28. Estimates of the future world market in 1987 suggest that 77 per cent of the world market will be that of telephone, record and data providing 14 per cent. Total market value $70 billion. Arthur D. Little quoted in *Financial Times*, 6 January 1986.

21. Cees J. Hamelink, *Transnational Data Flows in the Information Age*, Sweden, Studentlitteratur AB, Chartwell-Bratt Ltd, 1984, pp. 64–93.

22. I am indebted to Rob Van Tudler for pointing out the parallel between these developments in communications in Europe and those in the previous colonisation of Africa.

Bibliography

Akehurst, Michael, *A Modern Introduction to International Law*, London, George Allen & Unwin, 4th edition, 1982.

Anderson, James E., 'Economic, Regulatory and Consumer Protection Policies' in Theodore J. Lowi and Alan Stone, *Nationalizing Government. Public Policies in America*, New York and London, Sage, 1978, pp. 61–84.

Arnbak, Jens 'New Clothes for Old PTT Monopolies', *Intermedia*, **14**, 1, January 1986, pp. 22–7.

Babe, Robert E., 'Predatory Pricing and Foreclosure in Canadian Telecommunications', *Telecommunications Policy*, December 1985, pp. 329–33.

Barrett, R., 'Development and Use of Facsimile Systems in Japan', *Electronics and Power*, 12 December 1984, pp. 1118–1121.

Beesley, Michael and Stephen Littlechild, 'Privatization, Principles, Problems and Priorities', *Lloyds Bank Review*, July 1983, pp. 1–19.

Beesley, Michael, *Liberalisation of the Use of British Telecom's Network*, London, HMSO, 1981.

Beesley, Michael, 'The Liberalisation of British Telecom', *Journal of Economic Affairs*, **2**, 1, October 1981, pp. 19–27.

Bernstein, Marver, *Regulating Business by Independent Commission*, Princeton, N. J., Princeton University Press, 1955.

Bernstein, Marver H. and Horace M. Gray, 'In Practice is Regulation Consistent with the Public Interest?', Congressional Testimony to Hearings before the Antitrust Subcommittee of the Committee on the Judiciary, 84th Congress, 2nd Session, 1956, reprinted in Samuel Kristov and Lloyd M. Musolf (eds.), *The Politics of Regulation*, Boston, Houghton & Mifflin, pp. 223–30.

Bleazard, G. B., *Telecommunications in Transition—a Position Paper*, London, National Computing Centre, 1982.

Borchardt, Kurt, *Structure and Performance of the US Communications Industry. Government Regulation and Company Planning*, Boston, Mass., Harvard University, 1970, pp. 24–5.

Branscomb, Anne W., 'Communication Policy in the US: Diversity and Pluralism in a Competitive Market Place', in Patricia Edgar and Syed A. Rahim (eds.), *Communication Policy in Developed Countries*, London & Boston, Kegan Paul International, 1983, pp. 15–56.

Breyer, Stephen, *Regulation and its Reform*, Cambridge, Mass., Harvard University Press, 1982.

British Telecom, *Statistics 1981*, London, British Telecom, 1981.

Brock, Gerald, *The Telecommunications Industry: The Dynamics of Market Structure*, Cambridge Mass. & London, Harvard University Press, 1981.

Bruce, Peter, 'The High Price of a State Monopoly', *Financial Times*, 11 June 1985.

Cabinet Office, *Cable Systems*, London, HMSO, 1982.

Cable TV Expansion, Cmnd. 2866, London, HMSO, 1983.

Cameron, Sue, 'UK Privatisation. What the Managers Think', *Financial Times*, 20 July 1985.

Canes, Michael, *Telephones—Public or Private?*, London, Institute of Economic Affairs, 1966.

Carsberg, Bryan, 'OFTEL—The Challenge of the First Five Years', *Information Technology and Public Policy*, **4**, 1, September, 1985, pp. 1–11.

Carter Report, *Report of the Post Office Review Committee*, Cmnd. 6850, London, HMSO, 1977, p. 18.

Caruso, Andrea, 'Deregulation and Disorder in Satellite Communications', speech to Intelvent, 1984, 17 September 1984.

Colino, Richard, 'Global Satellite Communications: Winners and Losers', speech to Parliamentary and Scientific Committee of the House of Commons, 22 January 1985.

Colino, Richard, 'Questions and Answers', testimony to the Subcommittee on Arms Control, Oceans, International Operations and Environment, Senate Foreign Relations Committee, 19 October 1983.

Communications Industry Association of Japan, *Outline of Communications Industry*, Tokyo, CIAJ, 1984.

Computer White Papers, Tokyo, JIPDEC, 1982.

Conservative Party Manifesto 1979 reprinted in *The Times Guide to the House of Commons*, London, Times Books, 1983.

Cornell, Nina W., and Douglas W. Webbink, 'The Present Direction of the FCC: an Appraisal' *American Economic Review*, **73**, 2, 1983, pp. 194–7.

Corrigan, Richard, 'Intelsat Balking at Opening the Skies to Competitors', *National Journal*, 11 May 1985, pp. 1019–23.

Crandall, Robert W., and Bruce M. Owen, 'The Marketplace Economic Implications of Divestiture' in Harry M. Shooshan III, (ed.), *Disconnecting Bell*, New York, Pergamon, 1984, pp. 47–70.

Cripps, Francis and Wynne Godley, *The Planning of Telecommunications in the United Kingdom*, Cambridge, Dept. of Applied Economics, 1978.

Curtis, G. L. 'Big Business and Political Influence', in Ezra Vogel (ed.), *Japanese Organisation and Decision-making*, Berkeley, University of California Press, 1975, pp. 33–71.

Dang Nguyen, Geoffrey, 'Telecommunications: a Challenge to the Order', in Margaret Sharp (ed.), *Europe and the New Technologies*, London, Frances Pinter, pp. 87–133.

Davies, Glyn and John Davies, 'The Revolution in Monopoly Theory', *Lloyds Bank Review*, July 1984, pp. 38–52.

deButts, John Interview. 'Telephone Monopoly: Good or Bad?' *US. News & World Report*, 22 November 1976, pp. 42–4.

de Jonquieres, Guy & David Freud, 'BT: the 51% Solution' *Financial Times*, 27 September 1983.

de Jonquieres, Guy, 'The muddle that is slowing VANs', *Financial Times*, 10 September 1985.

Demsetz, Harold, 'Why Regulate Utilities?', *Journal of Law and Economics*, **11**, 1968, pp. 55–65.

Department of Industry, *The Future of Telecommunications in Britain*, London, HMSO, 1982.

Department of Trade and Industry, *Future Licensing of Value Added and Data Services: Revised Proposals*, 30 December 1985, (mimeo).

English, Maurice, 'The European Information Technology Industry', in A. Jacquemin (ed.), *European Industry: Public Policy and Corporate Strategy*, Oxford, Clarendon Press, 1984, pp. 227–74.

Eward, Ronald, *The Deregulation of International Telecommunications*, Dedham M. A., Artech House, 1985.

Evans, B. G., 'Towards the Intelligent Satellite', Guildford, Surrey University, unpublished Paper, 1985.

Fenton, Chester G., and Robert F. Stone, 'Competition in terminal equipment market', *Public Utilities Fortnightly*, 31 July 1977, pp. 25–71.

Fuchs, Peter E., 'Regulatory Reform and Japan's Telecommunications Revolution', *US–Japan Relations: New Attitudes for a New Era*, Program on US–Japan Relations, Boston, Mass., Harvard University, 1984, pp. 123–42.

Future Systems Inc., *The Impact of Future National and Regional Communications Satellite Systems on Intelsat*, prepared for the Office of Telecommunications Policy, Gaithersburg, Md., Future Systems Inc., February 1978.

Gabel, Richard, 'The Early Competitive Era in Telephone Communication 1893–1920', *Law and Contemporary problems*, **34**. no. 2, Spring 1969, pp. 340–59.

Gavin, Brigid, 'A GATT for International Banking', *Journal of World Trade Law*, **19**, 2, March/April 1985, pp. 121–35.

Geller, Henry, 'The New Telecommunications Act as a Regulatory Framework' in Eli M. Noam, *Telecommunications Regulation Today and Tomorrow*, New York, Law and Business, 1983, pp. 205–55.

Geller, Henry, 'Regulation and Public Policy After Divestiture. The FCC and Congress' in Harry M. Shooshan III (ed.) *Disconnecting Bell*, New York, Pergamon, 1984, pp. 94–6.

Glazer, Hal, *Birds of Babel. Satellites for a Human World*, Indianapolis, Howard W. Sams, 1983.

Goodhart, David, 'On the edge of a "black hole"', *Financial Times*, 12 October 1983.

Gregory, David, British Aerospace, 'Future Directions in Space Communications', *Information Technology and Public Policy*, **4**, 1, September 1985, pp. 12–22.

Guterl, Fred, and Gelnn Zorpette, 'Fiber optics: poised to displace satellites', IEEE Spectrum, 1 August 1985, pp. 30–37.

Hall, Robert C., president and chief executive, SBS, 'Remarks on Business Communications: The Business of SBS', in Alfred A. Green and Richard E. Wiley, *The New Telecommunications Landscape*, New York, Law and Business, 1984, pp. 21–33.

Hamelink, Cees J., *Transnational Data Flows in the Information Age*, Sweden, Studentlitteratur AB, Chartwell-Bratt Ltd, 1984.

Hatfield, Dale N., 'Remarks', in *Challenges in Telecommunications and Information Handling for the New Administration*, Washington, D.C., Center for Telecommunications Studies, George Washington University, 1981, pp. 204–9.

Heald, David, 'Will the Privatisation of Public Enterprises Solve the Problem of Control', *Public Administration*, 1985, **63**, Spring, pp. 7–22.

Heffron, Florence, 'The Federal Communications Commission and Broadcast Deregulation', in John J. Havick (ed.), *Communications Policy and the Political Process*, Westport, Conn., Greenwood Press, 1983, pp. 39–70.

Hills, Jill, 'Government Relations with Industry: Japan and Britain. A Review of Two Political Arguments', *Polity*, **XIV**, 2, Winter 1981, pp. 222–48.

Hills, Jill, 'The Industrial Reorganisation Corporation. The case of the GEC/AEI and GEC/English Electric Mergers', *Public Administration*, 59, Spring 1981, pp. 63–84.

Hills, Jill, *Information Technology and Industrial Policy*, Beckenham, Croom Helm, 1984.

Hills, Jill, 'The Industrial Policy of Japan', *Journal of Public Policy*, **3**, 1, 1983, pp. 63–80.

Hills, M. T., 'A Comparison of Switching System Development in Japan and the UK', *Telecommunications Group Report*, no. 116, Essex University, 1977, (mimeo).

Hollins, Timothy, *Beyond Broadcasting: Into the Cable Age*, London, BFI, 1984.

Hosoda, Akira, 'Telecommunications Administration in Japan' in H. Inose (ed.), *Telecommunications Technologies, Japan Annual Review in Electronics, Computers and Telecommunications* Vol. 14, 1984, pp. 305–21.

House of Commons Select Committee on the Nationalised Industries, *First Report on the Post Office*, London, HMSO, 1967.

Irwin, Manley Rutherford, *Telecommunications America. Markets Without Boundaries*, Westport, Conn., Quorum Books, 1984.

ITU, *The Missing Link*, report of the Independent Commission for World-wide Telecommunications Development, Geneva, ITU, 1984.

Janisch H. and Y. Kurisaki, 'Reform of telecommunications regulation in Japan and Canada', *Telecommunications Policy*, March 1985, pp. 31–40.

Johnson, Ben, 'By-passing the FCC: an Alternative Approach to Access Charges', *Public Utilities Fortnightly*, 7 March 1985, pp. 18–23.

Kaletsky, Anatole, 'Everywhere the State is in Retreat', *Financial Times* 2 August 1985.

Kaplan, Eugene, *Japan: The Government-Business Relationship*, Washington D. C., US. Dept. of Commerce, 1972.

Kay, John, 'The Privatization of British Telecommunications', in David Steel and David Heald (eds.), *Privatizing Public Enterprises*, London, RIPA, 1984, pp. 77–86.

Kerner, Tom, 'North Atlantic Fury', *Satellite Communications*, August 1985, pp. 23–5.

Kieve, Jeffrey, *The Electric Telegraph: A Social and Economic History*, Newton Abbott, David Charles, 1973.

Kitahara, Yasasuda, *INS: Telecommunications in the 21st Century*. London, Heinemann Educational Books, 1983.

Kitahara, Yasasuda, 'INS (Information Network System)—Telecommunications for the Advanced Information Society', in H. Inose (ed.), *Telecommunication Technologies*, Tokyo, OHMSHA, 1984, pp. 6–18.

Kobayashi, Taiyu, 'Hopes for an Open Policy in Telecommunications', *Keidanren Review*, no. 85, February 1984, pp. 5–9.

Koyama, Moriya 'The New Communications Age in Japan', *Telecommunications Policy*, September 1985, pp. 182–84.

Kuhn, Raymond, *The Politics of Broadcasting*, Beckenham, Croom Helm, 1985.

Kohlmeier Jr., Louis M., *The Regulators. Watchdog Agencies and the Public Interest*, New York, Harper and Row, 1969.

Lener, Norman C., 'Legislative and Regulatory Changes in International Telecommunications: an Evaluation of US and Foreign Impact', *Proceedings of 1st International Telecommunications Exposition* Vol. 3, *Telecommunications and Economic development*, Dedham, Ma., Horizon House International, 1978.

Lishman, R. W., '"Independence" in the Independent Regulatory Agencies', *Administrative Law Review* reprinted in Samuel Kristov and Lloyd M. Musolf (eds.), *The Politics of Regulation* Boston, Houghton and Mifflin, 1964, pp. 97–101.

Little Arthur D., Inc., *The Japanese Non-Tariff Trade Barrier Issue. American Views and the Implications for Japan—US Trade Relations*, Tokyo, National Institute for Research Advancement, 1979, p. IV–19; *Industrial Review of Japan*, Tokyo, Nihon Keizai Shimbun, 1977, p. 86.

Littlechild, Stephen C., 'Ten Steps to Denationalisation', *Journal of Economic Affairs*, 2, 1, October 1981, pp. 11–19.

Littlechild, Stephen C., *Elements of Telecommunications Economics*, London, Institute of Electrical Engineers, 1979.

Littlechild, Stephen C., *Regulation of British Telecommunications Profitability*, London, Department of Industry, 1983.

Loxley, Gareth, 'London calling: A Policy for Telecommunications after Privatisation', *Telecommunications Policy*, September 1984, pp. 178–80.

McLucas J. L. and C. Sheffield (eds.), *Commercial Operations in Space 1980–2000*, San Diego, American Astronautical Society, 1981.

Maeda, Kunji, 'Privatization of Japanese Telecommunications', *Telecommunications Policy*, June 1985, pp. 93–4.

Magaziner, Ira S., and Thomas M. Hout, *Japanese Industrial Policy*, London, PSI, 1980.

Magnant, Robert S., *Domestic Satellite, an FCC Giant Step. Toward Competitive Telecommunications Policy*, Boulder, Colorado, Westview Press, 1977.

Main, Jeremy, 'Waking up AT&T: There's Life After Culture Shock', *Fortune*, 24 December 1984, pp. 34–42.

McKnight, Lee, 'Implications of Deregulating Satellite Communications', *Telecommunications Policy*, December 1985, pp. 276–81.

Melody, William H. 'Efficient Rate Regulation in the Competitive Era', testimony to Joint Select Committee on Telecommunications, Washington State Legislature, Seattle, 11–12 July 1984.

Memorandum accompanying a statement by Sir Keith Joseph to the House of Commons, 21 July 1980.

Meyer, John R., and William B. Tye, 'The Consequences of Deregulation in the Transportation and Telecommunications Sector', *The American Economic Review*, 75, 2, 1985, pp. 46–51.

Meyer, John R., Robert W. Wilson, M. Alan Baughcum, Ellen Burton, Louis Caoulette, *The Economics of Competition in the Telecommunications Industry*, Cambridge, Mass., Oelgeschlager, Gunn & Hain, 1980.

Mintz, Morton and Jerry S. Cohen, *America Inc, Who Owns and Operates the United States*, London, Pitman, 1972.

Mitchell, Bridger M. 'Pricing Policies in Selected European Telephone Systems', in Herbert S. Dorick (ed.), *Proceedings of the 6th Annual Telecommunications Policy Conference*, Lexington, Mass., D. C. Heath, 1978, pp. 437–75.

Moran, Michael, 'Theories of regulation and changes in regulation: the case of financial markets', paper to Political Studies Annual Conference, Manchester, 1985.

Murray, Sir Evelyn, *The Post Office*, London & New York, G. P. Putnam's Sons, 1927.

Napier, Ron, 'International Services Trade: The Newest Dimension of Trade Tensions', in *US–Japan Relations in the 1980s: Towards Burden Sharing*, Cambridge, Mass., Programme on US-Japan Relations, Harvard University, 1981–2, pp. 63–76.

Noll, Roger, 'The Future of Telecommunications Regulation' in Eli M. Noam (ed.), *Telecommunications Regulation Today and Tomorrow*, New York, Law and Business Inc., pp. 41–71.

Noll, Roger G., 'Let Them Make Toll Calls: A State Regulator's Lament', *The American Economic Review*, **75**, 2, May 1985, pp. 52–56.

NTT, *NTT Telecommunications Bulletin*, no. 8, August 1984.

NTT, *NTT Procurement Update*, Tokyo, NTT, 1984.

OECD, *Telecommunications. Pressures and Policies for Change*, Paris, OECD, 1983.

OFTEL, *British Telecom's Price Increases—November 1985. A Statement Issued by the Director General of Telecommunications*, London, OFTEL, 16 January 1985 (mimeo).

OFTEL, *Determination of Terms and Conditions for the Purposes of an Agreement on the Interconnection of the BT Telephone System and the Mercury Communications Ltd System Under Condition 13 of the Licence Granted to BT under Section 7 of the Telecommunications Act 1984*, London, OFTEL, 1985.

OFTEL, *First Report 5 August—31 December 1984*, London, HMSO, 1985.

Ohashi, Ikuo, 'The Effects of Telecommunications Deregulation', in *US–Japan Relations: Towards a New Equilibrium*, Annual Review 1982–3, Mass., Center for International Affairs, Harvard University, 1983, pp. 85–97.

Patrick, Commissioner Denis R., 'On the Road to Telephone Deregulation', *Public Utilities Fortnightly*, 6 December 1984, pp. 19–21.

Peacock, Alan, (ed.), *The Regulation Game*, Oxford, Basil Blackwell, 1984.

Peltzman, Sam, 'Towards a More General Theory of Regulation', *Journal of Law and Economics*, **XIX**, 2, August 1976, pp. 211–40.

Pempel T. J., (ed.), *Policymaking in Contemporary Japan*, Ithaca & London, Cornell University Press, 1977.

Pitt, Douglas, *The Telecommunications Function in the British Post Office*, Farnborough, Saxon House, 1978.

POEU, *Making the Future Work. The Broad Strategy*, London, POEU, November 1984.

Poole R. W. Jr. (ed.), *Instead of Regulation*, Lexington, Mass., D. C. Heath, 1982.

PTTI, *Privatisation and Liberalisation of Telecommunications Services in the PTTI Asian Region*, PTTI Asian Regional Conference, Seoul, September 1984.

Quirk, Paul J., *Industry Influence in Federal Regulatory Agencies*, Princeton, New Jersey, Princeton University Press, 1981.

Report of Post Office Review Committee (Carter Report), London, HMSO, 1977.

Report on Present State of Communications in Japan, Tokyo, MPT & Japan Times, 1982.

Riddell, Peter *The Thatcher Government*, Oxford, Martin Robertson, 1983.

Roberts, Lawrence G. 'Data by the Packet', *IEEE Spectrum*, February 1974, pp. 46–51.

Robinson, P., 'Telecommunications Trade and TDF', *Telecommunications Policy*, December 1985, pp. 311–19.

Roman, James W., *Cablemania: The Cable Television Sourcebook*, New Jersey, Prentice-Hall, 1983.

Rutkowski, M., 'History of ITU and Current Developments' in Jane H. Yurow (ed.), *Issues in International Telecommunications Policy: A Sourcebook*, Washington D.C., George Washington University, 1983, pp. 51–84.

Sauvant, K. P., 'Transborder Data Flows and the Developing Countries', *International Organisation*, **37**, 2, 1983, pp. 359–71.

Schiller, Dan, 'Business Users and the Telecommunications Network', *Journal of Communication*, **32**, 4, Autumn 1982, pp. 84–96.

Schiller, Dan, 'The Emerging Global Grid—Planning for What?' *Media, Culture and Society*, **7**, 1, 1985, pp. 105–28.

Schiller, Herbert I, *Information and the Crisis Economy*, Norwood, N. J., Ablex, 1984.

Schmidt, Leland M., 'Telephone Service Pricing', in *Telecommunications and Economic Development. Exposition Proceedings Vol. 3*, Dedham, Ma., Horizon House International, 1978, pp. 219–27.

Schneider, William Jr., 'Competitive Challenges of Global Telecommunications', statement before the Subcommittee of Telecommunications, Consumer Protection, and Finance of the House of Reps. Energy and Commerce Committee, *Department of State Bulletin*, October 1984, pp. 43–6.

Sellars, O. P., J. J. E. Swaffield, J. F. L. Stubbs and S. Lunt, 'A Yen for Success', *British Telecom Journal*, Summer 1980, pp. 20–22.

Shackleton, J. R., 'UK Privatisation—US Deregulation', *Politics*, **5**, 2, 1985, pp. 8–15.

Shinto, Hisashi, 'Reform of the Telecommunications System in Japan', *Japan Quarterly*, **31**, 1984, pp. 380–83.

Shooshan, III, Harry M., 'The Bell Breakup. Putting it in Perspective', in Harry M. Shooshan III, (ed.), *Disconnecting Bell*, New York, Pergamon Press, 1984, pp. 8–22.

Silk, Leonard and David Vogel, *Ethics and Profits. The Crisis of Confidence in American Business*, New York, Simon & Schuster, 1976.

Smith, Michael, 'How Maggie sold us £2bn short', *Guardian*, 4 December 1984.

Steel, David R. and David Heald, 'Privatising Public Enterprise. An Analysis of the Government's Case', *Political Quarterly*, **53**, 1982, pp. 333–49.

Stigler, George and Claire Friedland, 'What Can Regulators Regulate? The Case of Electricity', *Journal of Law and Economics*, **V**, October 1962 reprinted in D. Grunewald and H. L. Bass, *Public Policy and The Modern Corporation*, New York, Appleton-Century-Crofts, 1966, pp. 147–67.

Stigler, George, 'The Theory of Economic Regulation', *Bell Journal of Economics and Management Science*, Spring 1971, pp. 3–21.

Stigler, George, *The Citizen and the State: Essays on Regulation*, Chicago, University of Chicago Press, 1975.

Tachikawa, Keichi, 'Information Network System: New telecommunications converged with computers', *Studies of Broadcasting*, **19**, 1983, pp. 49–69.

Taylor, Leslie A., 'Current Trends in Regulation', in Jane H. Yurow (ed.), *Issues in International Telecommunications Policy: a Sourcebook*, Washington D.C., George Washington University, 1983, pp. 86–102.

The Future of Telecommunications in Britain, Cmnd. 8610, London, HMSO, 1982.

Thomas, David, 'The Union Response to Denationalization' in David Steel and David Heald, (eds.), *Privatizing Public Enterprises*, 1984, London, RIPA, pp. 59–75.

Toffler, Alvin, *The Adaptive Corporation*, Guildford and Kings Lynn, Gower, 1985.

Trebing, Harry M., 'A Critique of Structural Regulation in Common Carrier Telecommunications', in Eli M. Noam (ed.), *Telecommunications Regulation Today and Tomorrow*, New York, Law and Business Inc., 1983, pp. 154–75.

United States International Trade Commission, *Changes in the US Telecommunications Industry and the Impact on US Telecommunications Trade*, Washington D.C., USITC, 1984.

Van Tudler, Rob and Gerd Junne, *European Multinationals in the Telecommunications Industry*, Amsterdam, University of Amsterdam, for Institute for Research and Information on Multinationals, Geneva, 1984 (mimeo).

Vickers, John and George Yarrow, *Privatization and the Natural Monopolies*, London, Public Policy Centre, 1985.

Vogel, Ezra, *Japan as Number One*, New York, Harper Row, 1979.

Weinberg, Steve, 'The Politics of Rewriting the Federal Communications Act' in John D. Havick, (ed.), *Communications and the Political Process*, Westport, Connecticut, Greenwood Press, 1983, pp. 71–89.

Whaley, Edwin T., 'Legal Protection of Software', in *US-Japan Relations: New Attitudes for a New Era*, Annual Review 1983–4, Boston, Mass., Center for International Affairs, Harvard University.

Wheeler, D., 'The Future of Communications Satellites', *Intermedia* **12**, 2, 1984, pp. 40–9.

Wiley, Richard E., 'Competition and Deregulation in Telecommunications: the American Experience', in Leonard L. Lewin, *Telecommunications in the United States, Trends and Policies*, Dedham Ma., Artech House, 1981, pp. 37–60.

Wiley, Richard E., 'The End of Monopoly. Regulatory Change and the Promotion of Competition', in Harry M. Shooshan III,ed., *Disconnecting Bell*, New York, Pergamon, 1984, pp. 23–46.

Wilson, James Q. 'The Dead Hand of Regulation', *Public Interest*, no. 25, Fall 1971, pp. 39–50.

Winnick, Joel S, 'Political, Institutional, Economic Constraints in International Telecommunications', *Proceedings of 1st International Telecommunications Exposition, Vol. 3., Telecommunications and Economic Development*, Dedham, Ma., Horizon House International, 1978, pp. 206–8.

Wolmer, Viscount, *Post Office Reform, Its Importance and Practicability*, London, Ivor Nicholson, 1932.

Yurow, Jane H., *Issues in International Telecommunications Policy, a Sourcebook*, Washington D.C., George Washington University, 1983.

US government publications

The Costs of Government Regulation to Business, A Study prepared for the use of the Subcommittee on Economic Growth and Stabilization of the Joint Economic Committee of Congress, 95th Congress, 2nd Session, 25–921, Washington D.C., Government Printing Off., 1978.

Majority Staff of the Subcommittee on Telecommunications, Consumer Protection and Finance of the Committee on Energy and Commerce, *Telecommunications in Transition: The Status of Competition in the Telecommunication Industry*, US. House of Representatives, 97th Congress, 1st Session, Washington D. C, Government Printing Off., 1981.

Hearings before a Subcommittee of the Committee on Government Operations, US House of Reps., 97th Congress, 1st Session, on International Communications Reorganization Act of 1981, HR1957, 31 March and 2 April 1981, Washington D.C., Government Printing Off., 1981.

Report to Congress by the Controller General, *Legislative and Regulatory Actions Needed to Deal with a Changing Domestic Telecommunications Industry*, CED-81-136, Washington D.C., General Accounting Office, 1981.

Joint Hearings before the Subcommittee on Telecommunications, Consumer Protection and Finance of the Committee on Energy and Commerce and the Subcommittee on Monopolies and Commercial Law of the Committee on the Judiciary, *Proposed Antitrust Settlement of US* v. *AT&T*, 98th Congress, 2nd Session, HR 97-116 26 and 28 January 1982, Washington D.C., Government Printing Off., 1982.

Hearing before the Subcommittee on Telecommunications, Consumer Protection and Finance and the Subcommittee on Oversight and Investigations of the House Committee on Energy and Commerce, *FCC Regulation of Common Carriers*, 97th Congress, 1st Session, 24 September 1981, HR 97-78, Washington D.C., Government Printing Off.,1982.

Hearings before a Subcommittee of the Committee on Government Operations, US House of Reps., 97th Congress, 1st & 2nd Sessions, *International Telecommunications and Information Policy*, 2 December 1981 and 29 April 1982, Washington D.C., Government Printing Off., 1982.

Hearings before a Subcommittee of the Committee on Government Operations, US House of Reps., 97th Congress, 2nd Session, *Impact of FCC Decisions on Local Telephone Service*, 7 April and 6 May 1982, Washington D.C., Government Printing Off., 1982.

Joint Hearings before the Senate Committee on Commerce, Science and Transportation and the House Committee on Energy and Commerce, *Universal Telephone Service Preservation Act of 1983, S1660, HR3621* , 98th Congress, 1st Session, Senate 98-30, House 98-39, 28 and 29 July 1983. Washington D.C., Government Printing Off., 1983.

Hearing before the Subcommittee on Telecommunications, Consumer Protection and Finance of the Committee on Energy and Commerce, US House of Reps., *International Trade Issues in Telecommunications and Related Industries*, 98-36, Washington D. C., Government Printing Off., 1983.

Hearing before the Subcommittee on Telecommunications, Consumer Protection and Finance of the Committee on Energy and Commerce, US House of Reps., 98th Congress, 1st Session, *Prospects for Universal Telephone Service*, 22 March 1983, 98-11, Washington D. C., Government Printing Off., 1983.

Hearings of Subcommittee of the Committee on Government Operations, *The Impact of the FCC's Telephone Access Charge Decision*, 98th Congress, 1st Session, HR 98-88, Washington D. C., Government Printing Off., 1984.

Local Telephone Rate Increases, report by the Committee Staff for the Committee on Energy and Commerce,US House of Reps., 98th Congress, 2nd Session, Committee Print 98-U, Washington D.C., Government Printing Off., 1984.

Subcommittee on Telecommunications, Consumer Protection and Finance of the Committee on Energy and Commerce, *International Trade Issues in Telecommunications and Related Industries*, 98th Congress, 1st Session, HR 98-36, 23 March, Washington D.C., US Government Printing Off. 1983, p. 9.

Hearings before Subcommittee of the Committee on Government Operations, *International Communications Reorganisation Act of 1981* , HR1957, 31 Marhc 1981, Washington D.C., Government Printing Off., 1981, p. 40.

Index